A 0/9 Q 4

A Loftier Flight

THE DE LA TORRE BUENO PRIZE / 1973

Charles-Louis Didelot
From an engraving by Reimond

A Loftier Flight

THE LIFE AND ACCOMPLISHMENTS OF

CHARLES-LOUIS DIDELOT, BALLETMASTER

BY

Mary Grace Swift

WESLEYAN UNIVERSITY PRESS

Middletown, Connecticut

———

PITMAN PUBLISHING

London

The publisher gratefully acknowledges the support of the Andrew W. Mellon Foundation toward the publication of this book.

The English versions of passages from *Evgenii Onegin* in this book were all translated by Babette Deutsch and are reprinted by permission from *The Works of Alexander Pushkin*, edited by Avrahm Yarmolinsky and published by Random House in 1936. Copyright 1936; renewed 1964 by Random House, Inc.

Library of Congress Cataloging in Publication Data

Swift, Mary Grace.
    A loftier flight.

    Includes bibliographical references.
    1. Didelot, Charles Louis, 1767–1838.   I. Title
GV1785.D54S94   792.8'2'0924 [B]   73-15007
ISBN 0-8195-4070-6

Published simultaneously in the United Kingdom by Pitman Publishing, 39 Parker Street, London.
U. K. ISBN 0 273 00849 8

Manufactured in the United States of America

FIRST EDITION

Contents

Illustrations

Preface

Balletmaster Charles-Louis Didelot was a competitive man and a perfectionist in his art. His artistic strivings were articulated in a phrase written to introduce the ballet *Sappho et Phaon*: "I venture a great work, and presume to take a loftier flight." My work is also a venture—to shed more light on the career of this man whose life was one of utter dedication to the art of dance.

Everyone who writes a book owes a debt of gratitude to others who have worked the field before him. My interest in Didelot grew from a remark once made by Clive Barnes, dance critic of *The New York Times*, that someone should translate the existing Russian biography of Charles Didelot, written by Yuri Slonimsky.* In reading Slonimsky's biography, I discovered that much of the material in it had been translated from French or English into Russian and that an investigation of those sources would have to be made even to translate it. This return to the sources brought to light much new information about Didelot and the milieu in which he flourished.

Thanks to a grant from the Academic Research Fund of Loyola University of New Orleans, I had the happy opportunity of visiting the towns in which Didelot worked. My book is an attempt to convey the excitement that was mine on various stages of this journey. It was thrilling to find vividly colored prints depicting Didelot's ballets in the Dance Collection of Lincoln Center and in the British Museum. Reading the rhythmic script of Dauberval's letters in Bordeaux and even the quaint wording of the critics' reviews in contemporary newspapers brought the era to life. What a revelation it was to find an

---

* *Dance News* (December, 1967), p. 4.

almost complete collection of the programs of Didelot's Russian works lovingly preserved in Leningrad libraries.

May the reader, too, venture upon "a loftier flight" of the imagination in following, with me, the exciting career of Didelot.

So many librarians and others have helped me in this work that I could never list them all. I gratefully acknowledge, however, the assistance of Birgitta Walin and the staff of Drottningholm Theatrical Library, the staff of the Royal Library in Stockholm, and Mary Skeaping, who generously shared information about Didelot's Swedish career with me. In France I had access to materials and kind assistance at the Bibliothèque de l'Opéra, the Bibliothèque Nationale, and the Bibliothèque de l'Arsenal in Paris. The Bibliothèque and Archives Municipales in Bordeaux yielded much primary material on Didelot's years there, and the British Museum's newspaper and print collections amply satisfied a researcher's quest. For Russian materials I used in Helsinki the University Library, in Leningrad the Public Library and the Lunacharsky Theatrical Library, and in Moscow the Lenin Library and the Central Theatrical Library. I was courteously assisted in all these institutions.

Finally, I had access to American libraries for laying the groundwork of the research: the Library of Congress, the New York Public Library's Slavonic and Dance Collections, the Harvard Theatre Collection, the Folger Shakespeare Library, and Tulane University Library. Mr. George Verdak assisted me with his private collection.

When various passages needed translating, I always found willing assistance from my colleagues at Loyola University: Rochelle Ross, Anthony Lala, Richard Franks, Charles O'Neil, and Ray Sabatini. I am very grateful for their assistance. Emily Clack assisted me with photography.

Many other people generously shared their knowledge with me, especially Ivor Guest, Jeanne Bruno, Edward Langhans, Philip Highfill, John Alexander, Joseph Giacobbe, Marvin Carlson, and Gerald Seamen. Sheila Steinberg gave much editorial assistance.

When I submitted this manuscript for the de la Torre Bueno Prize, my judges offered many helpful comments and suggestions. For these, and for their encouragement, I wish to thank Selma Jeanne Cohen, Genevieve Oswald, and Edwin Denby. Finally, I would like to thank

J. R. de la Torre Bueno, editor emeritus of Wesleyan University Press, who has encouraged me in my study of dance history.

Mary Grace Swift
New Orleans, Louisiana

NOTE: In transliterating Russian words and proper names, I have followed the system of the Library of Congress in the footnotes; however, for the sake of readability, I have used in the text the forms common in American dance publications, for example, Yuri Slonimsky for Iurii Slonimskii or Maya Plisetskaya for Maiia Plisetskaiia.

A Loftier Flight

CHAPTER I

Opening Steps

Prince Frederick, brother of the reigning monarch of Sweden, Gustav III (1771–1792), faced a problem. True, it was not a crisis of state, but it was a problem—centered around a coming masquerade ball. Little did he know that later, at such a masquerade, Gustav III would become the victim of an assassin's pistol, thus giving the world the plot later utilized in Verdi's opera, *Un Ballo in Maschera*. Now, however, Frederick was assembling his costume-ball regalia and wished to dress as a Savoyard. At that time, after outfitting themselves with a hurdy-gurdy and marmot,[1] Savoyards took to the road as itinerant performers. The outfit was no problem to the royal tailor, but finding someone to play the part of the marmot presented some difficulty.

Frederick therefore sought the aid of Charles Didelot, a teacher and second dancer of the Royal Opera House. The dancer, later styled Didelot the Elder, then had to find a boy with prematurely developed intelligence and agility, combined with retarded physical development, to play the part of the marmot. After vain searching, he thought of his own little son. Young Didelot was a full head smaller than the normal child of his years, and when costumed, made a beguiling marmot. At the supper table, Prince Frederick allowed him to cavort without a mask along the table. Didelot's marmotlike squatting, capering, and grimacing delighted the guests who exclaimed, "What a simpleton!" Frederick, seeing the performance of the unpolished little gem, defended him, saying, "He is not handsome, but there will be profit in him; I guarantee, that with time, talent will embellish the ugliness."[2]

This little lad, Charles-Louis Frédéric Didelot, was born in 1767 in Stockholm. The records of Stockholm's Santa Eugenia's Catholic Church reveal that in 1766, in the Chapelle Royale de France, his father, about twenty-eight years old and a native of Lunéville in

Lorraine, wed his mother, Magdelaine Maréchal, about thirty years old and a native of Metz. The Didelot couple were among the many French performers of the eighteenth century who brought the art of ballet to royal courts throughout Europe. Didelot's father had been a dancer at the Théâtre des Comédiens Italiens in Paris. Programs from this theater reveal that in 1759 a certain dancer named Didlot played such roles as a faun in *Télémaque dans l'Isle de Calypso* and the Aga des Janissaires in *Les Amants introduits au sérail.*[3]

At the age of two young Charles visited his mother's native Metz, where a case of smallpox almost cost him his eyesight. Though his vision was spared, his complexion was marred with ugly scars that proved to be only one more handicap toward achieving the stage career he coveted. At the age of six Didelot returned to Sweden. There his passion for dance developed into that veritable mania that only those so stricken can understand. He loved to visit rehearsals of the Royal troupe, and would mimic their steps and leaps while watching in the wings.

After he played the role of the marmot, the development of Didelot's talent was entrusted to Louis Frossard, a fortunate choice. This first pedagogue of Didelot had once been a member of a troupe of French dancers in Stockholm. When this troupe was disbanded in 1771, he went to the Comédie Italienne in Paris to serve as both dancer and choreographer. Gustav III recalled him to Stockholm in 1773. There he was noted especially for his splendid character dancing and pantomime. Contemporaries praised the strength and skill with which he danced in irons while representing a fettered slave. They likewise noted his lightness, his fiery liveliness, his elasticity, and dazzling pirouettes. Further, it was said he possessed "a considerable gift for invention and continual variation in his compositions . . . he always knew how to make use of what is comic and is most expressive in his dances." [4] Later in life Frossard's pupil Didelot would gain fame for attributes similar to those of his first master.

In his stage debut Didelot played the role of Cupid. According to his biographer Mundt he was so successful that thereafter he was always chosen for the role. The eighteenth-century stage was so surfeited with productions calling for cupids that Didelot no doubt gained a good deal of stage experience from his prowess in the role. Gustav III realized that he was destined for greater things than marmots and cupids, however, and sent him to perfect his dance art in Paris. While sailing from

Sweden, there occurred one of the many great calamities that periodically beset Didelot's life. During a storm at sea, near Norway, his ship lost its rigging and masts, and it found refuge in a cove near Christiania (Oslo).

Didelot arrived in Paris in 1776—a time when a colossal struggle was waging in the Opéra. Choreographic genuises were involved, and French ballet was eternally deprived of the creations of great men whose talents were shunted aside in power shifts. In the very year of Didelot's arrival, Jean-Georges Noverre finally achieved his long cherished goal of being appointed balletmaster at the Opéra. Certainly the Opéra needed Noverre more than he needed the Opéra.

By any artistic standards eighteenth-century France was a magnificent period. It was the age of compilers of the French *Encyclopédie*, of *littérateurs*, political philosophers, and art critics who seriously challenged former standards of morals and art. It was the era of ravishing Fragonard paintings and elegant Gobelin tapestries. Compared to other arts of the day, however, ballet was artistically underdeveloped and the critics of the age rightfully prodded it to bestir itself. An apt description of the poverty of ballet in this age of artistic splendor was written by Baron Melchior Grimm, one of the famous savants and critics of the day. He complained in 1765:

> All the ballets are composed of two lines of dancers who range themselves on each side of the theatre and who mix themselves, then form figures and groups without any idea. The best dancers nevertheless are reserved to dance sometimes alone, sometimes in pairs; for grand occasions, they form a *pas de trois*, or a *pas de quatre*, or even with five or six. . . . Sometimes in the ballet there is an idea, an instant of action, it is executed in a *pas de deux* or *trois*, after which the *corps de ballet* again does its insipid dance. The only difference between one *fête* and the others is that the opera's tailor sometimes dresses the ballet in white, sometimes in green, sometimes in yellow, sometimes in red. . . . It is only when the man of genius has perceived that he can make the dance an art of imitation, proper to express all sentiments and passions without using any other language than that of gestures and movements, that dance will have become worthy of being on a stage.[5]

For a few brief years, Noverre, "the man of genius," had his chance on the Paris stage, producing ballets which, added to his productions in Stuttgart, Vienna, and London, formed a total of over one hundred fifty works. In these, the art of ballet took a giant leap away from the former pretty, childish, rhythmic drills, and developed at least an adolescent's awareness of its ability to portray life, passion, themes of classical grandeur, and grief—as well as innocent joy. Young Didelot saw and absorbed much of Noverre's artistry, and perhaps he unconsciously imitated his methods of teaching and drilling his dancers. Noverre had a choleric, impetuous, proud, sometimes even brutal disposition, being known even to spit at his dancers in anger. One of his future London employers, the singer and opera director Michael Kelly, assured his readers that Noverre was indeed "a passionate little fellow" who swore and fumed so much behind the scenes that at times he could have been taken for an escaped lunatic. Once Noverre even resoundingly kicked director Kelly on stage for talking during a performance.[6] In this respect, Noverre was a bad example for young Didelot, and in later life, when Didelot became a master, his irascibility became no less infamous than Noverre's.

While, in Didelot's words, Noverre was the Corneille of ballet, he himself studied under the Molière of dance art, Jean Bercher, known as Dauberval.

Dauberval had made his debut at the Paris Opéra at the age of nineteen, where his vigor and good humor quickly made him an idol of the court and the public. His particular patron was Madame Du Barry, mistress of Louis XV. In 1770 Dauberval installed himself in a sumptuous hotel on the rue Saint-Lazare in Paris. In it he had constructed a salon, a marvel of taste and elegance, which could be transformed into a theater by means of special machinery.[7] However, Dauberval's extravagance brought debts and pursuit by creditors. Rather than face them he threatened in 1773 to leave Paris for St. Petersburg. Instead of really going to Russia, however, on April 29, 1774, Dauberval humbly wrote his famous patron, begging financial assistance. Du Barry promptly took up a subscription for him in which all the court, Louis XV included, contributed the sum of ninety thousand francs.[8] Further Dauberval and Maximilien Gardel were named to the position of *"maîtres adjoints"* of the opera ballet. In 1776, when the ruling balletmaster Gaetan Vestris stepped aside, Queen Marie Antoinette named her old dance instructor from the Austrian court, Jean-Georges Noverre, to Vestris' vacated post, bypassing the rights of succession of the *adjoints*, who became leaders of venomous cabals against Noverre. Finally weary of fighting to retain his position, and constitutionally unable to "play politics," Noverre retired in 1781 from the Opéra.[9] Dauberval, humiliated in the ensuing power struggle with Maximilien Gardel and his brother Pierre, left the Opéra himself in 1783 and married.

Though their collaboration was brief in his early Parisian days, Didelot established beautiful rapport with Dauberval. Didelot's Russian biographer N. P. Mundt affirms that Dauberval loved him very much and zealously taught him.[10] Time and again Didelot himself manifested his humble gratitude toward this man who apparently had been so kind to him as a poor student in Paris. In the preface to his ballet in Lyon in 1795, *La Métamorphose*, Didelot wrote a tribute to his master, saying:

> My Dear Friend,
> Will you accept this bagatelle? Gratitude is the sweetest of all duties; were it not so, I should never have dared to present you this work. Be pleased then to receive, under that respect, this feeble homage of the man whose friend you have ever been, whom you instructed in his profession, and who became only acquainted with it by having been your pupil.
> The ingenious Prometheus could steal a particle of the celestial fire with which he animated his work. Oh! that I could have, like him, stolen a single particle of the fire of that bright and inventive genius which perfuses and stamps with originality all your productions! Then should I not experience the timidity I feel in presenting you with this sketch of some pictures of mere imagination. . . . Adieu, my dear Friend. Be pleased still from your retirement, to give advice to your pupil, to your child. With what an avidity he will receive it! I stand in need, and ever shall, of your paternal, mild and instructive severity.
> Health, friendship, eternal and tender gratitude.
>
> > Your pupil,
> > Didelot.[11]

Fourteen years later, after his master had been dead three years, Didelot again recalled:

> It was the special talent of Dauberval to portray characters, and certainly that is one of the greatest difficulties of the art. No one has rendered pantomime better than he; he was true and profound in all. What a loss, if I may add, what regrets for the Opéra . . . not to have in its repertoire even one ballet of that grand master . . . dead

at an age when he still had all the means to work. O My Master, permit your infant to throw a flower, to shed a tear on your tomb. It is the transport of a heart penetrated by sadness at having nothing more, alas, than regrets to give to your memory.[12]

In order to maintain a miserable existence during these hard years of study, Didelot took various jobs. In 1769 Nicholas Audinot, an actor of the Comédie Italienne, had established a puppet show on the boulevard du Temple bearing the name of Théâtre de l'Ambigu-Comique, or later, the Théâtre Audinot.[13] Soon the puppets were exchanged for children, one of whom was young Didelot. There Parisians could see enacted hair-raising, blood-curdling melodramas portraying kidnapped infants and persecuted orphans. In 1779 their presentation of *The Siege of Montauban* or *The Four Sons of Aymon* brought tears to the eyes of spectators. This was followed by *The Black Forest, Captain Cook*, and *The Iron Mask*.[14] Though the theater obtained a rather unsavory reputation for the use of smutty jokes, it became the rage of the day, even among ladies of the court.[15] The experience possibly influenced Didelot's future career a great deal, for he gained practice there in the art of garish character dances and heroic pantomime in witty, topical farces. For this work Didelot received six hundred francs a year.[16] After an exhausting day of muscle-searing exercise in class, followed by an evening's exertion at the Ambigu, the lad returned to some shabby abode to eat an inadequate supper and rest his weary, growing adolescent frame. A year of this regime provoked nature to square accounts: he became ill. Didelot's health, perhaps even his life, was saved by his mother who came to Paris and found her exhausted son. She had tried to entrust him to the care of Parisian relatives, but they wanted nothing to do with him. The reputation of the Ambigu-Comique was not untainted—further, who wanted the expense of a growing boy? Though his mother managed to nurse him to health and insisted that he quit his job, these were the last maternal tendernesses the boy was to enjoy. Suddenly his mother died. If his father, who was a member of the Royal troupe of dancers in Stockholm from 1781 until 1792,[17] had any connection with his son, no source mentions it. When Didelot's financial plight again hit rock-bottom, help came from the father of a dance pupil, whom Didelot's Russian biographer Mundt called Brodeken. This gentlemen was apparently pleased with his son's progress and spared Didelot some of the ravages of poverty. Later in his life, though noted

for making tyrannical demands upon his own pupils, Didelot remembered those lean years, and his despotism was always tempered with a
benevolent willingness to aid his students in their physical hardships.

At some date, difficult to determine, Dauberval relinquished his
pupil to the tutelage of Jean Barthélemy Lany, whom Noverre
described as "a dancer who was knowledgeable in that which
concerned the mechanics of steps."[18] According to Mundt, Lany was
very much in vogue at the time as a teacher of high society pupils.
Didelot lacked the means to dress in the foppish, fashionable style of
the day, and because of this, Lany soon asked him in a very courteous
manner to leave his dwelling.[19] However, Lany did recommend him to
another competent teacher and member of a prominent family
connected with the Opéra—Monsieur Jacques-Francois Deshayes.

By at least the year 1782 Didelot's artistry had developed to the
point that he was hired by the Comédie-Française, where the performance of light operas and separate divertissements gave him ample
chance to display his youthful skill. There, Frédéric Didelot was listed
among the staff as one of the *danseurs seuls et en double.*[20] Also listed
among the dancers was a certain demoiselle named Marie Rose Paul
(Pole), whose stately elegance won her a place among the theater's
enfants et surnuméraires. They called her simply Mademoiselle Rose.
Rose had made her debut at the Opéra in 1782, but not having sufficient
strength yet for a career there, she had to continue instead at the
Comédie-Française.[21] Several years later, after winning fame that
sometimes seemed even to exceed Didelot's, she became Madame Rose
Didelot.

By 1783 Didelot was on the rolls of the Paris Opéra, being listed as
one of the pupils of the school who danced daily at the theater. The
master of this school, as well as that of the Comédie-Française, was
Didelot's teacher, Deshayes.[22]

In 1784 the king of Sweden, Gustav III, paid a visit to France.
Though he travelled under the lowly title of the count of Haga, Gustav
expected, and received, all the courtesies kings were afforded in that
age of grandeur. Gustav himself wrote plays, and had an irrestible
passion for the French stage, which he satisfied by attending two or
three performances almost each evening of his sojourn. Didelot was
presented to his monarch at a festival given in honor of the visit.[23] The
king was delighted to see this pensioner of his who would soon

embellish the Stockholm musical theater, which Gustav was zealously nurturing as a means of reinforcing the national spirit of his people. The monarch praised Didelot's progress and indicated that he soon expected him back in Sweden. No doubt Didelot bowed assent to his patron, but beneath the façade of submission, his heart cried to remain at Paris. In the beautiful French city he had known hunger, cold, illness, and rejection; later he would experience there shattering injustices. Yet like a rejected lover he always sought chances to return to his beloved Paris to try again to win her esteem and recognition.

It was not long, however, before Didelot received a summons from the Swedish ambassador to France, none other than Baron de Staël, who insisted that Didelot accompany him back to the homeland. Didelot could only obey; he returned to Stockholm in 1786. Actually Didelot had more opportunity there to test his ideas than he would have had in Paris. He appeared in a *pas de deux* of his own which was very successful. Further, according to the account of Didelot's pupil and biographer Adam Glushkovsky, he conceived a plan for the ballet *Diane et Endymion*,[24] though no account of this work exists in Swedish lists of the time. Didelot also took his place among the dancers gracing the opera productions. On May 11, 1786, he appeared in *Orpheus and Euridice*. Significantly Didelot was second on the list of Happy Shades who danced in the first act.[25] First on the list was a man whom Didelot feared would perpetually be ahead of him in Sweden: Antoine Bournonville. With a majestically proportioned body, handsome face, and extraordinary virtuosity in all forms of theatrical dancing, Bournonville had merited the title of first dancer in 1782. He projected an aura of inborn nobility, and was the idol of an audience which almost made a fetish of elegance. Small, sinewy Didelot, whose pock-marked complexion and harsh, prominent features betrayed the austerity of his youth, was better in demi-character dance than in the serious genre cultivated by his rival.

On January 24, 1787, the opera *Armide* by Gluck-Quinault was staged in Stockholm. This time, in the printed program, Didelot's name headed the list of Pleasures in the second act.[26] Further though Didelot, no doubt, was regarded by many in the troupe as just an ambitious upstart, to the credit of the administration, the twenty-year-old youth was allowed to stage the dances for the opera *Frigga* on May 31, 1787. The opera was based upon a mythological theme used in the poetry of the Swedish author C. G. Leopold, with music by O. Åhlström.

It is not hard to imagine the thrill of the young choreographer seeing printed on the back of the title page of the libretto, "Balleterne af Herr Didelot, Sonen." Bournonville was only a dancer in the production.

For the opera Didelot staged a Dance of Maidens, who, wearing white dresses bedecked with flowers, surrounded the goddess Frigga as she arose from a bed of more flowers. Another ballet included people of all classes who danced as they placed sacrifices before the goddess. There were also pantomimes, such as that of a ceremony in which warriors' weapons were consecrated by priestesses.[27] Though Didelot was happy for his choreographic experience, he knew that he would constantly have to compete with Bournonville's seven year's seniority and wide popularity, so Didelot soon decided to leave Stockholm for a return trip to Paris.

When Didelot resumed his studies in Paris in 1787, he added the Vestris family to his famed group of teachers. Gaetan Vestris the Father at age fifty-eight had passed the peak of his career, but he still gave lessons. While collaborating in Gaetan's teaching, his natural son Auguste was successfully building the reputation of being the first dancer in Europe in *"la danse forte."* The elder Vestris, who considered himself, in his prime, as *"le Diou de la danse,"* accepted with good humor the fact that his son's talent exceeded his own. Once, when someone was unkind enough to point out the fact, Gaetan only remarked, "I well believe it . . . I did not have the advantage of having such a good teacher as he!"[28]

According to one account, the Vestris teachers wanted to be the sole masters of their pupils, who were supposed to be supple and docile to their orders. In reality they terrorized their students at times by their authoritarianism. Added to that, it was rumored that their "good principles of choreography alternated with evil counsels of insubordination."[29]

In his future career Didelot had a difficult time living in peace with administrators. While it would hardly be fair to attribute Didelot's personality problems solely to this source, it can be said with certainty that in the sowing of seeds of insubordination, the Vestris teachers found fertile ground in Didelot.

At the same time Mademoiselle Rose was also studying with the Vestris masters (*Fig. 1*). She again made her debut at the Académie Royale de Musique in 1786 in the opera *Armide*. In spite of the group of excellent dancers already performing at the Académie, Rose received a

Figure 1. Madame Rose Didelot as Calypso in the ballet *Télémaque*, from an engraving by Charles Hénard in the Bibliothèque de l'Opéra, Paris.

most distinguished welcome at her second debut, and was lauded for her charming *taille*, her well placed head and arms.[30] The press remarked that all her movements were natural, especially since she shunned violent and unfeminine movements which should be reserved only for male dancers.

In spite of the fine training Rose received from Gaetan Vestris, her solicitous mother was unhappy about the unhealthy influence the Vestris family exerted over her daughter. The mother, Madame Delfevre, once a dancer herself at the Académie, took her complaints against the *mauvais conseils* of the Vestris teachers to the director. At the time she demanded strict secrecy concerning her appeal to higher authority, saying that if Le Sieur Vestris found out about it he would harm her daughter very much. Rose developed into a dancer capable of performing both *"le genre noble"* and demi-character roles, but it was in the former that she excelled and won enviable fame. With all her great successes, however, she bore the reputation of having a difficult, disagreeable, and capricious character, blamed in great part upon the influence of Gaetan Vestris.[31]

CHAPTER II

English Growing Pains

IN spite of his love for Paris, Didelot could be lured elsewhere by opportunities for artistic fulfillment and money. When word came to him in 1787 that Noverre, now retired from the Opéra, was engaged by King's Theatre in London as balletmaster and could use his services, the young artist was delighted to have a chance to collaborate with him. Further, Didelot was offered a sum for performing in London which overwhelmed him—four hundred pounds sterling.[1]

The British public was developing a taste for ballet in the mid-eighteenth century that prompted them to meet the relatively large cost of hiring foreign performers. In *The Gentleman's Magazine* in 1741 a mythical "Jack Briton" posed the question:

> What's the reason . . . our Fellows and Wenches cannot in their Dancing and Capers equal these French and Italians? Are they not as active, as strong, and as well made? These Questions seem at first rational enough, but on a little reflection we find, that the natives of all Countries, from the effect of the Climate and their own natural Humour, have their peculiar Genius. The French have more light, airy Dispositions than the English, and the Italians a more spirited Temper and refin'd Genius than the French. Experience has shown, that notwithstanding the public encouragement which has been given to Dancing, we have had but very few of our own Country, who have on the stage made any Figures in the Art; for there is so much of the Northern rough stiffness in the natural motion of a true Briton, that he will never arrive at the Capreols [sic] of the French, or the mimic Gesticulations of the Italians.
>
> Altho' I cannot think it unbecoming an Englishman to see the Entertainments which these Italians exhibit, I am sure it is beneath the Character of a Briton to wish to see his Countrymen endued

with such a Genius. Let us rather pay for such exotic Pleasures, than have them the Growth of this Island; Let the airy, sprightly French and Italians still excel in the Dance, but may Englishmen, like their forefathers, be still rough, strong, brave, and superior in the Battle.[2]

Several decades later "Jack Briton" might have been appalled to learn that the second reading of a Bill for the Retrenchment of Public Expenditures, sponsored by Edmund Burke, was postponed because of a ballet performance on Thursday, February 22, 1781. A certain Lord Nugent, urging the postponement, gave as the ostensible reason that Wednesday, the day previous to the proposed reading, was a day of fasting, which would prevent the gentlemen of the house from giving the bill due attention. Subsequent jottings in the journal of the House of Commons reveal the true nature of the delay:

[Burke] believed it was not on account of fasting, but of feasting, that the Bill was to be delayed. It was not because Wednesday was the fast day, but because Thursday was the benefit day of Mr. Vestris, the French dancer. This was the true reason. It would be shameful to think of their constituents, or to think of their country, when Vestris was to dance. It would be dreadful to set about retrenchment and economy, when Vestris had advertised for a benefit. What was the salvation of a state compared with the interest of Vestris! In the piping times of peace, he said, he would dance as willingly as any of them; he was fond of pleasure, in a season of joy: but now his mind was occupied by more melancholy considerations than dancing. But to a great part of that House, a dance was a much more important object than a war; and the Opera house must be maintained, whatever became of the country. For his own part, he was no enemy to merit of any kind, either of the heels or of the head; and he formed no design against Vestris, by moving for the second reading of his Bill on the day of his benefit: but the treasury-bench had taken care of that interest which he had forgotten. He promised the noble lord then, that if he would procure his Bill to pass, and the reform to take place, he would have no objection to make up to Vestris what he might suffer, by giving him the profits of one of the places to be abolished. The hon. gentleman concluded with a serious appeal to the House against that abominable spirit of levity which thus drove them from business of national importance to the entertainments of a theatre.[3]

Burke was overruled; the House postponed the reading of his bill until the following Monday by a vote of eighty-nine to seventy-seven.

In spite of the growing craze, however, by the time that Didelot arrived, England still had no established ballet school of its own, and the ranks of dancers at King's Theatre, as well as at the few other London theaters where ballet might be seen, were generally filled with artists imported from the Continent. Quite often they were contracted for only one season. In England, therefore, Didelot encountered many familiar faces. Auguste Vestris was there, and Didelot seemed to continue to enjoy cordial relations with him. One of the leading, upcoming ballerinas at King's Theatre in 1788 was Madame Hilligsberg. She, too, had been a pupil of the Vestris team in Paris, and her teachers' ambitious conniving won chances for her to perform. Others resented such machinations and Hilligsberg was described as "a pretty dancer, but still difficult because of the counsels of her master, Vestris the father." [4] Contemporary prints of her do not portray a face of ravishing beauty, but she became a darling of the English stage, and no doubt was one of the best dancers of her time in England. However, her popularity was also due to her willingness to stoop to a few tricks to please the less refined instincts of her audiences. Her appearances in men's trousers, risqué for her day, would always fill the house. Later Hilligsberg and Didelot's wife Rose were rivals in popularity, though they actually complemented each other. *The Morning Chronicle* was to describe their styles aptly as "the *Allegro* of Hilligsberg and the *Penseroso* of Madame Rose." [5]

There is another interesting name which appears on the roster of King's Theatre in the season of 1788: newspaper notices merely refer to him as Monsieur Chevalier.° His full name was Chevalier Peicam de Bressoles. It was not Didelot's first encounter with this dancer; he, along with Rose, had been *enfants et surnuméraires* at the Comédie-Française when Didelot danced there. By 1785, when Didelot headed the list of pupils of the Opéra school, Chevalier was listed as one of the children doing ordinary service.[6] Didelot's career was to be continually intertwined with the career of this man. In the future Chevalier Peicam was to earn the reputation of being one of the most disagreeable characters posing as a dancer in the opera houses of Europe.

° This man was a puzzle to research, because sometimes he was called either Chevalier or Peicam. His complete story has never been told. Perhaps the bit of information in this study may interest some future researcher in the bizarre careers of Peicam and his wife.

As the season opened in London on December 8, 1787, the public was offered a new divertissement composed by Chevalier. This was only an *hors d'oeuvre*, however, for the British public eagerly awaited great things from the master Noverre. In Noverre's subsequent production on the same evening of *Les Offrandes à l'Amour,* Didelot made his first appearance in England. Hilligsberg and Vestris also took part,[7] along with less well known members of the cast. On January 12 many of the same dancers took part in a work by Peicam called *The Military Dance.*[8] That season, rave notices did not go to Didelot but to Vestris or Pierre Gardel, who came at Easter. Though he failed to win plaudits from the Londoners during the season, Didelot did absorb much from his contact with Noverre, for in London in 1788 Didelot saw ballets whose themes he utilized years later in Russia. On January 29, 1788, *The Public Advertiser* announced the production of Noverre's *L'Amour et Psiché*, to the music of Mazzinghi. In it, Didelot played the part of Adonis. During the performances of the ballet Didelot experienced one of the worst trials that beset dancers on a British stage at the time—the actual presence on the stage of "gentlemen of fashion" who felt it their privilege to sport their familiarity with the dancers, and thus ruin the performance for all the rest of the audience. In historical retrospect, it seems ludicrous that such a situation was endured for so long by the British public, but at the time the greatest deterrant applied to the inconsiderate young men was a gentle notice in the newspaper, requesting all "who were not immediately interested in the performance of *L'Amour et Psiché* to keep clear from the stage during the representation, lest any accident should arise from the moving machinery, from the flambeaux to be used therein, and from the opening of the trap doors." [9]

On February 4 King's Theatre offered a masquerade party to highlight the carnival season. When the weary feet of dancing couples welcomed a break, there was entertainment by the professional cast. The evening's program included a *pas de deux* by Didelot and Mademoiselle Anne-Jacqueline Coulon, as well as a *pas de trois* with Chevalier added.[10] On February 21, at the end of the first act of the opera *Gli schiavi per amore*, Didelot and Mademoiselle Coulon again joined talents to dance a new number, a *Pas de Béarnois.*[11] On February 28, Londoners saw Noverre's *Les Fêtes du tempe* followed by his *Euthyme et Eucharis* on March 13.[12] Didelot took his place in both of these, playing the part of Mars in the latter. However, Londoners were more excited on April 3 by the *Pas de Quatre de Panurge* from *Euthyme et Eucharis* performed by Coulon, Hilligsberg, Vestris, and the guest dancer from Paris, Pierre Gardel. The Parisian guest star even prolonged his stay in London to repeat the *pas de quatre* because "several persons of the first distinction" had requested it.[13]

It was the custom in this era for top performers to gain the privilege of having their own special benefit performances. The profits, either in whole or in part, could be pocketed by the artist. Thus, in addition to the bountiful salary which Didelot received, he had also gained the right to have his first benefit, which took place on May 22. A few days before the event, London papers informed the public that tickets could be had from Mr. Didelot, No. 37, Silver Street, Golden Square. Undoubtedly he was glad for the income, but such a man as Didelot was much more delighted with the opportunity afforded by the benefit for creating two new ballets of his own. His first work was called *La Bonté du seigneur*, while the second was a grand ballet in five acts, *Richard Coeur-de-Lion*.[14] There were special attractions in the latter. In act two a new French instrument, Le Cistre, was used, and at the end of act four there was a concerto on the French horn. However, neither of the ballets gained any permanent place in the repertoire of the theater, for they were far overshadowed by the works of Noverre, who on April 17 presented *Adèle de Ponthieu*.[15] and on May 29 revived a favorite work of Dauberval's, *The Deserter*. Having danced in all of them, Didelot, enriched both with sterling and experience, crossed the Channel at the end of the season to return to Paris, where a golden opportunity for a fall debut had opened for him at the *Académie* in the opera *Le Devin du village*. The words and music were by none other than the famed author and political theorist Jean-Jacques Rousseau, who, obsessed by a hatred of French music, wrote this opera deliberately in the Italian style.[16] The *Journal de Paris* reported that Didelot obtained the most brilliant success in this production, and that he had abundant aplomb, grace, lightness, and expressiveness in his figure, as well as great aptitude for pantomime. In conclusion the *Journal* commented, "We can make no better eulogy than to congratulate the Opéra on this acquisition in a time when the art of the dance has attained so high a degree." [17]

Success in Paris at this time, however, was no guarantee of a permanent place in the Académie Royale de Musique. A lowly young artist such as Didelot could scarcely hope to withstand political cabals that had defeated Noverre and Dauberval. However, if Pierre Gardel, the ruling balletmaster since 1787, was unreceptive to his talents, London was not, and again an offer beckoned from across the Channel. This time the salary was six hundred pounds and a benefit during the 1789 season.[18]

He accepted, but to proud Didelot, the humiliations he would encounter during that season which opened on January 10, 1789, could hardly have been compensated by any salary. Didelot left Paris while the volcanic forces of discontent rumbled ever more loudly toward the day when the lava of revolution would erupt over all France. He came to an England noted in this period of history for corrupt government, where the gross, unrestrained, and unmannerly conduct of some elements of its high society would contrast sharply with the gentle manners the world has come to connect with Englishmen.

The season's new offerings included on January 10 the ballet *L'Embarquement pour Cythère* and *New Divertissement*—both by Didelot. *The Morning Post* remarked that "Didelot, since we last saw him, is much improved in his dance," to which *The Morning Herald* agreed.[19] However his hopes for a stunning immediate success were soon shattered by more hostile tones in the press. The *Post* later recalled that in 1781 they had seen the Vestris father and son, while now they saw only Didelot and his ilk.[20] Also recalling the former glories of Vestris and Hilligsberg, *The Times* philosophized that "since nothing better than Didelot, Adelaide and Normand are to be had—we must make the best of a bad bargain—depending on the genius of Noverre for something beyond the insipidity of a divertissement—something when the interest in the ballet may render the dancers interesting." [21] *The Morning Herald* was more unkind, remarking, "of the ballets—we will say little—the curtain cannot drop upon them too soon." [22] On the same day, however, the *Post* disagreed, remarking that, "The dances went off with much *éclat*. Didelot is now the best of them." [23] On January 31, Didelot danced in Noverre's *Les Fêtes provençales*. This failed to satisfy the public and during the first week of February, the ballet troupe was receiving such a hostile reception that the dancers resorted to kicking off their shoes to get laughs from the audience. The press reported that discontent prevailed, with one gentleman wanting to fight the manager, who "made a hasty retreat into quiet privacy." [24]

On February 9 the management was not so lucky. The concluding dance of the program had scarcely begun when discontent boiled over in the house. The conservative *Times* moralized that "the usual consequences of abdicated government ensued," and "the riot was general." [25] From all parts of the house the spectators began to call for the appearance of Sir John Gallini, the director of King's Theatre. While "young men of fashion" rushed up to the already crowded stage, Gallini fled the house, and few could blame him. A subordinate official was called to answer the irate audience's demand of "whether the subscribers might thereafter expect better dancers?" Receiving no answer, the young bucks then began to try "to beat an answer out of the scenery." While ladies screamed, the partisans of sweet reasonableness, led by none other than the Prince of Wales, tried to prevent the total destruction of the house.[26]

Gallini, the papers reported, had sent to Paris during the previous week to engage the best female dancer available, as well as a good male dancer, should one be available. The next day the press announced that Didelot had hurt his leg during the first dance on Saturday and would be unable to appear for some days. Such accidents were to become common during Didelot's subsequent career, but this time one is tempted to think his indisposition might have been due more to hurt pride than to a hurt leg. Gallini was called to the stage again on the evening of February 10 to account for his delay in engaging good dancers. In the picturesque account of *The World* he made the following announcement: "Gentilmin, I begs pardon. I hav sint for von vomans: I wil git her as soon as I can. I cannot do more." The reporter added that "this promised exertion . . . calmed the audience." [27]

On February 14 Didelot was again performing. *The Times* review was harsh, declaring that the extreme poverty and wretchedness of the dances classed them "in every respect below the lowest of those produced even at Sadler's Wells." [28] Didelot, the review added, might have agility, but he lacked the sort of expression and manner which would encourage Noverre to make him the hero of an interesting ballet.[29] While *The Times*'s estimate may have been true of Didelot at the time, distinct animosity already existed between *The Times* and Gallini, who had refused to run advertisements of his performances in *The Times*, possibly because the newspaper had reported the seizure of smuggled goods in Gallini's own house.[30] After complaining again about the wretched divertissements *The Times* revealed that Gallini had locked up all the stage scenery in anticipation of the audience's wrath.[31] On March 3 *Le Nymphe et le chasseur*, a ballet by Noverre's pupil

Coindé was offered, no doubt in the hopes of placating the angry public. Even before viewing it, however, the patrons asked why they had to watch Coindé's work when Noverre's was available. After viewing it the patrons declared that something better might have been expected from Noverre's pupil.[32] There were rumors that Noverre had been practicing a new ballet—"something about the jealousy of the sultan" in which he had the girls rehearse their movements repeatedly "till he seemed to be entranced into a state of Asiatic luxuriousness." [33] Where was this ballet that had been rumored, the press demanded? On March 7, a Saturday, (the favorite night for riots at King's Theatre), outright revolt again broke loose. Noverre himself was summoned to the stage to answer for his dilatoriness. He explained that the postponement was not his fault, for he had finished his plans for the choreography, but the delay was from the lack of everything accessory to the production. He had *"ni tailleur,—ni machiniste—ni musique—ni décorations."* [34] When Gallini, who had been watching the Frenchman with "a sardonic grin," began to explain his version of the story, five hostile young men surrounded the old director. Ladies screamed, "Don't kill him," while others fainted.[35] In the version of *The Morning Post*, "The unequal contention between a feeble old man against five young ones struck the audience with such indignation that hissing and groaning came from all parts of the house." However, the censure of the audience did not prevent the stage intruders from trying to kick Gallini into the orchestra, and only the assistance of a musician prevented him from falling. When Gallini escaped their grasp the young bucks "came to the verge of the stage with folded arms and contemptuous grinnings . . . [and] after standing in this indecent and insulting way some time, one of those heroic gentlemen began to kick the lamps into the orchestra pit, and his example was immediately followed by his associates." Like a schoolmaster, the *Post* scolded the English populace for its toleration of such behavior, saying: "It must occasion great regret that there should be so little spirit in an English audience as to permit what may be deemed a handful of boys, to treat them with so much insult and indignity, without making them severely feel the effects of their resentment . . . the tame sufferance of the audience at so gross an outrage exhibits a lamentable degeneracy in British spirit. The lamps fell upon the musicians. Some of the glass flew into the pit; but though thus insulted, not an individual had resolution enough to make the least attempt to repel so offensive an outrage." [36]

By March 17 the new ballet, *Les Jalousies du sérail* was shown. The *Post* told of its beautiful scenery, but said that the ballet itself was "hardly worthy of the great reputation of Noverre." The *Post*, however, was kind to Didelot, saying that Louis Nivelon, who also danced in it, "found a powerful competition in Didelot, who never shone with more *éclat*." The newspaper added that Nivelon "was not much improved since he was last in London." [37] On March 31 Londoners saw Didelot in a new allegorical ballet of Noverre called *Admète*.[38]

By April Gallini had engaged a ballerina who more than assuaged the tempers of the British balletomanes—the forty-six-year-old Madeleine Guimard, who shortly was to retire from the stage to enter on a long period of marital bliss. In her first appearance on April 28 Didelot had the pleasure of dancing with Guimard in the Minuet from Cherubini's *Iphigenia in Aulide* as well as in a new *Pas de Deux anacréontique* composed by Noverre. At the end of the program, they danced a new pantomime ballet, *Annette et Lubin*, also by Noverre. The press related that it was rare to have expectation of artistic treats so thoroughly gratified, and though Guimard was "by no means in the meridian of life," her dancing was "fraught with lightness, elegance, agility, and expression," and she had fired her partners "who never exerted themselves with so much spirit and effect." [39] The press begrudgingly accorded Didelot and some of the other dancers a bit of praise, while again Guimard, called the "grandmother of the Graces," received sufficient acclaim to lure the queen to attend a performance. In view of recent disturbances, Her Majesty had two sentinels posted at each avenue leading to the stage—an unusual prohibition, which according to the *Post*, "very highly disgusted John Bull, who seemed to think that he was conveyed into France, and murmured very strongly against this military intrusion." [40] All the murmuring against this insulting disregard of the rights of Englishmen was unheeded, however, by the queen, for her sentries stayed until she retired.

On June 18 there was scheduled a benefit that was to be quite special—"an entertainment of singing and dancing as performed with universal applause at the Court of Petersburg, called *Il sogno di Rinaldo*." Didelot and Guimard were to perform, along with others of the ballet troupe. While rehearsing a new ballet, *Le Tuteur trompé*, between ten and eleven o'clock in the evening of June 17, balls of fire dropped upon the stage immediately over the orchestra. Though many engines came to the rescue with abundant water, the avenues to King's

Theatre were so incommodious that the engines were ineffective, and the fire died more from a consumption of the materials than from attempts to extinguish it. A large and valuable quantity of manuscript music, as well as theatrical properties were destroyed.[41] On June 27 the company of King's Theatre moved to Covent Garden to resume their performances, where they were able to give divertissements and the ballet *L'Embarquement pour Cythère*, with Didelot dancing in both of them. The fire had done little to soften the antipathy of Londoners; they hissed during almost the whole of *Cythère*.[42] On June 30 Didelot danced in two divertissements. At the beginning of the first one, members of the gallery began to clamor for Guimard, who sat in the pit ready to dance only if the manager would meet her conditions. This time the clamorers were removed from the house. During the second ballet, partisans of the manager tried to show double approbation of the performance by applauding vehemently even the lowliest *figurante*.[43] The disastrous season thus ended on a happier note for Didelot, for the *Post* admitted that he and Pauline Duquesnay were particularly distinguished in their July 4 performance. However, the *Post* also reported that since the stage of Covent Garden was becoming as crowded with intruders as the Opera House had been, probably "puppyism would be triumphant there as in the original fops alley." [44] To the relief of many, and not the least to Didelot, the season ended on July 11, 1789.

After such a harrowing year, Didelot was only too happy to shake the dust of London from his feet, but news coming from Paris forestalled testing his fate again there. Many dancers were already fleeing the city, now being sucked into the whirlpool of revolution.

Didelot could have gone to Stockholm. Indeed, Gustav III was still on his trail. Gustav wrote to his roving theatrical administrator, Gust M. Armfelt, on July 15 that he had read that the London theater had burned and that no doubt the commitments of the dancers ceased when this happened. Thus, Didelot should be made to return home as soon as possible, because he did not see any reason for paying him while he danced in London. Armfelt replied on July 20 that Didelot had received precise orders to return by September 1.[45] Didelot, however, had other ideas: he never returned to the Stockholm troupe.

A subsequent Swedish dispatch declared that sometime before November 5, 1789, Didelot was married.[46] If this is true there is no indication that his wife accompanied him on the next stage of his odyssey, which took him not to Sweden, but to Bordeaux.

CHAPTER III

Faux Pas in Bordeaux

THE city to which Didelot turned after his miserable London months in normal times could have revivified spirits depressed from any cause. Bordeaux then was the first port in France. Ships swollen with the wealth of the Antilles emptied their cargoes of sugar, indigo, coffee, cocoa, and mahogany along her grand wharves. The surrounding land, ancient Aquitaine, had in ages past often provoked warfare between English and French monarchs, who mutually coveted the neat, golden wheat fields, the vineyards yielding abundant, sparkling wine both to gladden the heart of the Bordelais and to swell again the hulks headed anew for colonial ports.[1] The flamboyant ruler of the Province of Guienne, Le Maréchal de Richelieu, had decided that Bordeaux was to have a worthy theater. Sparing no pains to make it outstanding, Richelieu commissioned the architect Louis-Nicolas Louis to produce a civic cultural center. Louis' elegant building, graced by a façade of twelve columns, was erected at a cost approaching two and one-half million francs. (*Fig. 2*) Seeing it, jealous Parisians murmured, "It is too beautiful for a province,"[2] while an English visitor once made an unkind comparison: "L'Opéra de Paris est un parvenu, et le Grand Théâtre de Bordeaux un gentilhomme."[3] The dimensions of the stage approached those of the present Bolshoi Theater of Moscow.

The citizens of Bordeaux were passionate balletomanes. When Didelot arrived the chief balletmaster was none other than Dauberval, his beloved master, whose recent extravagant activities had even more drawn the attention of the citizens to ballet. Dauberval indeed had high standards for his art, declaring, "I conceive that a multiplicity of decorations and of mechanical effects can dazzle a multitude; but I dare to disdain this means when it does not hold essentially to the subject; I deal with pantomime and the dance; I wish to leave all the honor of

Figure 2. Le Grand-Théâtre de Bordeaux designed by the architect Victor Louis and constructed at the end of the eighteenth century. *Courtesy of the Syndicat d'Initiative, Bordeaux.*

success to these two arts; it is not sufficient for me to please the eyes, I wish to interest the heart." [4] Noverre himself, proudly referred to Dauberval as "my pupil, who fought constantly against prejudice, the commonplace, and bad taste." [5]

Dauberval had wed a dancer named Marie-Madeleine Crespé, who was known simply as Madame Théodore (*Figs. 3 and 4*). Her tastes were as elegant as those of her spouse. She was a true woman of the French Enlightenment, known to some as *le philosophe des coulisses*. Originally she had strong doubts about embracing a theatrical career, and was said to have written to the philosopher Jean-Jacques Rousseau to inquire how she should order her life in a fitting manner upon the stage. [6] Even Rousseau, who often seemed so sure that he knew the answers to most of the world's problems, responded that he was unable to counsel her in this matter. Théodore's subsequent writings and actions betray that she remained a true disciple of Rousseau, believing, as he did, in the nobility of the uncorrupted savage. In the Bibliothèque de la Ville de Bordeaux resides a pamphlet written by her—certainly one of the strangest pieces ever to be penned by a dancer. Théodore had visited a ship carrying some Indian Moslems, installed at the Bordeaux wharf. On the boat they had been dealt with harshly by Christians, she felt, so the humanitarian dancer took upon herself the task of writing a pamphlet to be offered for sale about them so that she might use the profits to relieve the financial plight of the Indians. In her eyes, *they* were the noble savage exalted by Rousseau. After telling of their trance dances and their ability to puncture their skin without bleeding, she described a visit these good men made to the theater. At that time James D'Egville, an English dancer then employed at Bordeaux, had shown the Moslems a certain Mademoiselle Rochette, and D'Egville had asked their chief if he would not like to embrace Rochette. The chief had answered politely, "It is not our custom," adding, "If a woman is not our wife, we only say '*salem*' (*bon jour*)." Madame Théodore was edified by their self control, marvelling, "Il faut être bien chaste pour refuser d'embrasser la jolie Rochette." [7]

In Bordeaux during these cataclysmic years there was a citizen named Pierre Bernadau who spent long hours in his study painstakingly recording and commenting on all the local news he thought might interest posterity. His voluminous notes are a precious historical source. While revolutionary tremors rocked France, Bernadau disgustedly noted that "the show-woman (*la saltimbanque*) Théodore has had the

Figure 3. Jean Dauberval and Madame Théodore Dauberval. *Courtesy of the Bibliothèque Municipale, Bordeaux.*

Figure 4. Madame Dauberval, an oil painting by Lonsing in the collection of the Baronne de Gervain.

audacity to have a medallion made of herself, like an empress (*Fig. 5*)."
Around her picture was the motto *Honorer les talens que la vertu décore
c'est rendre hommage à Théodore*. However, Bernadau himself, whose
chief delight seemed to be to ferret out scandal, begrugingly admitted
that Théodore was "one of our fashionable women about whom
scandalous chronicles keep silent." [8]

Noverre called Théodore "the image of Terpsichore," saying she
had ease, facility, and brilliance. Her *balloon* rendered her execution so
light that even without leaping, only by the elasticity of her insteps, she
seemed no longer to touch the floor.[9]

After leaving the Opéra in 1783 the Daubervals were too young, too
creative, and too accustomed to a large income to enjoy their period of
inactivity. When an offer came to head the Bordeaux ballet, they
accepted. Dauberval, born in Bordeaux, had worked in the Grand
Théâtre early in his career, having produced *Le Déserteur* there in 1772.
Being an excellent hunter, Dauberval soon became a leading *gentilhomme* in the fashionable society of Bordeaux, fitting in well with the
class of men there who regularly sent their dress linen to the colonies to
be laundered because the tropical sun bleached it just a shade whiter.[10]

At the Bordeaux theater Dauberval was able to create works which
he never would have been allowed to produce in Paris. A creditable
critic, Carlo Blasis, remarked that during his stay in France, he noticed
that the best pantomime performers came from provincial theaters.
"They were more industrious," he said, "and their stock of pieces was
greater than at the capital. . . . At Bordeaux, Marseilles, and Lyons
every ballet that has succeeded is performed; at Paris, on the contrary,
only those are performed that have been introduced by private interest
and favour," meaning the ballets of the Gardels.[11]

In February of 1785 the debonair Théodore made her debut in her
spouse's first production at Bordeaux, *Le Bonheur est d'aimer*. However,
their life was anything but peaceful thereafter. Their days were blighted
by the same sort of low, theatrical cabals which had driven them from
their positions at the Opéra—and certainly in both places, Jean
Dauberval was a bit more than a passive victim of intrigue. Actually,
many problems stemmed from the fact that the Grand Théâtre suffered
continual financial problems, and Dauberval had to fight not only for his
luxurious salary of twenty-eight thousand livres, but for the funds to
produce his ballets. The Bordelais, in turn, were no more long suffering
than Londoners had been. In October of 1787 the management spoke of

Figure 5. Madame Dauberval, from an engraving in the Archives Municipales, Bordeaux.

releasing Théodore for want of funds. The public became irate and during a performance showed their feelings by beginning to dance themselves and chanting *rondeaux*. After that the city fathers saw fit to grant the necessary funds.[12] By 1788 good manners and tolerance were completely out of mode among the "conceited, quarrelsome, and immoral" youth of the city. It was fashionable to arrive at the theater intoxicated, to molest the occupants of the loges, and to throw nails on the stage during the ballets.[13] This was actually done by a discontented observer in mid-February of 1788. A week later Dauberval was ready to present his new ballet, *Psyché*. The audience, impatient to see it, did not like the preceeding number and showed it by tearing off the doors of the loges. On the stage, during the performance, a thoroughly discombobulated devil, while attempting to *cabriole* lost control of his torch, which sailed into the parterre and burnt the coiffures of some spectators.[14]

To add to all the disturbances that erupted from a jittery French society, real problems beset Dauberval when a certain native of the city returned to seek a career as dancer upon the Bordeaux stage. This was the mercurial Chevalier Peicam, who made his reentrance with customary fanfare and flourish. According to Bernadau Peicam was at the time a pensioner of the court of Modena (Italy). On September 20, 1788, a fulsome letter appeared in the local *Journal de Guienne*, signed by Peicam. He was returning to his native city after seven years, he said, "to offer to my citizens the respectful homage of my feeble talents, to admire those of the grand-master [Dauberval] and to gather his advice." He was presenting two works of his own: *Les Plaisirs de la campagne*, a pastoral divertissement, and *Le Naufrage des Français, ou Les Corsairs vaincus*, a ballet pantomime.

Peicam somehow succeeded in winning fervent partisans who, comparing his genius to that of Vestris, agitated forcefully to keep him at the theater. However, in Bernadau's judgment, which resembled that of later critics, Peicam was "a cabrioler, noisily announced, whose talents were practically nill." In his view the two ballets displayed "neither taste nor verity, nor knowledge of the theater." Bernadau also noted that it was bruited about that Dauberval detested him.[15]

In the midst of the tension mounting between Peicam and Dauberval, Théodore had her little problems too. She had lost her beloved cuddly lap dog with a reddish brown spot on its tail and on each ear. In a long letter to the *Journal de Guienne* she bemoaned her great loss. "That which affects me the most, Monsieur," she explained, "is that my little dog is subject to a thousand infirmities, and it is necessary by the most great care to forestall them." She promised not only a reward of two louis, but added that if it was the beauty of the animal which tempted some cruel purloiner, the thief would be assured of the first little pup which would be born to her *petite bichonne*. Her letter evoked gales of laughter in the town, and was even eulogized in poetry in the *Journal de Guienne*.[16] However there were greater troubles on the horizon for the couple. In December of 1788 a ballet named *Dorothée* by Dauberval was so unsuccessful that extensive changes had to be made in it—which scarcely relieved the boredom of it in Bernadau's eyes.[17] On February 12, 1789, the audience was deprived of the ballet which normally terminated Grétry's comic opera, *La Rosière de Salency*. This provoked open revolt from the spectators. Dauberval came forward on the stage to defend himself, but some spectators yelled, "Keep quiet," while others whistled and tossed apples at his head. To calm the public Dauberval reassembled some of his dancers to execute steps to bizarre airs.[18]

While Dauberval's luck seemed to wane, his adversary Peicam went busily about building a little power base of his own. Dauberval had little to fear from him as an artistic rival, but what Peicam lacked in talent he could compensate by intrigue. The Bordeaux theatrical public divided into *Peicamistes*, chiefly in the parterre, and *Daubervalistes*, who occupied the more expensive loges. Dauberval tried to force the director not to hire Peicam for the coming season, at the same time that he levelled demands for a salary of thirty thousand livres for himself, with a promise that he could control the company without interference from lesser officials. Peicam's partisans then turned to brute tactics. One spring evening four unknown men accosted Dauberval under the peristyle of the Grand Théâtre to ask if he really opposed the hiring of Peicam. Further, they wanted a written response from him within four hours. In the face of such intimidating tactics, as well as more disruptive conduct from the parterre, the director hired Peicam, whereupon Dauberval, temporarily defeated, left Bordeaux. The matter of Peicam's conduct did not rest there however; word reached the court of King Louis XVI, who responded April 4, 1789, with a beautifully inscribed *lettre de cachet* exiling Peicam at least twenty leagues from Bordeaux.[19] Incensed to a high pitch at this new monarchical thrust, the *Peicamistes* then threatened to use their clubs on anyone who attended a theatrical performance in the Grand Théâtre. However, Bernadau assured his diary that "the menace intimidated no one." [20]

Once Peicam was gone the self-imposed exile of Dauberval did not last too long. Bernadau cycnically observed that "the love of money triumphed over delicacy in the heart of the Dauberval couple. He has reappeared in Bordeaux, which he called a detestable city, and which he said he was leaving with joy." He noted also that Madame Théodore never had harvested such applause as when she appeared in *Annette et Lubin* in her initial appearance after the return to Bordeaux. Disgusted, Bernadau berated the audiences's softness, saying, "I blush for you, my benign compatriots." [21]

Dauberval's career reached its apogée at this time, for on July 1, 1789, he brought forward his most enduring work, *Le Ballet de la paille*, which was to bring delight to audiences almost two centuries later in London, Paris, Moscow, and Peking under the name *La Fille mal gardée* or *Vain Precautions*. The ballet dramatized a high point in the history of France. Feudalism was toppling; the Third Estate of middle class citizens had asserted its power over the nobility and the church, promising themselves that they would form a constitution for France. At the end of the ballet couplets about these contemporary events were sung, based upon the refrain *Il ne faut désesperer de rien, il n'est qu'un pas du mal au bien*, the latter half of which became a part of the ballet's French title. During the repast of the harvesters in the ballet, the first dancer gave a salute to the Third Estate. The toast was applauded frantically and the ballet enjoyed great success.[22]

As revolutionary events rolled forward on their inexorable course, it became more important to listen to the demands of the parterre in French theaters—no doubt altering Dauberval's attitude toward Peicam. As the tide of revolution swelled, Peicam had much in his favor, for he was a victim of despotic government. He had suffered from a hated *lettre de cachet*, an instrument of monarchical despotism which reformers of the day were determined to crush. Whatever prompted him to write it, a letter of Dauberval to Peicam in neat, rhythmic script still lies in the Bordeaux archives, telling the latter that he did not object to Peicam's return to Bordeaux and firmly denying being the cause of Peicam's exile. In gnarled script, lacking the facility of expression of Dauberval, Peicam then wrote to the French secretary of state, asking to be allowed to return to Bordeaux, signing the letter "First dancer of the Académie Royale de Musique." [23] Peicam's efforts were at last rewarded, and he was eventually allowed to return to Bordeaux, performing in Dauberval's *Le Déserteur* on October 10. The press, reviewing the performance, commented on his svelte build, his interesting figure, his grace, intelligence, and sensibility in the perform- ance of the pantomime.[24]

Such was the train of unhappy events that preceded the arrival of Didelot in Bordeaux in the fall of 1789. It is not hard to picture the emotional Frenchman's kiss on each cheek during the meeting between Dauberval and his chauvinistic pupil. Didelot appeared on October 21, 1789, in a new divertissement by his master and then in the ballet, *Amphion, élève des muses*. The press warmly praised Didelot's build, his grace, aplomb, precision, ease, and lightness. Not satisfied with its initial generous praise, on the following day the *Journal de Guienne* printed another review of Didelot's performance, emphasizing his great dexterity, mellowness, and precision.[25] The sour Bernadau took a dim view of Didelot's debut: he complained that Didelot's attitudes were forced, that he lacked ease, showed no expression in his physiogonomy, and in general had a physique too strongly pronounced for the delicate and sentimental subjects he portrayed. Bernadau berated the *Journal* for overdoing its praise, remarking: "To men without taste, all is sublime or tedious. We have remarked," he said, "that in it there was no denouement, and the mythological title which the ballet carries is only erudite charlatanry on the part of the composer." [26] *Amphion*, however, must have pleased the public, for it played ten times in the 1789–1790 season, ceding in popularity only to *Le Bonheur est d'aimer*, and *Il n'ya qu'un pas*, which ran eleven times.[27]

As the months passed, the Bordeaux theater, like theaters all over France, increasingly reflected revolutionary passions and sentiments. However, at this point the revolution was still in a moderate stage, and though nobles had denounced their feudal privileges in the summer months, Louis XVI was still the reigning monarch. Further, Dauberval still had many royal friends whose heads would later roll in the streets of Paris during the time the radical Jacobin terrorists were to control the revolution in 1793. On January 4, 1790, Dauberval presented a new work called *Le Ballet national*, which depicted the king and queen carrying their son the dauphin, "surrounded by numerous people prostrate with love at their feet, contrasting with officers and soldiers of the national guard who, in a warlike posture, formed with their naked shields a rampart of steel around that precious family for which they were prepared to shed their blood." [28]

In March of 1790 Didelot performed a *pas de deux* entitled *Sylvie* with Madame Dauberval. The *Journal de Guienne* enthusiastically praised their performance in verse, saying that even a mediocre talent would be electrified by Madame Théodore, but Didelot's talent was worthy in itself. Its critic emphasized Didelot's outstanding grace, suppleness, his intelligent and animated pantomime, adding that "the first subjects of the dance have made new efforts and deployed new talents to underline the ingenious production of the composer [Dauberval] which make us love each day more that part of our performances." [29] This was one of the last columns praising the Daubervals, for they left Bordeaux in April for travels taking them to Spain and England. As for Peicam, he still was fighting in April of 1790 for a job with the company, which had again refused to rehire him. In that month he circulated a printed four page *Mémoire* advertising to the populace his plea. An attorney carefully prepared his case, pompously supporting his claim to a job in the Bordeaux ballet with pedantic Latin legal maxims and quotes from the work entitled *De Jure Belli et Pacis* of the eminent legalist Grotius.[30] Apparently, not even the authority of Grotius could convince the management of the theater to retain him, for he was not numbered in the cast for 1790–1791. During this season Didelot became acquainted with a more successful dancer, Salvatore Viganò, who joined the ballet troupe with his wife Maria Medina. The position of balletmaster, vacated by Dauberval, was taken by Eugène Hus, who founded the first school of dance at the Grand Théâtre.[31]

In June Hus presented his version of Maximilien Gardel's ballet *Le Premier Navigateur*. The press tactfully remarked that they "could not pretend that the execution had left nothing to be desired by spectators accustomed to the astonishing precision of M. Dauberval." However, they agreed that "M. Didelot rendered the principal role with that grace which accompanies all his movements." [32]

The army of the French patriots waged war against foreign enemies of the revolution in the summer of 1790. When they returned victorious, public sentiment found expression in a solemn, emotion-packed performance of a work called *La Partie de chasse de Henri IV*. Like many revolutionary spectacles it was composed of chants and dances, interrupted to give a toast or perhaps to crown a current hero who might be in attendance. Didelot and a male dancer, Monsieur Rochefort, danced a *pas de quatre* with two mesdemoiselles named Granger and Chouchoux. Their appearance was warmly applauded. The press remarked in general that the dances had such elegance and variety that one would not suspect the speed with which they had been prepared.[33] It was a harrowing time for choreographers such as Eugène Hus who were called upon to compile works on short notice to commemorate victories or to rouse the population to support an issue which a ruling clique of the moment might wish to have propagandized.

In July when *Premier Navigateur* was given for the fifth time, the press was ecstatic over the ballet in general but particularly over Didelot's part in it, saying, "M. Didelot, for a long time in possession of the esteem of the public, has deployed in this ballet all the brilliant means nature has so prodigally endowed him. His suave and gracious manner, always engaging, always applauded, proves that art has not depraved the work of nature. It seems that nothing can be added to the charm of his execution, not having here . . . any rival to fear. M. Didelot will not lose view of the fact, without doubt, that the flattering reception which he continually receives from the public must excite him to attain the degree of perfection to which his talents seem destined to us." [34] In the summer of 1790 Didelot was given a chance to stage the ballets for the opera *Chimène*. His joy at the chance was blighted by the jealousy of his collaborators. After the initial performance he received an anonymous letter, which he promptly sent to the local *Journal de Guienne* with a refutation of its contents. The letter read: "As it is just to render to each person his due, M. Didelot should, the second time that *Chimène* is given, have the printer substitute for his name, that of Mr. Nivelon, the true composer of the charming *pas de trois* danced to the air and variations of the *Folies D'Espagne.*" Didelot begged the editor to insert his response, since he could not answer an anonymous letter. He said that he thought the editor would not refuse "a young *artiste* commencing his career the means to justify himself of a calumny which attacks his honor, his feeble talents, and above all, his respect for a public which deigns to honor him with its good will."

Didelot explained:

The air and the variations of the *Folies D'Espagne* belong to every poet, artist, or composer who wishes to avail himself of them. That pretty production was at first rendered in dance in London by

Monsieur Le Picq, whose rare talents are known. Not having ever had the pleasure of knowing him . . . nor even of seeing him dance, I could not then be his copyist.

At Paris, M. Nivelon, whom they accuse me of aping, mounted alternately a *pas de trois* on the air of *Folies D'Espagne* in the opera of *Le Roi Théodore* and in *Chimène*. Monsieur Hus the father, wishing to avail himself also of the same in this opera, offered to let me mount the dance of Nivelon, but since each dancer has his manner of feeling and executing, I believed, without wishing to insult the talents of the Parisian author, whose merit is generally recognized, that I could try, while following the lessons and the principles of a great master, (M. Dauberval) also compose a *pas de trois* to the air, which alone has caused the indiscreet anonymous note. That person who gave this opinion, without having the goodness to designate who he was, should have awaited the execution of the dance which is in question; then he would have seen that I am not culpable of plagarizing, and he would have without doubt participated in the infinite pleasure I felt while the public had the goodness to encourage me.

I would have kept silence on this bagatelle, if it did not attack so strongly the sentiment of respectful gratitude with which I am penetrated for the public. . . . Several persons who know the dance of Nivelon and mine can attest to the truth that I advance.

Didelot [35]

There were other indications that all was not completely well for Didelot in Bordeaux. When Bernadau first introduced Didelot in his diary, he referred to him as a "pensioner of the King of Sweden." Didelot would have liked to forget that this was still his position. As word filtered through to the court of Sweden about his accomplishments, King Gustav became more agitated about his long absence. On October 31, 1788, he wrote to A. N. Clewberg (Edelcranz), who later became head of the Stockholm Royal Academy of Music: "I am going to write to Baron de Staël to reclaim Didelot. He is my subject, born in Sweden, educated at my expense, engaged in my service, and in every respect I have rights over him. The directorship must write to Paris to make him return. . . ." [36]

While Didelot proceeded to grace the boards of stages in London and Bordeaux, Gustav III remained equally resolved to snare his stormy petrel so that his talents could once again adorn the Stockholm Academy. Edelcranz journeyed about Europe in 1790, explaining to his monarch that during the long voyage he could perhaps "trap the fugitive Didelot." [37] Didelot was equally anxious to evade him, but the adamant Edelcranz seemed to enjoy an excuse for more sightseeing. He explained to Gustav III on October 11, 1790:

> Since the dancer Didelot has not responded either to Baron de Staël nor to me, I set out for Bordeaux to find him. . . . Warned of my arrival and wanting, evidently, to avoid explaining things, he had spread the rumor that he had parted for Paris. It was by the merest chance and with great trouble that I deterred him and succeeded in speaking to him. He appeared very surprised and piqued that anyone would doubt an instant that he would return to Sweden, [saying] that he had been absent only by virtue of different leaves and extensions accorded him by the directorship or Baron de Staël. Finally, he had asked a new leave of the ambassador and had interpreted his silence as consent. He and his wife are engaged at London next year for eleven hundred guineas. I was stupefied at all his falsities, pretexts and stories with which he regaled me during the conversation, which was long enough. He finished by telling me that to prove his zeal for the service of His Majesty, he was entirely prepared to break his engagement in England and leave at the same moment if someone would pay the deficit of five hundred fifty guineas. . . . I could not obtain any other response from him, but I have an appointment with him in Paris fifteen days from now, where he wants to indicate his final decision. He is very much in debt here, in spite of the good conditions they gave him. He has quarreled with his comrades and has not danced at Bordeaux since four months. He complains a lot to the direction at Bordeaux, just as at Stockholm; to the Swedish consul; to almost everyone." [38]

Edelcranz was a bit wrong in his estimate of time, and in spite of Gustav's pursuits, Didelot's next employment was not to be in Stockholm, but in London. Edelcranz later wrote that sometime before December 16, 1790, Didelot made a trip to Paris on his way to England, and though he remained there eight days, he reported neither to Edelcranz nor to the Swedish ambassador.[39]

Probably Didelot went to Paris to rejoin his wife, for she had been climbing steadily to fame there. By 1789, Rose had passed from the ranks of *remplaçants* to become a *premier sujet*.[40] On December 14, 1790, Rose played the part of Terpsichore in Pierre Gardel's highly successful ballet *Psyché,* with Auguste Vestris dancing the role of

Amour. To the profound regret of the Parisians, this ballet soon had to be suspended for a time because of the absence of Rose and Vestris. Actually, Vestris, Rose, and Didelot had been lured to London. When *Psyché* was again staged in late January with replacements, the critic of the *Chronique de Paris* commented, "To replace Rose as Terpsichore was a perilous enterprise." [41]

As for Bordeaux, ballet continued to be popular, and in 1791 the citizens saw interesting productions directed by Hus, such as a *ballet d'action* in four acts, *La Mort du Capitaine Cook*. The scene took place, according to the *Journal patriotique*, on the famous island Cook discovered, O-Why-E.[42] Though treated to such exotic wonders, the Bordelais still nostalgically recalled the days of Dauberval, Théodore, and Didelot, while the local press at times poignantly noted their subsequent successes in London.[43]

CHAPTER IV

Revolutionary Ballet

W HEN Didelot left England in 1789, he probably did not anticipate returning soon to the audience which had treated him so shabbily. After the hectic months of living amidst petty theatrical intrigue and national revolt in France, however, an offer from the Pantheon Theatre in 1791 again beckoned to him from across the Channel. Besides, he felt things would be different; this time not only was his wife with him, but Dauberval and Théodore had also come to London. For the manager of the Pantheon, Robert Bray O'Reilly, it was to be a nightmarish year. The old King's Theatre, which burned down, reopened again at the Haymarket, headed by a determined manager, William Taylor. Consequently both the Pantheon and Haymarket Theatres felt they had special rights to royal patronage and to the peculiar privilege of calling themselves "King's Theatre." Taylor, it seems, had engaged his performers without determining whether they could obtain a license to perform. It was believed that proceedings against the Haymarket players were pending for an unlicensed dramatic performance. As Taylor was a protégé of Richard Brinsley Sheridan, the famous playwright and member of Parliament, the dispute became a *cause célèbre*, with the prince of Wales supporting the Haymarket Theatre and the Tories and George III backing the Pantheon. The whole situation was too ludicrous to escape the vitriolic pen of the caricaturists. Thomas Rowlandson issued two etchings entitled *The Prospect Before Us*, on January 13, 1791. In one the dancers and musicians of the Haymarket were shown as vagrant strolling players appealing for charity in the less distinguished neighborhoods of London. Just as begging sailors in England sometimes carried a model of their ship, one of the performers carried a model of their yet unfinished opera house. In the second Didelot and Théodore were shown dancing as Amphion and Thalia at the elegant Pantheon (*Fig. 6*). As Rowlandson viewed the performance from the back of the stage, he filled the picture with homely details. Pompous, high-wigged females leaned over boxes poised on the very stage itself. Heads and shoulders of the orchestra appeared behind the stage, while a very old man holding a 'cello put an ear trumpet to his ear. In the royal box, King George III, the theater's patron, peered through an opera glass, while the queen sat sedately.[1] Rowlandson was not the last artist to utilize the theme however.°

Figure 6. The Prospect Before Us, a cartoon of 1791 by Rowlandson depicting Didelot dancing with Madame Théodore in *Amphion and Thalia*, "Respectfully dedicated to those Singers, Dancers & Musical Professors, who are fortunately engaged with the Proprietor of the King's Theatre, at the Pantheon." *Courtesy of the British Museum, London.*

On February 17, 1791, O'Reilly presented the ballet *Amphion and Thalia*. In it, Didelot danced the part of Amphion, and Rose played the part of the Muse of Tragedy.[2] *The Morning Chronicle* dryly remarked that "on a stage deficient in space, and with only two dancers above mediocrity, to shorten must be to improve the ballet." The *Chronicle* further bemoaned the injustice of the fact that the Pantheon was being given crown patronage, and pointed out that never before had the audience been so sparse when their Majesties were present. *The*

° In the twentieth century Dame Ninette de Valois created a ballet entitled *The Prospect Before Us*, which commemorates the same grotesque affair.

Morning Post, on the contrary, reported that the ballet met with an uncommon amount of applause, and that Didelot had greatly improved.[3] Madame Rose was dropped from the bills by February 26.

On March 19 the Pantheon audience saw Dauberval's production of *Télémaque*. It was marred by the incompetency of the machinist, who failed to produce quick transitions of scenery, but the *Chronicle* was kind to the balletmaster, remarking that "a good workman is not answerable for the poverty of his tools." Further, its critic hailed the *pas seul* of Théodore and the *pas de deux* of Didelot and Théodore. Didelot was suffering from a wound in the heel, yet he still "exerted himself in a very uncommon degree." However, the *Chronicle* added that it would be idle to talk of their dancing in comparison with that of Vestris and Hilligsberg, who were presently performing at the competing Haymarket Theatre.[4] Dauberval proceeded to stage more of the ballets he had previously produced at Bordeaux, and Londoners soon saw *La Fille mal gardée*, *La Triomphe de la folie*, and *Le Siège de Cythère*. In the critics view, *Cythère* had such beautiful scenery and such appropriate dances, that it was hoped the siege would not very shortly be raised.[5] The season closed on July 19 with the ever popular *Fille*.

Didelot had finally won the respect of the London public, but he knew that success in London, though lucrative, was nothing in comparison to the status that acceptance in Paris might bring. He correctly sensed that the future of English ballet did not reside in the Pantheon, for it, too, burned to the ground on January 14, 1792. However, by that time Didelot had left London. When the management of the Paris Opéra unexpectedly presented him with an offer, Didelot hastened to France. On the advice of Dauberval he made his debut on the Paris stage on August 31, 1791, in the last act of *Le Premier Navigateur*, one of the more popular productions of Gardel. In it he partnered Madame Miller, whom Noverre praised as "the Venus de Medicis of the dance," from whose feet diamonds sprang forth.[6] Later, she became known as Madame Gardel. The *Chronique de Paris* affirmed that Didelot had enjoyed a decided success, that he showed a very distinguished talent for the serious genre, and that when his talent would have been fortified by the example of his rivals, then no doubt he would become one of the first dancers of Europe.[7] In November of 1791, when Didelot took his place in the dances of the opera *Diane et Endimion*, he joined a cast which the press hailed as uniting all perfection. On November 24 he danced the principal role in *Le*

Déserteur. The *Chronique de Paris* raved about his nobility and expressiveness, but added that he was somewhat inclined to exaggerate.[8]

By December 1 his beloved Rose appeared on the Paris stage after an absence unexplained to the Parisians of more than eight months. Perhaps she had suffered a miscarriage. Along with Didelot, she danced in the opera *Castor et Pollux*.[9] On December 29 she played Terpsichore again in Gardel's *Psyché*, which was attended by Marie Antoinette herself. Some thought it was scandalous that the queen should appear in public when France was on the verge of war with her brother's Austrian realm.[10]

Also, on December 11 Sébastien Gallet, a pupil of Noverre and a competent balletmaster, succeeded in winning a chance to stage the ballet *Bacchus et Ariadne*. Gallet had fought hard to break through the monopoly held by the ruling clique of the Opéra, and the ballet was a great success. However Gallet, like Noverre, could not stand the disagreeable state of affairs at the Opéra and soon took his talents elsewhere.[11] The *Mercure de France* commented that the performance of Didelot and his fellow dancers was veritably magical.[12] Further the costume which Didelot wore in *Bacchus et Ariadne* has numbered him among the ranks of the important innovators in dance costume. In eighteenth-century ballet, no matter what part the dancers portrayed, they customarily wore costumes modelled on the contemporary dress of the nobility, including buckled, heeled shoes, powdered wigs, farthingales or panniers for the women, and knee breeches for the men. It is true that others before Didelot had tried to reform stage costume. The dramatic actor Larive, who claimed to be the first to appear in the French theater in true classical Roman costume, said that as a result, he was treated as an "audacious rioter." [13] A regulation of 1714 forbade actors of the Opéra to change the required costume. Marie Sallé was one of the first dancers to appear in a Greek tunic, without hoops, with her hair gently flowing naturally, while appearing in *Pygmalion* in 1734. She also danced the part of Cupid in male habiliments.[14] However, these innovations remained her private, unimitated foibles at the time. Noverre preached the necessity of forsaking the hoops and farthingales and actually did so in such ballets as *La Toilette de Vénus*, in which dancers appeared dressed as fauns, without hoops.[15] However, lasting changes in costuming only became acceptable when the tide of revolt began eroding previously accepted canons in all phases of French life.

The revolutionary Committee of Public Safety commissioned the painter Jacques-Louis David to design costumes for the population of newly liberated France. Sketches by David, inspired by Greek and Roman models, were also used for costumes in mass theatrical pageants.

With such general reforms fomenting society, Didelot mustered sufficient courage in *Bacchus et Ariadne* to appear in flesh-colored tights, with a light tiger's skin thrown over his shoulder, grape leaves in his hair, and a staff of Bacchus in his hand.[16] During a performance of this ballet on December 19, 1791 Didelot suffered a sprain which kept him from performing many months.[17] By May, however, he was again dancing in the opera *Tarare*, and the *Chronique* welcomed his return because, they said, his talent was *si aimable*.[18] In July he and Rose were acclaimed for their part in the opera *Corisande*.[19] In it Didelot played the part of a sylph, and again dared to appear in a light gauzy tunic,[20] which was still novel enough both to shock and to delight a good part of the audience (*Fig. 7*). In this instance, his partner Mademoiselle Chévigny dared to appear also in a Greek-type costume, when the other women still wore their traditional farthingales. Before too long many members of the cast were converted to wearing tunics, togas, and sandals.

These years of revolutionary upheaval which Didelot passed in Paris were some of the most astounding and significant times in theatrical history. Many actors, dancers, and singers at the time had honest grievances against the old monarchy and actively supported the revolution. Under the French kings, performers who refused to act were subject to imprisonment. Dauberval and Auguste Vestris were once confined by a dreaded *lettre de cachet* in the For-L'Évêque, a famous Parisian confinement spot, for refusing to dance in the ballet *Armide* and for taking part in a charitable event sponsored by Madeleine Guimard. It seemed to royal authorities that Guimard was parodying a similar court project.[21] Such punishments were not at all uncommon. Théodore spent four days in the prison called La Force, for similar obstreporousness.[22]

Further, small theaters in general had great grievances against the *ancien régime*. A law of November 26, 1716 had granted to the pompous Opéra the privilege of selling rights to the use of music in popular theaters.[23] In June of 1769 letters patent made it necessary for theaters to apply to the director of the Opéra for permission to use

Figure 7. Watercolor of dancer in classical costume, possibly in the role of Zéphire. *Courtesy of Harvard Theatre Collection.*

music and dances. Audinot, for one, had to pay the Académie Royale an annual tribute of twelve thousand livres.[24]

Living under such conditions it is small wonder that the theatrical world welcomed the forces which promised to abolish this yoke. A law of January 13–19, 1791, declared that any citizen could erect a theater and present all types of performances, provided he notified the municipal authorities. Preventive censorship was abolished, but comedians and actors were still individually responsible for their actions on stage.[25]

For their part the people flocked to the theaters. Families divided into two groups: one part would stand in line for bread rations while the others queued up for the theater tickets.[26] The theater itself became a political arena, a schoolroom for instilling moral principles and political

Figure 8. Carmagnole during the French Revolution, from Charbonnel's *La Danse* (Garnier, Paris, 1916).

attitudes. Revolutionary leaders lived by the theory that "performances must purify morals, give lessons in civic duty; they must be a school of patriotism and virtue." [27] Actually, theaters became arenas where the deep cleavages between moderates and radicals became openly manifest. A play showing sympathy for the old regime would be jeered, and at times radical bands of hoodlums themselves invaded the stage singing revolutionary songs and dancing the carmagnole (*Fig. 8*). The moderate revolution of 1789 soon gave way to the tide of radical Jacobin terrorism, headed by Maximilien de Robespierre, which engulfed France in 1793–1794. Theaters then found that they had merely changed despotic masters. It was truly said, "The Terror makes the theater its accomplice. By it, the Terror injures those that it kills. By it, the Terror ridicules the armies that it fights. In its hands the theater becomes a tribune without decency or dignity . . . that swallows up in mire its enemies, still warm, while the populace applauds. . . ." [28] On August 2, 1793 the National Convention decreed that any theater which presented works tending to deprave the public or to awaken loyalty to the old regime should be closed and the director punished accordingly. Further, those dissenting against revolutionary terrorism could not hide behind a cloak of silence: three times a week there were to be presented works which depicted the glories of the revolution and the virtues of the defenders of liberty and equality. One such performance was to be given each week at the expense of the republic for the general populace.[29] Modern totalitarian governments which use theaters for propaganda have merely copied many of the devices used in revolutionary France, such as the employment of masses of extras for portraying the people as the moving force of the revolution. To accomplish the goals of instilling civic virtue and enthusiasm for revolution, the eighteenth-century French theater leaned chiefly toward the style of revolutionary classicism, where actors garbed in Grecian robes personified Liberty, Equality, Fraternity, or any virtue deemed worthy of emulation by the savants of the era. One observer compared an evening at the theater to attending a church service, because in the end all had to get down on their knees and intone a hymn to liberty in a drone-like chant.[30]

A typical performance at the Opéra in this revolutionary style was given October 2, 1792 by Pierre Gardel, a political weathercock who was sufficiently interested in holding his job to placate the demands of nine different changes of government.[31] Working with the composer François-Joseph Gossec, he produced a monumental vocal and choreographic staging of the "Marseillaise" in an event described as a *scène religieuse*. The production, entitled *Offrande à la Liberté*, utilized the large cast of the theater. The "Marseillaise" was chanted, with stirring pageantry inserted between couplets to ignite the patriotic fervor of the audience. At one point, the participants, including twenty well mounted cavaliers, all knelt before an actress portraying Liberté. Dances were staged to celebrate victories of the people in their struggles.[32]

After satisfying the ruling patriots with this work, Gardel produced one of his greatest ballets on March 6, 1793, *Le Jugement de Paris*. The *Gazette national* waxed eloquent over the work, declaring, "All that magnificent luxury, all that blissful imagination can conceive of grace and voluptuousness, all the marvels that the combined arts can produce and the most celebrated artists can execute most perfectly—all that went into the making of the ballet *Le Jugement de Paris*." [33] Didelot's performance in it, along with those of Vestris and Laborie, was styled "distinguished." The *Chronique de Paris* agreed, singling out as a chief adornment of the production the grace and nobility of Didelot and Rose.[34] However, this was to be one of their last triumphs at the Opéra during this stage of their careers. At this time Didelot did not enjoy great stature at the Opéra. In a list compiled in 1792 of the male dancers, headed by Gardel, Vestris, and Nivelon, Didelot was the last of the *remplaçants*.[35] It was probably with few regrets that he and his wife left the Opéra in 1793 to join an enterprise begun by a woman rare and intelligent for her day—Marguerite Brunet Montansier.

A notice dated August 15, 1793 in the *Journal de Paris* announced that "progress and a reasoned love of the art of the stage, have inspired the Citizeness Montansier and the Citizen Neuville to dare to erect a monument worthy of the majesty of the French." This was a vast, new beautiful theater built opposite the Bibliothèque Nationale on the rue Richelieu. It bore the name Théâtre National, and was intended for developing "tragedy, grand comedy, opera, dance, and grand panto-mime." [36] The splendid building by Louis, the same architect who built the Bordeaux theater, had Doric pillars, a marble foyer, and boxes with crimson and gold drapery. Much to Didelot's liking, there were no loges adjoining the stage. The press extolled the size and general facilities for the production of ballets.[37] This grand theater opened with a varied program which included *La Constitution à Constantinople*, described as a *pièce patriotique*, a divertissement of chant and dances. To modern tastes the plot was a strange mélange centered around an acceptance ceremony of the new French constitution in Constantinople, wherein a Mohammedan Turkish damsel strove and won the right to marry a Frenchman. In the tableau depicting the feast of acceptance of the constitution, there advanced on the stage eight horses attached to a triumphal chariot. On it the tables of the new law were placed, preceded by a calvalry corps, infantry, old people, mothers, and white robed virgins, who executed their march with wondrous precision. Above all this, however, the press extolled the troupe of fine dancers who performed a varied group of entries and steps under the inescapable Tree of Liberty. In particular, those "emigrés from the Opéra," Didelot, Rose, and Laborie, were praised for giving great pleasure to the audience, wherever they deployed their talents.[38]

On August 29, 1793 the theater presented another type of patriotic performance called *La Fête civique*, a divertissement in one act by Sébastien Gallet. Though his works were well received, it is significant that balletmaster Gallet received a salary of only twelve thousand livres, while Didelot and his wife received twenty thousand livres.[39] On October 5 an opera entitled *Selico, ou Les Negres* was presented. It was based on a revolutionary plot, newly published by a certain Citizen Florian. Coindé composed the ballets to the music of Mengozzi, while the lyrics were by the revolutionary leader Louis de Saint-Just. The press declared that the decisive factor in the success of the opera was the terminating ballet, in which Didelot, Laborie, Rochefort, and Rose displayed their suppleness and grace. The ballet was subsequently given, detached from the opera, under the title *La Liberté des negres*.[40]

The very success of Montansier's venture, combined with the fact that important actors from the large theaters were being lured to her troupe, helped determine her downfall. Further, the spacious beautiful theater stirred the jealousy of the Opéra, which for twelve years had resided in a less commodious building on the boulevard Saint-Martin. Robespierre, too, felt the Opéra should have this new theater. It thus happened that on November 14, 1793 Robespierre's henchman Anaxagoras Chaumette rose in a meeting of the Commune of Paris, saying, "I denounce the citizeness Montansier for having built the theater in order to start a fire at the Bibliothèque Nationale." Others then rose to frame a case against the proprietress. They said that Marie Antoinette contributed to the cost of the building, that Montansier had connived with General Dumoriez, one of the revolutionary army officers who had defected to fight with Austria against the republic, subsequently leading an army against revolutionary France. Montansier, it was said, had also decredited the value of the revolutionary currency, the assignats, by charging double the price for tickets bought with assignats compared with those purchased for silver currency. For all these transgressions, Montansier's detractors declared, she should be arrested as a *femme suspect*. Further, there would be no passports issued to the performers of the company until they had passed the purifying scrutiny of the Conseil Générale.[41] Fourty-eight hours later Montansier's theater was closed and she and her partner Neuville were arrested.[42] The building itself was given to the Opéra and was renamed the Théâtre des Arts. On November 19 Chaumette announced to the Commune that the closing of Montansier's theater had reduced a group of good citizens to mendacity.[43] On his recommendation they were allowed to reopen in a theater constructed for the Comédie-Française, whose troupe had been incarcerated since September of 1793. After Montansier's cast agreed that they would not use any *grand feux* in their productions, and would submit to constant censure by the Conseil, the theater opened under the title Théâtre de l'Egalité in the new building in the faubourg Saint-Germain. The theater operated under a Society of Artists made up of certain members of the company, such as Didelot, Gallet, and

Coindé, who drew up a charter establishing a type of primitive communistic rule for the company.[44] Didelot and the other dancers were abashed when they saw their new quarters, and wrote a formal letter protesting the small stage they had inherited, which was inadequate for performing the large ballets designed for Montansier's building. In answer to the protest signed by Didelot, Rose, Gallet, Laborie, and others, promises were made to them of expanding it, but the company had to open in their new quarters June 27, 1794, making the best of facilities which were quite incommodious.[45]

Mundt's Russian biography of Didelot declares that the whole troupe of Montansier was jailed temporarily. There is no evidence for this in French sources. Sébastien Gallet, Laborie, and Coindé had the decency to sign a petition to try to free Montansier. Didelot and others of the cast did not risk antagonizing the powerful Jacobins. When an attempt was made against the life of Robespierre the artists of the Théâtre de l'Egalité sent the following declaration to him:

> Liberty, equality, fraternity or death!
>   The artists of the Théâtre de l'Egalité as representing the people to Robespierre:
> Permit the artists, always mindful of the important services that you render to our common motherland share the frightful sadness they experienced at the first news of your assassination. You will easily be convinced of our profound and vibrant joy when we learned that Providence, protector of all happy destinies, has preserved you, so necessary to the health of the Republic, from the hand of parricides. Accept this feeble tribute of our recognition and be assured that there is not one of us who would not want to be your protector if the least danger would seem to menace you again.
>   Long live the Republic and its defenders!
>   Signed,
>   Didelot, Gallet, and other artists of the
>   Théâtre de l'Egalité.[46]

In the margin of the document, Robespierre inscribed scornfully: "Flatterers."

While Montansier languished in irons the cast proceeded to charm the Parisian audience with such works as the ballet by Gallet, *La Journée de l'Amour*. The production, styled an anacreontic divertissement, brought to life a painting entitled *Le Serment d'Aimer* by Fragonard. In it Love descends from Olympus to spend a day on earth, arriving in a country experiencing a Golden Age. The people erect a temple to Love, in whose outer court lovers come to swear eternal fidelity. A hunter, rebelling against Love, tries to upset his altar, but the god overpowers his adversary, pierces his enemy with an arrow and returns in triumph to Olympus. The *Journal de Paris* was prodigal with praise of the brilliant execution by Didelot, Rose, and Laborie. The *Journal des Théâtres* expressed the regret that the three artists had abandoned the Théâtre des Arts (the Opéra) and had isolated themselves at the moment when the interests of art demanded that they should draw more closely together with their comrades. Gallet, too, enjoyed well earned moments of triumph when the audience applauded warmly and demanded his appearance.[47] Ticket sales were good, with the house often sold out at an early hour. In short, during the summer of 1794, Montansier's theater was thriving while its owner spent her days in prison, furiously writing letters to right the injustice that had been dealt her.

The same summer saw the end of the harsh rule of the Jacobins in Paris, with Robespierre finally falling a victim on July 27, 1794, to the revolution he had excited to its highest pitch. When the titan fell many political prisoners were finally freed, among them Montansier and Neuville, who fell weeping into each other's arms after their release on September 16, 1794.[48] However, in spite of its successes, the theater itself was forced to close in December of 1794 and Didelot had to find employment elsewhere.

Didelot and Rose next were engaged to perform in Lyon, which considered itself second only to Paris as a center of French culture. Didelot's earliest teacher Frossard was born in Lyon and had been balletmaster there in 1784–1785, even organizing a troupe of about forty children under the title L'Ambigu-Comique.[49] When Didelot came to town the chief balletmaster was also a native son of the town and coworker of Didelot's in Paris—Coindé. Didelot and Rose appeared in Coindé's version of *La Siège de Cythère*, at the Théâtre des Terreaux in September of 1795. The *Journal de Lyon* was delighted with many aspects of the production, judging it to be worthy of the second city of the republic. Weariness with the rudeness of the radical fringe of their society, which by now had lost its political grip of the country, was evidenced in the paper's comment that the ballet was "enriched . . . by the rare talents of Monsieur Didelot and Mademoiselle Rose Paul, which the parterre, emerging from a long period of vandalism, does not perhaps appreciate enough." [50]

At Lyon Didelot finally had his chance on a French stage to produce a one-act ballet of his own, entitled *La Métamorphose*. This was the seminal work which blossomed in later years under other titles—*Zéphire et Flore*, or *Zéphyr inconstant*. As if seeking a refuge from revolutionary strife, he used a form completely divorced from contemporary life—the anacreontic. In the last half of the eighteenth and early years of the nineteenth century, the anacreontic genre had become an approved and admired popular art form. The poetry of Anacreon, of sixth century Grecian fame, had extolled a life where wine and love were the only treasures worth seeking, with the idyllic pursuit of them usually occurring in sylvan dales or dreamy meadows. The tenor of an anacreontic ode was blissfully carefree:

> Now with roses we are crown'd,
> Let our mirth and cups go round,
> Whilst a lass, whose hand a spear
> Branch'd with ivy twines doth bear,
> With her white feet beats the ground
> To the lute's harmonious sound[51]

It was not difficult to convey this aura of Elysian delectation in ballets; Noverre himself laid down artistic canons for it. "Anacreontic ballet demands varied scenes, agreeable situations and tableaux. Sentiment and love must sketch them; ingenuous grace must paint them; all must be light in these ballets, and bear the character of delicate pleasure and of artless love." [52]

In his new work Didelot acknowledged Ovid as his inspiration. Actually, he had planned a more spectacular ballet but it could not be presented because there was not sufficient time to prepare adequate machinery. Unfortunately, the programs of the envisaged production had already been prepared. In the prologue to the program, Didelot articulated several points of his artistic credo. First of all, he declared his intention to develop the art of mime. He believed that by mime one could question and respond in ballet, and in this respect he affirmed "I search to instruct myself." Further, he believed in forcing ballet artists to try to discover expressions and gestures to depict the written word, and by thus obliging the artists to search for means of expression, he felt the art could naught but gain.

He stated his implicit belief that ballet could teach moral lessons, declaring, "Finally, I wanted to convey [in *La Métamorphose*] the idea that misfortunes were almost always the lot of a man carried away by his passions, that a woman who loves you for yourself is a precious treasure, and a passionate and disordered youth is often only a morning storm which the most beautiful of days follows." [53]

He tried to forestall criticism of the costumes, which no doubt followed earlier styles he himself had worn in Paris, declaring: "If someone criticizes the innovations in the costume of my satyrs, I will only reply a word: I have followed the truth. Is that wrong?" He justified his act further by citing the Théâtre de la République and their practice of using similar "truthful" costumes. At the end of his remarks the young artist commended his work to the public, saying, "Certainly if zeal could take the place of talent, I would have nothing to fear."

La Métamorphose was Didelot's swan-song at Lyon, but as he declared later, it was an important milestone in his career, for it was, he said, a "sketch" for his later supremely important work, *Zéphire et Flore*. In late 1795 London again beckoned. There this time he would truly find opportunities for satisfying his passionate urge to create.

CHAPTER V

Lofty Flights in Britian

As the year 1796 dawned in an England thoroughly war-weary from its three-year contest with France, the hottest news in the ballet world was that Madame Hilligsberg was scheduled to appear in *Paul et Virginie*, in which she would dance in men's clothes.[1] Consequently on February 6 the audience nearly rioted when Hilligsberg, who tried to excuse herself because of indisposition, did not appear in her trousers. With even the ladies in the audience "kicking up the row," both Hilligsberg and Michael Kelly, the director, were called from the wings for further explanation.[2] Happily, Kelly had quite a few treats up his sleeve this season to placate his unruly clientele. One of them, he produced a few days later—the beautiful teen-aged Mademoiselle Parisot. Her balance, *The Morning Chronicle* affirmed, was "positively magical, for her person was almost horizontal while turning as on a pivot on her toe." Another fact commended her to the British audience. The beautiful dancer was the daughter of Parisot the dramatic poet who, "for his integrity," had fallen a victim of Robespierre.[3]

On February 11 the following exciting announcement appeared in *The Morning Chronicle*: "Didelot and Rose have arrived—Didelot yields only to Vestris in elasticity and power; and who is his superior in action and grace? Rose is incomparably the finest female dancer in the world. With such a company as the Opera now possesses, they may bid defiance to all the theatres of Europe to rival them." [4] Didelot and Rose advertised that they were very tired from their two-week voyage on a packet boat, and besought the indulgence of the spectators for their fatigue.[5] Nevertheless, on February 20 they opened with a *pas de deux* composed by Didelot within a work entitled *A Divertissement*. To end the evening's entertainment, they performed Onorati's *Soliman II, ou Les Trois Sultanes*. It was Didelot's first performance in the new King's

Theatre. Apparently forgetting her brief stay in 1791, the press declared it was Rose's first appearance in England. The triumph of the young couple was complete that evening. All were curious about Rose, who, it was said, "has had no competition at Paris for several years but Millard, and she is generally acknowledged to be her superior in elegance and power." [6] Their coming raised so much excitement that all avenues to the Opera House were crowded at a very early hour. *The True Briton* declared, "We never witnessed more genteel mobbing in our lives . . . Didelot and Rose were the magnetic objects of curiosity . . . [and] public expectation has seldom been more fully gratified. We never witnessed anything of a kind so admirable as the management, by Madame Rose, of her arms, and the upper parts of her body. Grace, ease, and dignity seem contending for preeminence. Didelot is likewise highly graceful and active." [7] Unfortunately, however, the stage was more than half filled with spectators who impeded the changing of scenery and the working of stage machinery. Once during the season the stage was so crowded that Rose "in throwing up her fine muscular arm into a graceful attitude, inadvertently levelled three men of quality at a stroke" [8]—so said the press. However, knowing Rose's disposition one is tempted to believe the action might not have been so inadvertent.

Subsequently the couple took part in various divertissements with Parisot and Hilligsberg. Didelot composed a *pas de deux* and a *pas de trois* which were performed as part of Onorati's demi-character dance *Le Bouquet* on March 1. The *pas de trois* "electrified the house." Rose continued to reap rave reviews. A critic observed that "the enchanting grace with which Rose uses her arms, the chaste and delicate attitudes into which, without any violent exertion, she throws her figure, the neatness of every movement, and the steadiness of the step, are charms which have a most powerful influence on the heart." [9] Such success was no doubt doubly sweet for Didelot, who well remembered the wrath of the 1789 audiences. However, applause was not their only compensation: Rose and Didelot were now making the stupendous salary of eighty pounds a performance.[10]

On March 8 they performed a *pas de deux* "of a Polish character." [11] There were bigger productions in store for them, however, and on April 2 the couple appeared in a new ballet by Onorati, *Alonso e Cora* with a plot based upon *The Incas* by Jean-François Marmontel. Though the mime in the work was considered tedious, their *pas de deux* was hailed as "the prettiest thing that year." [12] In the name of patriotism a special *pas de trois* was inserted in this ballet to the music of "God Save the King." *Alonso e Cora* secured a place for itself in the London theater, and many years later Didelot mounted the same ballet in St. Petersburg. The ballet also won a place for itself in art history, for two famous British caricaturists of the day left pictorial records of it. James Gillray produced a beautifully colored print entitled *Modern Grace, or The Operatical Finale to the Ballet of Alonzo E Cora (Fig. 9).* The print showed Didelot dancing between Rose and Parisot, whose right breast was unashamedly bare. In the background two buxom choristers twirled on their toes. The feet of all the women were clad in Roman cothurns and their dresses were of flimsy material.[13]

Figure 9. Modern Grace, or the Operatical Finale to the Ballet of Alonzo e caro [Cora], a cartoon of 1796 by James Gillray showing Didelot dancing between Madame Rose, on the left, and Madame Parisot. *Courtesy of the British Museum, London.*

Thomas Rowlandson portrayed King's Theatre as a spectator looking from its depths would view small figures dancing on the stage. The similarity of arrangement of the dancers to that in Gillray's picture points to the fact that it, too, portrayed *Alonso e Cora*. In 1796 Gillray also produced another colored print of Rose alone, entitled *No Flower That Blows, Is Like This Rose (Fig. 10).*[14] She was poised on one toe, with hand held aloft, holding a long garland of roses. Gillray took special delight in showing Rose's angular profile. She again wore a

"No Flower that Blows, is like this Rose.."

Figure 10. "No Flower that Blows, is like this Rose", a caricature of Madame Rose done in 1796 by James Gillray. *Courtesy of the British Museum, London.*

pseudoclassical costume, which did little to conceal a figure obviously judged by Gillray to be "dumpy." The length of Rose's skirts provoked some criticism this season, for the *Chronicle* commented, "By the bye, the pleasantries about her dress have lengthened her petticoat." [15] In this respect, however, the worst was yet to come for daring Rose.

On April 21 Didelot produced for the benefit of Hilligsberg a work which became a constant favorite of London audiences. It was styled simply "a new dance in the Scotch style, called *Little Peggy's Love.*" A critic remarked that it might as well have been called Russian instead of Scotch, but nevertheless, he had never seen such a trifle produce a finer effect. While the playful Hilligsberg took the lead in *Peggy*, another ballet the same evening, *L'Amant Statue*, showed the talents of Rose to advantage. Didelot appeared in the work as a statue which was supposed to move according to the direction of the sculptor, but which was at last completely animated by the charms of a nymph who danced about him.[16] As the season progressed the *Chronicle* affirmed of Didelot and Rose: "Every night, they advance in public favour." [17] For Parisot's benefit on May 12 they danced in a new ballet by Onorati, *La Villageoise enlevée, ou Les Corsaires.*

On June 2 Rose had her first benefit in London. She did it in grand style, even having a special ticket engraved for the night, separate from the one used at the door (*Fig. 11*).[18] The evening included two ballets by her husband. One called a new Indian divertissement, *The Caravan at Rest*, drew the comment that it was an amusing little ballet which showed the sports of the Arabs, but that no caravan was visible. In it, Didelot played the role of Nair, a Malabar officer, while Rose was a Malabar woman. The second, a two-act *ballet episodique* entitled *L'Amour vengé, ou la Métamorphose* was a more elaborate presentation of his Lyon production. In the Londoners' view this ballet was an unprecedented wonder. It was the first blossoming on the London stage of the style for which Didelot was to become famous, and the sheer amazement and delight of the British public bore comparison with the world's comments while watching the first moon landing. In the view of *The True Briton*, "the most interesting part of the spectacle was the aerial passage of Cupid, who flew about the stage with great ease, with a retinue of little Loves, 'sailing on the bosom of the air.' The whole of this part excited much pleasure," the paper added, "mingled . . . with some degree of anxiety, lest an accident should happen." [19] *The Morning Chronicle* wholeheartedly agreed, saying that "it was the most

Figure 11. A complimentary ticket for benefit of Madame Rose, engraved by L. Legroux. *Courtesy of the Victoria and Albert Museum, London.*

bewitching dance we ever witnessed for novelty of idea, charm of fancy and delicacy of passion." [20] However the same paper voiced discontent over a chronic problem, saying, "It is impossible to imagine an effect more delightful than the magical appearance of the floating cupids. . . . The illusion of the scene would have been complete, had it not been for the number of Cornhill Cupids and Broad-street *Beaux* who mixed with the dancers, and unhappily recalled the fancy from the Temple of Love to Lloyd's Coffee-house!" [21]

In the eighteenth-century theater many productions involved descents from heaven by the gods or other characters. Huge machinery, often masked by decorative clouds or chariots, was used to produce these aerial effects.° Didelot did much to popularize the use of wires, corsets, and mobile wings attached to the spines of performers to create flights of his otherworldly creatures. He did not invent these devices. In his early experience at the theater of Audinot, he had witnessed the manipulation of puppets, and Slonimsky believed that ideas for similar manipulation of his dancers stemmed from this experience.[22] Didelot also took much of his inspiration from contemporary prints and engravings. He admitted that an idea for one episode in the ballet came from an engraving of Bartolozzi's, *La Marchande d'Amour*, which depicted groups of little caged cupids being sold (*Fig. 12*).

For Didelot's benefit on July 7 he produced two more pieces in his own aerial style. The first emerged as a one-act production. Later, when expanded to two acts, it was considered his greatest ballet: *Flore et Zéphire*. The story, he declared, was simple: "Heathen mythology tells us that Zephyrus [the west wind] loved Chloris, a nymph of the Fortunate Islands, that his passion was returned; he married her, and gave her the name of Flora, queen of flowers. From this subject my piece is taken." [23] Didelot himself danced the part of Zephyrus with Rose, his Flora.

In the critics view, it was "one of the most captivating entertainments of the kind we have ever witnessed. By an airiness of fancy, he makes all his personages literally fly—for they are borne on the bosom of the air, in a vey new and extraordinary manner." [24]

The second work, *L'Heureux naufrage, ou Les Sorcières écossaises*, was of a different mold. The ballet was noteworthy for its use of local

---

° Present day viewers can see an authentic production in this style at Drottningholm Court Theater in Stockholm. After the untimely death of Gustav III, the theater was closed in mourning. When it was rediscovered in 1922, its scenery was quite usable.

Figure 12. The Market of Love, an engraving of 1795 by F. Bartlozzi. *Courtesy of the British Museum, London.*

color and of simple people, contrasting to the well worn anacreontic popular modes dealing with gods, fauns, and satyrs. In the program Didelot dedicated his work "to the Manes of Shakespeare." He then acknowledged his debt to the great dramatist for inspiration, saying:

> Illustrious bard, permit a young artist to pay your memory the homage which is due to you. I have seen *Macbeth.* Alas! how unhappy for me not to speak or understand your language! however, that truly tragical impression which is perfused in the whole drama, that stamp of originality engraved on every character, that mystic style which you have so eminently given to your witches; in a word, that concatenation of scenes so clearly framed, that even, without having recourse to the words, the mind may follow the whole of the action; all has affected my soul with a thousand different impressions of grief, terror and despair. The three antic witches,° have aroused in me an idea to compose a drama with three modern witches. Permit, O Shakespeare, that I attempt that line for the first time under your auspices; it will be a good omen for me: and if the

° *"Sorcières gothiques"* in Didelot's original French. The program was printed in both languages.

indulgent public should favour this new work with as kind reception, as my *Métamorphose*, encouraging still my feeble talents, permit that I may go to your tomb, and there adorn with a fresh garland your immortal crown.[25]

In the rather simple plot a young peasant named Jamie loves Jenny, a daughter of a solid Scotch farmer named MacDonald. The father does not want his daughter to marry Jamie until he seeks a fortune, so Jamie enlists as a sailor. Before he sets foot on his ship, Jamie gives a love note for Jenny to a passer-by, who is actually a witch. The witch then invites Jenny to her home to help regain her lover. Then occurs the fortunate shipwreck, during which Jamie is tossed on shore near the witch's lair. When Jenny comes to the witch's abode, she finds her lover there. Meanwhile, however, a wicked robber has entered the MacDonald farmhouse, and upon the return home of the two lovers, Jamie helps to overpower the intruder, thus winning MacDonald's approval of the marriage.

Within the plot the common romantic balletic device of the danced dream was used, with the reflection of a character being played out in the background. Another scenic arrangement, uncommon in ballets before Didelot, was the use in the last act of a stage divided into two parts. One side depicted action within the house, while the other showed simultaneous action in the garden. Didelot's cup of good fortune overflowed the brim that night. "The history of the theatre cannot produce an instance of so great a benefit at so late a season of the year," said the *Chronicle*. "Every part of the theatre was crowded. The tribute thus paid to his talents, seemed to give to every spectator a sentiment of pleasure, as if he were personally interested in his success. Such is the powerful influence that merit in any line always has upon liberal feelings." [26] *The True Briton* also bestowed an unusual tribute upon Didelot, saying:

> To talents, in whatever line exercised, we feel a peculiar happiness in paying tribute of our praise. Didelot, whose execution as a dancer has for some time been the admiration of the town, has taken more than one opportunity of proving that he has a head as well as heels, and that the former merits an equal share of applause with the latter. In praising Didelot we praise not the fool who highest lifts his heels, but a man who had a head to contrive, and a power to execute scenic representations that charm the eye, captivate the fancy, and interest the heart.[27]

On July 23, Didelot showed Londoners dances he composed incidental to the opera *Zémire et Azor*. Like most of his productions in that happy year these dances were well received. In fact, there was such abundant applause, according to *The True Briton*, that Michael Kelly resolved to finish the season with another performance.[28] This second one took place on July 30, 1796.

On November 26 King's Theatre opened a new season, again presenting *Zémire et Azor*. Again, the press was rapturous, saying "The band of dancers was received with the most flattering welcome, and never we will venture to say, did the English stage see such a female dancer as Madame Rose shewed herself to be. Having recovered the full vigor of health, she displayed talents that drew forth the most vehement bursts of applause; and Didelot, enchanted with the music of praise, emulated the exertions of his wife." [29] *Flore et Zéphire* was also given, with beautiful new scenery by Thomas Greenwood. The management was determined to try to stop some of the abuses on the part of the audience, asking that ladies dressed in bonnets and gentlemen in boots should not be admitted into the pit of the opera house.[30] When "an obtrusion of foppery" came onto the stage at the first performance, "the disapprobation of the audience was so forcibly and resolutely expressed that the herd of Coxcombs, so ambitious to display their pretty persons, were compelled to retire." [31]

In late November a new "import" from France came to serve as balletmaster in London. After a long delay in the port of Calais, due to a wartime embargo, Sébastien Gallet arrived. The press noted that the *coryphées* and *figurantes* of the theater were especially delighted.[32] Gallet began work on several noteworthy ballets, but meanwhile, on December 13, a ballet of Noverre, *L'Amour et Psiché*, was recreated by Mr. Barré. In it the performances of Didelot, Rose, and Hilligsberg were judged so good that it was impossible to speak with sufficient praise of them. Their groups and combinations were so aerial and elegant that they brought forth rapturous emotions of applause.[33] A scene depicting hell, produced by the artist Greenwood, was judged by the renowned engraver Bartolozzi to be "the greatest masterpiece of the art of painting ever exhibited in this country." [34] Furies brandishing torches and swords of fire produced such an effect that a part of the audience was petrified, and the use of these was later curtailed. Didelot played the part of Cupid and his *pas seul* was highly praised. However, *The*

True Briton complained that Barré might indeed have found greater scope for the fine talents of the Didelot couple.[35]

On December 27 Gallet produced a divertissement entitled *Apollon Berger*. The *Chronicle* was optimistic about Gallet's talent, saying that if his subsequent productions were as good, the public would have no reason to regret the absence of Dauberval. Didelot played the part of Apollo, with the Three Graces played by the captivating Parisot, Rose, and Hilligsberg; in the cititcs view, "the God of Music never had more captivating reasons to be delighted with them." [36]

The year 1797 was not to be such a triumph as the previous one for the Didelots. On January 17 Rose, Hilligsberg, Parisot, and a dancer imported from Russia named Marcadet took part in a new divertissement called *Les Délassements militaires*. In February Sébastien Gallet finally showed his true talents with the production of the ballet *Pizarre, ou La Conquête du Pérou*. The *Chronicle* declared that it did

> infinite honor to the talents of M. Gallet . . . the groups form so many living pictures and we have nothing on our stage comparable in expression and taste to the *pas de deux* of Didelot and Rose in the first act. It electrified the house; and indeed the plan of the ballet is so happily digested, that the dancing returns at intervals so naturally as to enliven the heart without abating interest; and the attention is not suffered for one instant to deviate from the scene until it comes to its affecting and pathetic close. It is perhaps the only ballet we ever saw from which we would not wish a single scene to be removed.[37]

On March 11, 1797 King's Theatre indulged in a grand show of national pride. A victory over the Spanish fleet in a naval battle off Cape St. Vincent on February 14 had lifted the sagging spirits of the war-weary population. In celebration of this a cantata called *Le nozze del Tamigi e Bellona* was produced. In the pageantry and dancing staged for it by Gallet, the Genio d'Africa was portrayed by Didelot and the Genio d'America by Parisot. Parisot, it was advertised, would make her debut in breeches—a drawing card which would fill the house more certainly than the patriotic motive. In the ballet succeeding to and analogous to the cantata, Didelot played the part of Nerid and Rose that of Doris. The *Chronicle* later reported that *Le nozze* "was not the most happy illustration of the event," [38] but no doubt it served a bit to bestir British patriotism.

Rose had another benefit on April 6, 1797. Tickets could be bought at No. 8, Haymarket, and again she distributed a souvenir that was considered by the *Chronicle* "one of the most charming things we ever saw." [39] The ballet produced for the occasion was a monumental one called *Sappho et Phaon* with Rose and her husband dancing the title roles. The program, published and delivered with the tickets, was said to be "written in so masterly a stile" that the "expectation of the audience was wound up to the highest point of eager curiosity." [40] They were not disappointed.

In the program, Didelot explained: "Loaded with the favours of the Public, emboldened by the flattering manner in which my productions were received last year. . . . I venture a great work, and presume to take a loftier flight." He was basing his work, he said, upon the life of the poet Sappho, who left nothing to posterity but a few pieces of poetry. She loved Phaon, who was ungrateful, and he left her for one of her pupils. In the end Sappho followed her lover to Sicily, where, being unable to gain his heart, she threw herself into the deep from the Rock of Leucadia. In his remarks, Didelot hopefully expressed the wish that the public would not refuse their indulgent benevolence to this new child of a father they deigned to protect. He hoped the audience would forgive him if he had represented his characters too strongly, adding. "Woe to the artist, who does but unleave roses, without daring to gather any for fear of the thorns. . . . I chuse rather to over-pass my aim, than not to be able to obtain it, and if I have gone too far, I can soon correct my mistakes." Finally, once again he paid tribute to his teacher Dauberval, saying, "May I, oh! my master, inspired by thee, retain still in my Sappho a spark of thy genius! my thankful heart would enjoy it but as thy gift." [41]

The press extolled the results:

A more delightful spectacle we never saw on any stage. In the contrivance and structure it is full of imagination. Not a moment is wasted. The progress of the fable is enriched with a variety of incidents, the most bewitching; and we see throughout the whole the effects of rapturous fancy. . . . It sets Didelot high as an Artist; and he has shown in this performance that it requires no ordinary endowments of classical knowledge and taste, of inventive mind, and luxurious imagination, to compose a ballet of this kind. [42]

Several factors, however, marred the triumph of the Didelots. *The*

Monthly Mirror reported that although Madame Rose was admittedly the best dancer in Europe, "the house was extremely thin, owing, we suppose, to the notoriety of the circumstance, that the profits were compromised with the manager previously for 600 pounds." [43] Also, during the performance, Didelot hurt himself so much in a leap from the Rock of Leucadia that he was unable to function at his peak for many months. Further, there were new unpleasantries brewing among the Didelots, Hilligsberg, Gallet, and Taylor, which were to become open scandals. Didelot wanted to postpone the second performance of *Sappho* to the day on which Hilligsberg's benefit was planned because he needed time to refurbish it. In the press he declared that if he was not furnished with all that he wanted in machinery and decorations he would take his case to the nobility and public, thus causing embarrassment to the management. The management answered his allegations and demands on May 6. After summarizing the evidence and concluding that the problem of guilt lay with Didelot, the manager berated his conduct, saying: "Mr. Didelot has, from motives which it will become him to explain, excited by addresses and appeals to the public, tumults in the Theatre whose interests he is employed to serve." Kelly then described the considerate treatment afforded the difficult couple. In the course of fourteen months, Didelot and his wife had earned in salary and benefits upward of five thousand pounds. Though engaged to arrive in November of 1795 they did not arrive until February of 1796, yet they had received salaries for the whole season, and in every other instance they had been treated with a liberality that demanded a more grateful return.[44] The public became a little tired of the bickering, and *The Monthly Mirror* expressed the general disgust by saying, "Why those continual broils between Mr. Gallet and Mr. Taylor, Mr. Didelot and Madame Hilligsberg? Surely as we visit those places for our entertainment, we ought not to be pestered in the public prints with a ridiculous correspondence between a ballet master and a dancing master." [45]

On April 25, Didelot and Rose performed in Gallet's new ballet *Le Trompeur trompé*. For his own benefit on June 15 Didelot presented the ballet *Acis et Galathée* with a new score by Cesare Bossi. The most charming part of it was said to be a *pas seul* by Rose.[46] *The Monthly Mirror* thought it was "certainly a charming little dance," but criticized it from a humanitarian point of view, saying:

> It grieves us to the soul, nightly to hear the complaints of the dear little infants behind the scenes against the manager. These flying

and dancing cupids, whose astonishing exactness entitles them to our support, have not received a shilling salary during the season. The whole concerns of this magnificent theatre, for want of system and regularity, are rapidly going to destruction. The subordinate performers expostulate with the treasurer, than whom there is not a more able or worthy man, but he is debarred the means;—the cash is laid hold of by higher powers, and that which would satisfy the cravings of nature and the wants of the necessitous, is perhaps appropriated to bribery and corruption for the purpose of obtaining a seat in parliament, and that being at length accomplished, bills, bonds, and ejectments become waste paper.[47]

On May 25, Londoners saw the Didelots dance in *Le Triomphe de Cupidon, ou Les Nymphes vaincues par l'Amour*. The season closed at King's Theatre on July 29.

After a summer's vacation to pacify the frazzled nerves of the company, King's Theatre again opened on November 28 with a Gallet production entitled *L'Offrande à Terpsichore*. Along with the Didelots, the dancers included the Laborie couple, Madame Hilligsberg and a younger Hilligsberg named Janet, who, the *Chronicle* affirmed, "Though evidently overcome by her terrors . . . had adopted the style which Madame Rose has carried to its point of perfection"—a judgment which was probably not at all appreciated by the elder Hilligsberg.[48]

On December 20 Britain was still celebrating its earlier naval victory. This time a production by Gallet entitled *Le Triomphe de Thémis* bestirred the patriotism of the Britons. Though the firing of guns in it obscured the audience's view for several minutes, it was considered a beautiful allegory, "an unabated attraction." Rose and Didelot, who danced the parts of America, were praised for contributing to the success of it.[49] Other unlisted performers who played the roles of Discord and Jacobinism were, no doubt, properly hissed.

Sébastian Gallet produced another divertissement entitled *La Chasse d'Amour* in which Rose and Didelot did a *pas de deux* on January 2, 1798.[50] However, on February 6 he brought forth another work in which the Didelot couple were allowed an opportunity of displaying the whole extent and variety of their powers. This was *Constante et Alcidonis*, based upon Marmontel's allegorical tale, *Les Quatre Flacons*. Didelot was the hero, and the critic of the *Chronicle* declared he had never seen Didelot to so much advantage, though "his superb Oriental habit concealed much of his person." [51]

It is ironical that Didelot's costume was deemed too voluminous in February, for exactly the opposite problem became a central issue in a forthcoming farce that shattered the dignity of the very House of Lords itself. At a regular meeting of the august body on March 2, 1798, the topic of discussion was an act to dissolve the marriage of a certain James and Harriet Esten, for in that day, divorce cases were dealt with on a high level. There rose to speak a certain Barrington, bishop of Durham. No doubt he rued his action later, considering the manner in which the press made jolly good sport of his talk for several weeks to come (*Figs. 13 and 14*).

The bishop, disturbed by the low moral tone of society that begot such cases, blamed England's current wartime enemy France for her moral problems. He deplored the evil that must attend the introduction of French morality into these kingdoms, declaring that

> the French Rulers, while they despaired of making any impression on us by the force of arms, attempted a more subtle and alarming warfare, by endeavoring to enforce the influence of their example. In order to taint and undermine the morals of our ingenuous youth, they sent among us a number of female dancers, who by the allurements of the most indecent attitudes, and most wanton theatrical exhibitions, succeeded but too effectually in loosening and corrupting the moral feelings of the people—and indeed if common report might be relied upon, the indecency of those appearances far outshamed anything of a similar nature that had ever been exhibited . . . he would not say on any Christian theatre, but even upon the more licentious theatres of Athens and of Rome. [Further, Durham declared], If their Lordships did but seriously attend to the sad consequences that must result from the exhibition of such spectacles before the eyes of their wives and daughters . . . they would doubtless feel the necessity of arresting *in limine*, not only the progress of such scandalous immorality, but also of preventing it in the future; and indeed unless an immediate stop were put to it, the inevitable consequence must be, that the malignant influence of such contaminating example must finally corrupt both sexes, and their lordships' time and sitting would henceforward be wholly engrossed by cases of divorce.[52]

A member of parliament proposed that the skirts of dancers could not be shorter than the stated length of the regiment of Scottish highlanders.

Figure 13. Durham Mustard too Powerfull for Italian Capers, or the Opera in an Uproar, a cartoon of 1798 by I. Cruikshank. Bishop Barrington of Durham is shown climbing onto the stage, saying: "Avaunt the Satan I fear the not assume whatever shape or form thou wilt I am determined to lay the thou black Fiend." *Courtesy of the British Museum, London.*

Figure 14. Modern Modesty Clerical Improvements ro [*sic*] Wigs a l'Eveque, a cartoon of 1798 by I. Cruikshank[?] showing Bishop Barrington of Durham striding off stage while a dancer uses her wig to screen herself. The Bishop is saying: "There, now you may go on. I would not have had my Wife seen you so, for the World, why you should be as choice of your charms as I am of my Claret." To which the dancer replies: "Oh, this was transplanting of de wig indeed, I suppose I shall not be allowed to shew my face next." *Courtesy of the British Museum, London.*

Figure 15. A M[rebus eye]nute Regulation of the Opera Step, or an Episcopal Examination, a cartoon of 1798 by Woodward showing a dancer, possibly Madame Hilligsberg or Madame Parisot, being inspected by Salisbury, the Lord Chamberlain, and Bishop Barrington of Durham. Salisbury is saying: "My Dear Madam if you raise your foot one quarter of an Inch higher it will be impossible for me to grant you a Licence." The Bishop is saying: "No! No! No! Not a hair's breadth higher for the World; such sights as these is the cause of so many Divorces." To which the dancer replies: "Vat! you see enof." On the wall hang pictures of Thaïs flourishing two firebrands, the temptation of St. Anthony by a courtesan, and Durham Cathedral. *Courtesy of the British Museum, London.*

The Morning Chronicle lampooned the speech for days to come. "A century and a half ago," it remarked, "a judge said on the bench that poisoning was a popish trick, but the Jacobins in our days have a much greater variety of tricks than the papists. Thus, for instance, dancing is pronounced by a Reverend Prelate to be an invention not of the Devil, as some Divines maintain, but of the French to propogate levelling principles." [53] Meantime as the press had its fun, King's Theatre made a change of schedule: *Bacchus et Ariadne*, wherein the offensive costumes were seen, was postponed for a time, and finally the ballet reemerged with new dress.[54] Further, white stockings henceforth replaced flesh-colored ones (*Figs. 15 and 16*).[55] This, the *Chronicle* likewise burlesqued, saying: "Everything which, in the dresses of the dancers, at the

Figure 16. Ecclesiastical Scrutiny—or the Durham Inquest on Duty, a cartoon of 1798 by Ansell[?] showing Bishop Barrington of Durham and two other bishops supervising four female dancers dressing for a performance of *Bacchus and Ariadne.* They are putting on striped stockings and clumsy shoes with buckles. One is saying: "I really now think it a shame to disguise such a leg as this why my fortune will be ruin'd." Bishop Barrington is saying: "Aye the upper part will do very well, many a husband will bless me for introducing these stays." Another dancer is saying: "Pa Pa don't tell me these things must not be shown but to private parties." *Courtesy of the British Museum, London.*

Opera approached to carnation, is fading away to vestal white. Nothing prurient will now be visible *sub rosa,* and the Turkish trouser conceals those graceful genuflections, which were so many excitements to idolatry. The interference of the dignified clergy with the dresses of dancers is certainly no departure from the strict line of their duty. Cloathing [*sic*] the naked is a Christian precept." [56] The *Chronicle* affirmed it would be necessary for the bishops "to attend the tiring room in person and to inspect the preparations for a new Ballet. The criterion of purity may be easily ascertained. If the men of God feel any unholy thoughts, surely the audience will be set in a flame!" Further, the press said "it will be absolutely necessary in future to put the *corps* of female dancers under certain Right Reverend Licensers, previous to their appearance in public. Their Reverences, judging from their own feelings, will then be able to determine what portion of loyalty and constitutional spirit there is in each posture, and using the freedom of all Theatrical Licensers, will take care to scratch out everything that has a tendency to the levelling system." [57] Rubbing salt into the wounds of the bishop of Durham, the *Chronicle* then printed the following letter:

DEMOCRATIC DANCING

Mr. Editor: Our vigilant statesman, previous to, as well as since the commencement of the war, have busied themselves in discovering every supposed or real plot which tended to the introduction of French principles into this country, and although they have hitherto been rather unfortunate, insomuch that one man only has been hanged, and he one of their own spies (and therefore not underserving of his fate), it must afford vast consolation to every lover of his country that their zeal is not damped, nor their vigilance abated. They still are employed in stopping up every channel by which French principles can be conveyed, and baffling all attempts of our enemies both external and internal. The threats of an invasion, indeed, must naturally make them more diligent.

But, Sir, I confess I read with some degree of astonishment in the papers of last week that after every other channel of communication had been damned up, the French have had the art to cut a canal through passages, by which, I believe, political principles were never before conveyed, and by a sort of new contrived Grand Junction, are whisking Democracy in the cadenza of a *pas seul*, and propagating Jacobinism in the evolutions of a pirouette.

What are we to understand by all this? Is this a metaphorical or a literal discovery? Not long ago we were told that Buonaparte was to ride here in the WIND, and afterward that he was to come over by WATER—What are we to think now? I protest, Sir, I never was more puzzled between difficulties in my life. I should suppose the crown lawyers must likewise feel a little awkward in the business. Give them a pamphlet and they can make anything out of it, but lay an information against a petticoat, and how will you make out the innuendos? I have a great respect for the ingenuity of our crown lawyers, but I fancy they will have some difficulty in unripping the seditious parts of a petticoat, in explaining the xxxxxx and in filling up the blanks and dashes so as to bring the crime home to the party.

For my part, dancing has so long been my favourite amusement that I have rather taken the alarm on the present occasion; and it is become so fashionable an amusement that I know not what our people of quality will do without it. However, I say, "Perish our Petticoats, let the Constitution live." It is time to be on our guard when the enemy has changed his tone from the loud roar of the cannon to the gentler notes of warbling flutes in unison with the "many twinkling feet." Yet, Sir, allow me to start some doubts on this subject.

Every man judges best when he judges from his own feelings. I have not the feelings of a learned Prelate, not by some thousands a year, yet in all my observation of our best dancing, I must say that when they vaulted the highest, and went round the quickest, I never had a single thought of politics in my head. On the contrary, all such considerations vanish the moment the leader of the band draws his bow; King, Lords and Commons are no longer in imagination—I think only of the scene before me, and at that moment would not give half a crown to revolutionize the whole empire of China. Being somewhat near sighted, I use my opera glasses on such occasions. So do many Noble men and Gentlemen of the first rank. Now, Sir, do you think they do this as spies who have discovered a small print piece of sedition which they wish to make more legible? I should suppose not—I speak for myself—I think the proceedings of the petticoat propagandistes are fair and open. They affect no secrecy. They seem to have no concealments which people that are meditating plots generally have. If they do then publish sedition and French principles in this way, they are open to refutation, and what I think is a material point here, what they deal in, be it seditious or not, is not calculated for the lower classes of people. It cannot, as was said of Paine's works, be wrapped [around] sweatmeats, dropped down in areas, or sent in waggon loads among country bumpkins.

These I humbly offer as objections to the discernment of persons who think they have made the discovery that the French mean to make the first attack in the Haymarket. It appears to me doubtful. The French are certainly an ingenious people, but I cannot think that they would descend from the mighty rafts they have constructed, in order to invade us by mere crannies. There is a departure here from the grand plans of the great nation which their pride can never allow of. Besides there is a regularity in every movement of our dances which is the farthest possible from the anarchy which we are told French principles introduce, and which is so prevalent in the Opera house in Paris, that if we may credit the learned and well informed Editors of our Ministerial papers, all the performers there dance upon their heads, and the musicians, in order to keep time, are as deaf as posts. I am, Sir, yours,

FANDANGO[58]

As if this were not enough, cartoonists likewise had a field day over the petty controversy, with noted artists such as Gillray, Cruikshank, and others producing at least five prints ridiculing the beleaguered bishops (*Fig. 17*).[59] When King's Theatre scheduled a benefit for the defense of the country, which sadly needed funds to support England's unpopular war against France the *Chronicle* suggested that the bishops would wave their objections in this performance against nakedness of performers, because surely there could be no danger of treason on a night when every step and attitude was inspired by loyalty.[60] At the same time the *Chronicle* affirmed that with the nobility contributing their wealth and the bishops their advice, the performance should produce a very *decent* sum. Actually, the receipts from the performance amounted to the decent sum of seven hundred seven pounds, which was paid to the Bank of England in aid of Voluntary Contribution for the Defense of the Country.[61]

Figure 17. Operational Reform, or la Dance a l'Eveque, a cartoon of 1798 by James Gillray. Madame Rose is the figure shown in profile on the right. The inscription reads:

     " 'Tis hard for such new fangled orthodox rules,

       That our Opera-Troop, should be blam'd,

       Since like our first parents, they only, poor fools,

       Danc'd Naked, & were not asham'd!" —, *Morning Herald*,
Courtesy of the British Museum, London.

During the benefit on March 22, Gallet produced a new anacreontic ballet entitled *La Vengeance de l'Amour*. In it, Didelot, Rose, Laborie, and Hilligsberg danced the *Pas de Quatre de Panurge*, a favorite with the audience. The *Chronicle* thought it an elegant and tasteful composition, but commented that it had less action and more dancing than normal.[62] During a performance on March 25, Didelot suffered a contusion which kept him off the stage for some days, but at Rose's benefit on April 19, he danced with his wife in Gallet's *Énée et Didon*.[63] Many members of the cast of King's Theatre, the Didelots included, performed at Drury Lane Theatre on May 9 for Michael Kelly's benefit. On the next night, however, they were at home at King's Theatre for Hilligsberg's benefit. That evening Gallet produced *Elisa, ou La Triomphe de la nature*, in which Didelot, Rose, and the Labories exerted themselves very successfully on behalf of their theatrical collaborator.[64]

All in all, the Didelots experienced a harrowing season in 1798. Didelot had his own benefit on June 14, and though the audience which attended it was elegant, it was not as numerous as expected. The ballet *Le Déserteur* was revived by Gallet, and "it met with that sort of reception to which an old friend is entitled after a long absence," [65] since it had not been staged since the destruction of the Pantheon by fire. While Didelot played the part of Henry in it, Rose was incapacitated from mid-May until June 26 and did not dance for her husband's benefit.

When the winter season began on December 8, 1798, the most important work scheduled was a revival on March 26, 1799, of Dauberval's *Télémaque*. This ballet, which had gained great popularity in France, was staged by James D'Egville, who had taken Sébastien Gallet's place in King's Theatre. Didelot knew D'Egville from their days together at the Grand Théâtre in Bordeaux. The British audience welcomed D'Egville, a native son, and soon Didelot had to share top honors with him in the press. For Didelot this was not easy. Reviewing *Télémaque, The True Briton* declared that "As a *ballet d'action* it may indeed rank with the best works of the kind. Rose gives increased interest to the character of Calypso, and the grave dignity of her manner is finely in contrast with the light elegance of Hilligsberg in *Eucharis*. The same contrast, and in a still more striking way, is observable between Didelot and D'Egville, the one in the animated fire of *Télémaque* and the other in the austere energy of Mentor. D'Egville indeed is uncommonly impressive, and possesses all the oratory of action." [66] Another report affirmed that D'Egville "decidedly took the lead: He was truly the sage and august Mentor. We are glad to see this able performer restored to his proper station in the theater." [67] On April 18 for Hilligsberg's benefit D'Egville produced *Hylas et Témire* as well as his own version of Dauberval's *La Fille mal gardée*. The latter was called in the British press by the name which was the motto of the respectable British Order of the Garter: *Honi soit qui mal y pense*.[68] On May 2, 1799, D'Egville presented *Tarare et Irza* for Rose's benefit.

A third Dauberval ballet opened the winter season on January 11, 1800—*Les Jeux D'Egle*. In it danced André-Jean-Jacques Deshayes, a member of the family of Didelot's Parisian teacher. No doubt Didelot swelled with pride at the judgment of *The True Briton*, which noted that although Deshayes was "a very good dancer, he was not qualified to eclipse Didelot." [69] However, Deshayes' manner of escaping the stage by a spring was something novel and admired by the audience.

Didelot danced in D'Egville's *Le Mariage mexicain* and his *Hyppomène et Atlante* in February and March. Rose, however, danced only sporadically in early spring, and she was conspicuously absent from the stage from mid-April until late June of 1800. According to Russian biographies, Rose was said to have given birth to Didelot's son Karl on May 2, 1801. If so, English newspapers were greatly deceived, for Rose was listed in *The Morning Chronicle* as dancing on that very day. It seems more probable that the son was born during this time of her absence from the stage in 1800. Didelot took part in a *New Bacchanalian Divertissement Ballet* on April 15 by Gallet and on May 8 Didelot staged *Laura et Lenza, ou Le Troubadour*. The plot of this work was completely divorced from reality. In it Sir Edward, the baron of a manor, attends a wedding at which he becomes infatuated with the peasant Laura, who was played by Madame Hilligsberg, who has eyes for none but Lenza. Sir Edward follows Laura to her hut, where his attempts to seduce her are interrupted by Lenza, who instead of fighting the lord, disguises himself as the girl's grandmother and pretends to be aroused from sleep by the baron's visit. Embarrassed, the baron formally proposes to Laura. Lenza is overcome by trepidation that his lover might accept the baron's offer when Aline, the Fairy of Benevolence, appears to him, whereupon he falls asleep. In slumber, a Genii tries to make Lenza extinguish the fire of love in his heart, but in vain. In the morning he betakes himself to Laura, but the baron does likewise, capturing Lenza and imprisoning him. Aline then leads Laura through an underground passage for a visit to her lover in prison. When Sir Edward discovers the united lovers, he binds Lenza to a column to be axed. As the fatal blow is about to fall, the fairy Aline transports all three to the palace of the Genii, where the nuptials of Laura and Lenza take place amid general entertainment, with a divertissement finishing the ballet.[70] The part of Aline, the solver of impossible problems, was played by the young Janet Hilligsberg.

The problem ever remained of the young society gentlemen constantly inhabiting the stage during the performances. *The Monthly Mirror* commented in April of 1800 that the stage's race of locusts, with which it had long been infested, had taken flight.[71] However, their absence was not permanent. During *Laura et Lenza*, a group of the usual "coxcombs" invaded the stage and were saluted first with oranges, then with a stone thrown at them. The manager appeared on stage in a state of *déshabillé* trying to persuade them to leave. When this failed he ordered the curtain to be let down. In doing so it hit one of the young nuisances, and the rest "took flight and scampered away like a terrified flock of geese." [72] On June 17, for their joint benefit, Rose again joined her husband in *Laura et Lenza* and in *Télémaque*.

On January 3, 1801, D'Egville produced the ballet *Pygmalion*. Though Didelot's acting was "exquisitely fine," and Bossi's music was a credit to its composer, a critic declared that the progress of the fable was too slow, and that English spectators did not have patience for "a slow and gradual working of the passions. They desire to be roused by a more rapid movement than is used on the foreign stage." [73] The Didelots danced in February in a work called *Barbara and Allen, or The Orphan*, but Didelot's supreme opportunity of the year came with his benefit on March 26, 1801, when he produced a ballet version of the well known gory, romantic tale, *Alonzo the Brave and the Fair Imogene*, by Matthew Lewis, author of *The Monk*. *The Morning Chronicle* was impressed, affirming that "Mr. Didelot . . . with the license which an artist of his superior powers has a right to exercise, has materially altered the plan of the fable, and given it new incidents and a moral, though a most striking end. It is not easy for the mind to conceive anything more sublime and impressive than the denouement as he has managed it." It was reported that the music, by Dragonetti, "Speaks to the soul on the appearance of the spectre, and the whole scene is full of magical act. It justly added to the fame of Didelot." [74]

Figure 18. Madame Hilligsberg in *Ken-si and Tao*, a print in the Bibliothèque de l'Opéra, Paris.

For Hilligsberg's benefit on May 14, 1801, Didelot staged his last ballet in England for many years to come. This was *Ken-si and Tao*, based upon the story of Grétry's opera, *Zémire et Azor (Fig. 18)*. In it a wicked young Chinese woman named Yio-Ha tries to seduce her sister's fiancé Tao and even to kill him, but he is saved by virtuous Ken-si, a part played by Hilligsberg. Didelot played the part of a khan.[75] *The Morning Chronicle* reported that it was well received, and though the pantomime had little to interest the feeling, the dancing would make it a favorite with the public.[76] The last new part taken by Didelot during this stage of his career was in a ballet staged by D'Egville, *Heliska, ou La Fille Soldat*, to the music of Bossi. In the story a Polish girl follows her lover to camp, enlists in the army, and eventually saves his life in battle. Didelot played the part of Baron Gorlitz, the governor of a Polish province.

For the London public, which had indeed been gracious to the Didelot couple, it probably came as a shock when *The Morning Chronicle* carried the announcement on July 28, 1801, that "Didelot and Rose quit the Opera House at the end of the present season, having had very advantageous offers from Russia. Their time is not expired; but the Manager liberally parts with them upon a promise of return."

Many factors probably entered into the decision. For one, Didelot was never able to live in happy peaceful coexistence with the young roughnecks who habitually made the English stage their abode during performances. This he would not have to suffer in czarist Russia. Further, the machinery at his disposal in England left much to be desired. There were many critical reviews telling of performances marred by slow changes of scenery or general awkward management of stage devices. Though the arrival of the Didelots in England in 1796 brought them more notoriety than any other performers, the ardor of the British press, which was probably a reflection of the public's attitude, was becoming less glowing, and the Didelots were having increasingly to share the limelight with D'Egville, Deshayes, and Laborie. Didelot's chances for creation of original ballets would have been enough to satisfy some men, but not one with his superabundance of restless, creative energy. In addition, he had suffered many sprains and could see the day approaching when he would have to curtail his performing activity and engage more in teaching and choreography. He longed for a school where he could train his own dancers. Thus when an offer came from the very rich Imperial Theater of St. Petersburg, Didelot was willing to listen. With his young infant and wife in precarious health, he boarded a ship for Russia in the summer of 1801.

CHAPTER VI

Loftier Flights in Russia

IN the spring of 1799 the Russian ambassador in England, Prince Semyon R. Vorontsov, was greatly flustered, to say the least, by a letter he received from the director of the Russian Imperial Theaters, Count Nikolai P. Sheremetev. In French he answered Sheremetev:

London, April, 1799

Monsieur Count,

I have received the letter that you have taken the pains to write March 15, by which you charge me to have dancers come to my house, to negotiate engagements with them for the theatre which you direct, to inform myself of their morals and principles, and to have them sign the contract that you have sent, which only lacks their names. You remark also in your letter that you wish that a certain Didelot and his wife be given preference, and that in case they are engaged here, I should make the same proposition to a certain Laborie and his wife.

I am very mortified not to be able to comply with what you desire of me. Your predecessor in the direction of the theatre, Monsieur Prince Yusupov, since I have come to England, has troubled me with similar commissions, and I have excluded myself, because I am the most inept man for affairs of this type. I love music, but I do not love ballet and do not comprehend it in the least. My health is so feeble, that although I love the first, there are not 10 days in the year when I am able to go to the opera, at the end of which I leave without attending the grand ballet which terminates the perform- ance. I have paid singers to come to my house from time to time for concerts, but I do not have any liaison with them, having always detested the society of theatrical people. Negotiations, engagements, and contracts of the type that you wish that I make, are never made by ministers: it is the business of bankers, of negotiators and of consuls, and I would have left this task to the house of commerce, which has had the order to remit the money, if one passage of your letter had not held me back. It is that where you say to me: if on account of their morals and principles you judge them worthy of that favor.

Never in my life will I take upon myself such a responsibility; never will I be the guarantor of morals and principles of theatrical people, and above all when they are French. Where do you wish, Monsieur Count, that I should be able to get such information? It would be necessary that I would live with them, that I would pass my life in the taverns and cafés that these people frequent. My age, my birth, my grade, the post that I occupy, and my personal character do not permit me to lead such a type of life. I must warn you also that I see news at times in the papers that such or such a dancer or musician has been chased out of England for his principles, or for having been discovered to be a spy of France. . . . For all these reasons you will find it good, Monsieur Count, that I dispense myself of a commission so above my capacity to fill well, and so below my manner of thinking. From here to the month of August you will have all the time necessary to address yourself directly to some banker, negotiator or some other person who assiduously frequents the theatre. Whoever it will be, he will be a thousand times more capable of satisfying you than he who has the honor to be, Monsieur Count, your excellency, the very humble and obedient

S. R. Vorontsov.

P.S. Not being able to make any use of the contract that you have sent, because of the reasons herein mentioned, I am returning it to you, included here, Monsieur Count. *Ut in litteris* S. R. Vorontsov

Sheremetev replied to Vorontsov with the following letter:

Pavlovsk, 1799

I beg of you a thousand and thousand pardons for the liberty that I have taken, in remitting to your care a commission that you judge so below your fashion of thinking.

I would have believed quite frankly, that, as grand chamberlain, having been charged by the Emperor with the direction of his theatres, that I would not be able better to address myself than to his own ministers in foreign countries in order to obtain subjects capable of satisfying the rare taste that His Majesty has for fine performances. I would have equally believed by doing so to have furnished you with an occasion to make our August Master happy, who merits well, I think, a bit of recreation, since he is so seriously occupied with our well being and that of all Europe. But I see that I was wrong in my calculations, and I would have committed a thousand times the same blunder, without the lessons full of sense that I received from you, for which I am infinitely obliged. I did not pretend at all Monsieur Count, to render you responsible for the morals or the principles of individuals that you would have judged worthy of being engaged in the services of the Emperor; because, as it is impossible to read to the depth of hearts, one can only in such a case give preference to those whose public conduct is not notoriously scandalous: and I would have imagined, that it would not have been too difficult to obtain sufficient information without assuming any responsibility, without lowering one's dignity. That is the true sense of the passage that you have cited in my letters, and it can have no other.

In effect, a theatrical director, who by his position is obliged to have business with that type of men, despised for their profession, but always esteemed for their good qualities, is only himself held responsible for scandal to a certain point. Then so much the worse for the guilty one; he falls into the claws of the police. . . . Because, after all, we would only know in these persons the talents that they deploy in the theatre, and not the character that they deploy in our antichambers, without having with them other liaisons capable of compromising, as you put it very wisely, our age, our birth, our grade and our charge. We would be very much exposed, if it would be otherwise.

Thus, Monsieur Count, I beg you to pardon that pain that you have taken to reply to me, and believe that in this I have acted in all the simplicity of my heart, particularly because of the intimacy that has reigned between Monsieur your brother and myself.

I will not fail to address myself subsequently either to a consul or a banker, or to some negotiator, and if it will please His Majesty, to exempt me from the direction of his theatres, which lately come under the charge of the grand marshal of the court.

I have the honor to be with particular consideration, Monsieur Count, the very humble and very obedient servant of your excellency.

N. P. Sheremetev[1]

Sheremetev's letter is even more interesting when viewed in light of his own background and the other role is played in Russian theatrical history. For his time, he was an "enlightened" member of society who had studied at Leyden University and who read Voltaire, Rousseau, and other French *Encyclopédistes*. Further, he translated foreign works, played the violincello well, and gathered the best collection of books on art in Russia. While being an avid reader of enlightened political theory, however, he was master of more than seven hundred sixty thousand *desiatins*° of land, on which lived more than two hundred thousand serfs. At Ostankino, near Moscow, he had a theater staffed by one hundred sixty-six serfs, twenty-six of whom were dancers in 1789. It rivalled the Imperial Theaters in repertoire and excellence of performances.[2] In an age in which even free theatrical people were considered on a low level of society in Russia, he himself married a serf actress, Praskovia Zhemchugova, who died early in life from tuberculosis. Sheremetev employed balletmasters such as Charles Le Picq, who had come to St. Petersburg in 1786 after gaining fame in Paris and London.

Later Didelot's own ballets were performed at Ostankino. In 1799 Sheremetev actually was replaced as director of the Imperial Theaters by Alexander L. Naryshkin, who began renewing talks with Didelot in 1801, the year in which Emperor Paul I was assassinated. Apparently Didelot passed the test of morality, though certainly if it had been known in the Russian court that his signature graced a letter of sympathy sent by the cast of Montansier's theater to Robespierre, it is doubtful if he would have been admitted, for the Russian court greatly feared Jacobin revolutionary influences coming into their country. In the end, the contract was signed by a negotiant named Ferlin de Tactei. According to its terms, the Didelot couple had to serve in the Imperial Theaters three years, receiving a sum of twelve thousand rubles.

Didelot's arrival was a landmark in the history of Russian ballet, and the first quarter of the nineteenth century is justifiably called "the epoch of Didelot." He found in Russia aids to his creative growth scarcely available anywhere else, save in Paris, where Gardel held a complete stranglehold on them. There were three theaters where ballet might be seen in St. Petersburg, including the Bolshoi Kamenny Theater, located in the spot now occupied by the Leningrad Conservatory, and the Maly Theater, located near the present Pushkin Theater of Drama. While these two were open to the public, the third, the

---

° A desiatin equals one hundred ten acres.

Hermitage Theater, was for the exclusive use of the imperial family, the court, and foreign guests. All three theaters, as well as the theatrical school, were supported by the state. Their workshops for producing wardrobes and scenic decorations surpassed those in London and Bordeaux by far.

When Didelot arrived on September 8, 1801, both new and old faces greeted him. One of his chief collaborators was Prince Alexander Alexandrovich Shakhovskoi, who in 1802 was made a member of the theatrical committee in the Directorate of the Imperial Theaters (*Fig. 19*). He was the author of about one hundred plays, a *régisseur*, teacher of theatrical arts, and general leader among the literature-loving intelligentsia of St. Petersburg. In the words of P. A. Karatygin, a comedy actor and author of vaudeville works, the prince was "just as much a fanatic in his profession as Didelot, just as ready to tear his hair out, to go into ecstasy, or to weep from tender emotion if his pupils, especially the girls, truly carried out his energetic direction." [3] Didelot frequently visited his home, where he could ordinarily have met and conversed with authors such as Pushkin, Griboyedov, Ivan Krylov, the Russian Aesop, and Vasily Zhukovsky, a translator of classical verse and tutor of the future emperor Alexander II.

Didelot's most faithful musical collaborator was Catarino Alberto-vich Cavos. Born in Venice, Cavos spent forty-three years in his adopted country, and is classified as "a Russian composer." [4] In addition to being director of the opera since 1806, he was a singing teacher and a prolific composer. One commentator noted that Didelot's relation to ballet in St. Petersburg was the same as that of Shakhovskoi to dramatic art and Cavos to the teaching of singing, adding, "this was such a triumvirate that art grew not by days, but by hours." [5]

Happily for Didelot, one of his former acquaintances had just left Russia; unhappily, however, the new balletmaster had to try to dispel some of the bad will engendered by the antics of his fellow Frenchman. This was the same dancer who had blighted the life of his master Dauberval in Bordeaux—Chevalier Peicam de Bressoles. In the intervening years Peicam had gained the reputation of being a violent Jacobin, a friend of the French revolutionary terrorist Collot d'Herbois, whom he had assisted in massacres perpetrated at Lyon. [6] After leaving France, Peicam had spent some time running a gambling house in Hamburg. From there, he and his wife, a charming and talented singer, wended their way by April 1, 1798, to St. Petersburg, where she gained

Figure 19. Prince Alexander Alexandrovich Shakhovskoi, from M. Borisoglebsky's *Materialy po istorii russkogo baleta.*

quick fame at the French Theater. According to the discriminating taste of the painter Madame Vigée-Lebrun, Madame Chevalier was "the prettiest actress of the St. Petersburg theater." [7] Though it was rumored she was in the pay of Napoleon Bonaparte's police in St. Petersburg, she gained entrance to the highest circles by her disarming talent and beauty.[8] One of the most privileged members of Emperor Paul I's entourage, Count Ivan Pavlovich Kutaisov, installed her in a mansion near his own on the Neva River. Subsequently, the count was driven to the depths of despair when the emperor himself took a fancy to the charmer. A man of many absurd contradictions, Paul I was known to have donned the insignia of the Order of the Knights of Malta when he called on her. Thanks to such connections, by the year 1799, it was said that "all the empire was at the disposition of three women," one of whom was Madame Chevalier.[9] Apart from her husband Madame Chevalier herself was praised by some for her *"moeurs irréprochables."* [10] However, in Russia she and her unscrupulous spouse flagrantly engaged in the practice of selling their patronage to gain ranks, orders, and posts. She received clients like a queen; he like a pasha. A word from them to Kutaisov settled many a problem—for a price, while one victim of their disfavor endured the knout, mutilation, and exile in chains to Siberia.[11] They further enriched themselves by intimidating others to buy tickets to their benefits. In ordinary practice loges were subscribed by the season in St. Petersburg, but, as in Western Europe, at special performances the chief artists were allowed to reap profits from their own benefits. For a seat which ordinarily sold for twenty to twenty-five rubles, a patron might pay the Chevaliers three hundred to six hundred rubles. Lists of purchasers were submitted to Kutaisov as well as to the emperor himself, and to refuse to buy a ticket would have been to court imperial disfavor. On the other hand, a high price paid for such a ticket might yield rich returns. One noble who gave Madame Chevalier a piece of jewelry worth twelve hundred rubles for a ticket was rewarded a few days later by Paul with a regiment garrisoned near St. Petersburg.[12]

Peicam himself soon gained the imposing title of *assesseur de college*. While holding the rank of an infantry major, he wore Paul's favorite uniform of the Order of Malta. One observer remembered that he pranced about decked in a gold embroidered court coat, a sword, and a three-cornered hat with plumes, but that to the degree that his wife was a good actress, Peicam was a terrible balletmaster.[13] August von Kotzebuë, the noted German playwright and director of the German Theater in St. Petersburg, confirmed this view, observing that "he was one of the worst balletmasters that ever lived." [14] It seems only Paul I liked his work, but indeed Paul liked it very much for the military marches that Peicam incorporated into his ballets. As a result, the emperor awarded him the title of balletmaster in perpetuity on November 9, 1799, shoving aside the reigning balletmaster, Charles Le Picq.

While he was balletmaster, Peicam produced at least four works. One, given at Gatchina, was *Les Amours de Flore et Zéphyr* (1800). This ballet was not recorded in the Archives of the Imperial Theaters; apparently the royal historians wanted to forget about it. However, a copy of the program remains, attached to the score.[15] Others were *L'Enlèvement* (1798), *Gaston de Foa* (1800), and *L'Heroine villageoise* (1800). In the latter, twenty-four supers were employed, including four noncomissioned officers and two drummers—no doubt for the military evolutions Paul I liked so much.

Theatrical director Naryshkin would give orders that Peicam was to be given everything needed for his uninteresting productions.[16] As a result they were embellished with beautiful, expensive decorations by the scenic artists Gonzago and Dranché, but their choreography was so bad they were seldom repeated. Without Peicam's sanction no other ballet could be staged. The artists of the Imperial Theaters suffered in many ways from the balletmaster, but perhaps their greatest and most justified grievance was his ability to bring about the banishment of Italian and Russian performers from the emperor's theaters.

Besides allowing Peicam's despotism, Paul I inaugurated other unpopular policies in the ballet world, which were short-lived, but troublesome. He proscribed the performance of the waltz, and ordered that only women dancers should perform in ballets, since healthy men would be more useful in the army. The dancers were commanded by him to attend guards' parades,[17] probably to train them to perform the marches and evolutions he liked. Indeed, these and other indignities perpetrated by a sick mind made his memory so despised that a century and one-half later Soviet ballet took sweet revenge by lampooning his reign in a comic satire entitled *Lieutenant Kizhe*. Needless to say, Paul's assassination in the spring of 1801 evoked few genuine tears from the imperial dancers. His death brought the end of Peicam's Russian sinecure, whereupon he fled the country after receiving two thousand rubles from the imperial treasury for his voyage. According to one account his beautiful wife remarried in Cassel;[18] a Russian acquaintance, however, reported that she entered a convent in Dresden and there lived a strict life.[19]

Whatever fate befell the couple, when Didelot followed the charlatan "balletmaster," the dancers were prone to look with jaundiced eyes upon another Frenchmen who might treat them in the same contemptible manner.

The chief balletmaster with whom Didelot had to share the limelight in the beginning of his stay in Russia was Ivan Val'berkh, considered to be the first native born Russian to occupy the post. During his career Val'berkh mounted thirty-six ballets and renewed ten productions of other choreographers. Some of them were based upon Russian folk life or contemporary themes, a fact which has been praised by Soviet dance historians, no doubt with the aim of urging present day balletmasters to imitate this facet of his creativity. However, Val'berkh's own contemporaries were often less kind. The St. Petersburg critic Rafail Zotov had little use for him. When Didelot left Russia in 1811, Zotov bemoaned the loss saying that there was left now "only the half-baked balletmaster Val'berkh" to replace him.[20]

During 1802 Val'berkh was sent by the administration of the Imperial Theaters to Paris to perfect his art. There some of Didelot's French rivals did their best to poison Val'berkh's mind against his coworker. The man whose ballet Didelot was accused in Bordeaux of copying and claiming as his own, Louis Nivelon, entertained and gave "a great present" to Val'berkh. During the visit Nivelon also told him many unsavory facts about Didelot. Val'berkh was impressed with Nivelon's disclosures and confided to his diary on April 17, 1802, "Ah, pock-marked, dry Didelot. What a fine fellow you are. Everywhere you love to be first and rule under a mask of modesty. Thanks to Nivelon, I now know you. You lack force, are haughty, and think yourself to be twice what you are worth. You would be worse than Chevalier if you had been in his place during his time . . . now I know you. And so I am obliged to go along with you." On the following day, he again vented his feelings against Didelot, affirming his intention "to beat down Didelot's arrogance and manage well upon arrival." Before Val'berkh left Paris Gardel himself also tried to turn his mind against Didelot. Val'berkh assured his diary that he would never dance for Didelot and that he must remember that he was an envious creature and wished to become what Peicam was.[21] Upon returning home Val'berkh maintained quite a remarkable state of peaceful coexistence with Didelot, considering all the facts of the case. Once in 1808 Madame Val'berkh wrote to her husband, telling of a personal favor Didelot had done for her. When their daughter was playing the role Dido she had gone to Didelot to beg the use of a diadem from him. Didelot, without offering a word of resistance, sent sandals as well as the jewelry, and even showed the daughter how to wear her costume. Madame Val'berkh added, "He also asked whether you were healthy, and asked me to convey his regards to you." Suspicious Val'berkh replied to his wife, "What you write me of Didelot pleases me. One must not always look on people from the dark side. . . . His attention to my family is worthy of gratitude from my side." For that reason, Val'berkh asked his wife to convey his gratitude and regards to him.[22]

Didelot's first printed word to the Russian public, in the preface to a program from *Psyché et l'Amour* (1809) publicly praised Val'berkh, pointing out that he was "justly esteemed as a distinguished artist in several genres, as well as a good father, an upright man and excellent comrade." Further, he said, "when these qualities so essential are found united to talent, they seem to double themselves and add luster, moreover, to merit." [23]

When Didelot came to Russia, there were two other *premiers danseurs* in St. Petersburg besides Val'berkh and himself: Charles Le Picq and Vasily Balashov. Le Picq had come to Russia in 1786. He married the dancer Gertrude Rossi, the mother of the well known architect Carlo Rossi, whose name was given to the tiny street in Leningrad, unofficially known as "Theater Street," on which the Leningrad Choreographic Institute is now located. Didelot referred to Le Picq as a dancer with distinguished talent, "certainly one of the patriarchs of our art." [24] Le Picq's career, however, was drawing to an end, for he died in 1806, while Balashov moved to Moscow in 1803.

Among his other collaborators in Russia Didelot had high esteem for Auguste Poirot, who had made his debut in St. Petersburg in 1798. Poirot, usually called simply "Auguste," was the brother of Peicam's wife, but managed to maintain a respected position in Russia in spite of his notorious relatives. While employed as a first demi-character dancer he was obliged by contract to fill all roles assigned to him except that of a tyrant. In addition he often aided Val'berkh and Didelot in the role of balletmaster or teacher. Didelot's pupil Adam Glushkovsky said that

Auguste "chiefly played pantomime roles; in divertissements he danced superbly in the Russian style. He ennobled Cossack, Russian, Gypsy, Hungarian, and Polish Mazurka dancing." [25] With his unusually sensitive appreciation of Russian artistry, Poirot found that the Russians reciprocated. "Auguste was handsome, a real Russian fellow, with intelligent, charming looks," [26] a Russian commentator recorded. Both the public and the royal family warmly accepted him; he taught dancing to the Czarevitch and lived in Russia until his death in 1844.[27] In the later years of his career Didelot dedicated one of his greatest ballets, *Raoul de Créquis* to Poirot, saying, "Dear Friend! Friendship does not need many words. This ballet was compiled for your benefit, and I dedicate it to you. If possibly it achieves success, then all the more may it be a worthy expression of the warm friendship and esteem of your friend, C. Didelot." [28]

Among the ballerinas in St. Petersburg, Didelot found one who was, truly, a dancer's dancer. This was Yevgenia Kolosova (*Fig. 20*). She was the daughter of a *figurante* named N. D. Neelova, and had appeared in dramatic, operatic, and ballet productions long before finishing theatrical school in 1799. "With the expressive lines of her face, beautiful figure and majestic bearing," one critic remarked, "Kolosova could speak by glances and movements better than by speech." [29] Glushkovsky sensitively recalled, "I have observed dance art for forty years, and many times I saw wonderful ballet artists who came to Russia, but in none of them did I see talent equal to that of Yevgenia Ivanovna Kolosova. . . . Each movement of her face, each gesture was so natural and understandable that it decisively replaced speech for the spectator." [30] Kolosova played many important roles in Didelot's ballets, and he once declared that "her beautiful physique, the effectiveness of her dancing, her superiority as a mime made her a precious subject and pride of her master, Val'berkh." [31]

The Russian audiences were especially charmed by Kolosova's Russian folk dancing, when her partner was Auguste Poirot. The critic Thaddeus Bulgarin commented, "No one, before or after her, understood Russian folk dance to such a degree. Each of her steps, each glance, each movement brought forth loud, rapturous, unceasing waves of applause, forcing her to repeat the work several times." [32] She is greatly credited with giving Russian folk dance an honorable place not only on the stage, but also on the parquetry floors of the grand ballrooms of the day. For a time folk dance had been looked down upon

Figure 20. Yevgenia Kolosova, an oil painting by A. Varnek in the Russian Museum in Leningrad, from Slonimsky's *Didlo.*

by the French salon-oriented upper class of Russia. When Princess Amalia of Baden, the sister of Alexander I's wife, came to live in Russia, she was entranced with its folk dance and asked Kolosova to teach her. Soon Kolosova had more requests for giving lessons to the aristocracy then she could fulfill.[33] Along with her beauty and talents, Kolosova was also considered to be "an intelligent and truly good woman," [34] generous and motherly toward the young artists.

Since Emperor Paul I had ordered that no men should dance in ballets, for a short time before the arrival of Auguste Poirot another well known dancer, Nastasia Berilova often served as Kolosova's partner. Though Didelot was not confronted with a complete dearth of talent, most of the other great names among ballerinas of the first half of the nineteenth century were those who, several years after his arrival, would emerge from the master's training.

In regard to Didelot's own performing ability in Russia, Glushkovsky recalled that "he was a graceful dancer; he produced each step with great purity. He did many entrechats and pirouettes, but did not have great elevation in his entrechats and leaps. He created for himself a special form of dance with graceful poses, smoothness, purity and speed in gliding steps (*pas à terre*), pleasing positions of the arms and lively pirouettes." [35] However, not all Russian critics found Didelot so pleasing as a performer. A description of his appearance by Stepan Zhikharev, an official who kept a theatrical memoire, noted that he had seen a *pas de deux* representing Apollo and Diana danced by Didelot and his pupil Ikonina. "This Didelot," he commented in December of 1806, "is now recognized as the best contemporary choreographer in Europe, but in appearance, he is truly the last. Thin as a skeleton, with a huge nose, wearing a light red wig with a wreath of laurel on his head and lyre in his hand, in spite of the art with which he danced, he was closer to a caricature of Apollo than of the brilliant god of song." [36] Another acquaintance drew a similar picture: "He was of middle growth, lean, pock-marked, with a small bald spot, a long aquiline nose, with gray, quick eyes and a sharp chin . . . in general his looks were not handsome." [37]

After half a year of careful rehearsal of the troupe, Didelot made his debut as a balletmaster by mounting the anacreontic work *Apollo and Daphne* in St. Petersburg in 1802. Seldom were complaints ever voiced against his choreography. Glushkovsky remarked that *Apollo and Daphne* "enthralled the St. Petersburg public by its charming dances and groupings, so like a painting." [38] These same features were to constitute the outstanding delight of many of his productions in the future. The ballet followed the ancient myth in which the god Apollo pursues his beloved Daphne, who asks the other gods to save her from her pursuer. They promptly oblige by changing her into a tree.

At Pavlovsk, the lovely imperial palace not far from St. Petersburg, Didelot presented the last act of the ballet *Roland and Morgana*. Although the ballet was intended to be a five-act production, Pavlovsk Theater lacked the facilities for presenting the total work. The production was used again on March 16, 1803 at St. Petersburg as part of the celebration commemorating the one hundreth anniversary of the founding of the city by Peter the Great. For this, all places in the brilliantly lit theater were occupied by the highest government officials and members of the diplomatic *corps*.[39] Didelot would make several attempts in the future to stage this same work, but it seems it seldom lived up to his expectations.

In March or April of 1803, death claimed his wife, the elegant Rose, in the prime of her life. No cause has come to light, but the harsh Russian climate was difficult for even the hardy to bear and Rose's health was not rugged when she arrived. By her death Didelot lost a partner whose suave art gave him tremendous pride, who had no minor part in the success he obtained as a performer. Later engagements in London were scarcely as successful as those from 1796–1801 when Rose Paul was his wife and partner. Didelot, six years after her death, reminisced that "Vestris the father, Le Picq, and my wife had neither strength nor extreme vivacity; they pirouetted little, with difficulty, because their genre would not permit it. Nevertheless, they were not less beautiful models of the dance because of it." He then uttered a panegyric about his dead wife: "Beautiful was your talent, O Rose! My art—must it give me only sad souvenirs?" [40]

Rose's loss was also sorely felt by the Russian audience. Commenting on a performance at the Hermitage, a member of the court, Princess Dorothée Lieven, confided to her diary, "Rose Didelot is dead, a great loss for us. Also, we did not have her husband yesterday, but in his place, that blockhead Val'berkh." [41]

Though greatly downcast at his wife's death, Didelot took the chief role of his own ballet, *Le Pâtre et l'hamadryade* on December 1. The part of the Hamadryad was performed by Marie Rose Colinette, a French dancer who had come to St. Petersburg in 1799. She was considered the rival of Nastasia Berilova.[42] Colinette danced in the traditional manner of the old school in the epoch of French classicism, with body erect, feet carefully turned out, and arms rounded affectedly.[43] Lonely Didelot soon married this new Rose, either in 1805 or 1806. According to Glushkovsky, "she was rather good looking, had outstanding talent, and was adored by the St. Petersburg public." [44] After her marriage, Rose left the theater, and gained an excellent reputation as a teacher of ballroom dancing. She taught her students beautiful, original ballroom dances specially composed by Didelot. Her clientele included grand dukes, as well as students of the Smolny Institute, a finishing school for aristocratic young women, who were proud to be able to show their friends the same dances the grand dukes were doing. The widowed empress Maria Feodorovna often visited classes at the institute and became a confirmed patron of Madame Didelot. Young Glushkovsky, who often accompanied Rose on her pedogogical rounds in order to distribute tambourines, veils, castanets, and other necessary accroutrements, remembered that when she gave one of her two-hour lessons to eight noblemen, Rose received one hundred assignat rubles.[45] There were other compensations which were received, no doubt partly because of Rose's connections. For awhile during his early Russian years, Didelot lived in Mikhailovsky Palace. This huge fortress had been built by the unpopular emperor Paul I, who felt safer living in it than in other imperial residences. However, its deep moats and especially picked guards could not save Paul from members of his own entourage, who, sick of his arbitrariness, strangled him there in his bedroom on March 10, 1801. The royal family then immediately vacated the castle, and the Didelots were allowed to live there with the caretaker and a few servants. Many of its huge rooms were adorned with marble fireplaces, great mirrors, and gilded ceilings and door knobs as well as floors with parquetry wood patterns of flowers, birds, and animals. Glushkovsky, who lived there with the Didelots, was enthralled with its general aura of romance, and especially with its secret passages, where, in his child's imagination, the ghost of poor Paul I no doubt roamed.[46]

Justifiably, Didelot gained the reputation of being a strict disciplinarian in the Imperial Theaters, but his dealings with Glushkovsky and other artists betrayed a heart of gold inside the stern master. Noticing young Adam's talent, and knowing that he was homeless, Didelot asked the director, Naryshkin, to take the boy into his own household. When the treasurer of the theaters wanted to give Didelot five hundred assignat rubles for Glushkovsky's upkeep, Didelot was indignant, asking, "Do you really think I asked to educate *le jeune Adam* for money?" [47] The treasurer told him that the money was for his clothes and other necessities, and if Didelot did not want to spend it, he could keep it for Glushkovsky. This is what was done; when Didelot later left Russia for England, he gave his student the sum accumulated from the five-hundred-ruble annual allotment.

Didelot's second contract was concluded ahead of time on March 31, 1804 with Naryshkin. According to the new terms Didelot agreed:

to fulfill all first roles in ballets;

to serve as chief director of the dance school, educating soloists, perfecting the existing *corps de ballet*, and forming a new one;

to mount ballets and divertissements and to make use of all his talents for the good of the Imperial Theaters;

to follow the troupe wherever it would be directed;

to attend all meetings and rehearsals decreed by the director;

to wear the dress required by the costumer, and to submit to all other rules governing the performances. [48]

The clause signifying that he must form a new corps no doubt delighted Didelot. He envisioned works demanding a staff comparable to that of the Paris Opéra, whose staff in 1800 numbered ninety-three, while St. Petersburg had only about forty-five members. [49] Further, the Russian staff completely lacked two categories of performers: *coryphées* and soloists. With no intermediate positions between the *corps de ballet* and the first dancers, the youthful members were deprived of a chance for artistic growth which a more graduated system would allow.

In 1805 Didelot hurt himself quite seriously. In a letter to Emperor Alexander I he explained that "he lost his talent as a consequence of wounds which took place in the Hermitage Theater." [50] Time after time in London, Bordeaux, and Paris he had suffered the agony of severe muscular strain. In Russia, after years of grueling work, by 1809 he declared that he could only appear in those genres of dance which did not demand virtuoso technique. This decline in his performing talent gradually forced Didelot to channel his energy elsewhere. While Le Picq and Val'berkh were still active, he could not hope to be named balletmaster officially. Therefore in these years of his first Russian period, Didelot became immersed in teaching duties.

At the turn of the century the key concept dominating the St.

Petersburg Theatrical School seemed to be thrift. Pupils were often recruited cheaply from a local factory in which Gobelin tapestries were made by the labor of serfs whose services were bought from their landlords.[51]

The head of the school, Antonio Kazacci, was determined to utilize the talents of the students fully. He made the following proposal to the directorate concerning their education:

Theatrical students must all study music, dancing, Russian, writing and reading, and if thought fit, French . . . if some students play comedy or operatic roles, then, having changed their dress, they appear in the ballet; also, if they are not appearing in the present performance, maybe they will play in the orchestra, so that they will always be occupied. In this way, if the student, having studied dramatic art, is found not suitable, then perhaps he will dance not badly, or failing that, become a musician. Thus, the directorate can be assured that everything studied in the school will not be in vain. An honest man will be able to earn a living, because he has had no time to spare during his study. I propose that for two hours each morning the students study Russian, later, dancing for two hours, after dinner, music for two hours, and then dramatic art for two hours. Any free time can be usefully occupied by playing symphonies amongst themselves. Sometimes they can go out walking and since they will have no free time, evil thoughts will not arise. If at the time when students are allowed to go walking the weather is not fit, then for an hour they must do multiplication, which I can supervise. With all this study, I shall be able to keep good order. . . . If, also, some student cannot apply himself to the science that is to be his livelihood, then at least he will be able to read and write well, so that he can obtain some position (if he is honest) as a music copyist, clerk, etc.[52]

Prince Yusupov approved of Kazacci's plan completely, and under such a regime, the teaching of dancing understandably declined.

Val'berkh had been under contract as a teacher in the school since 1794 and was in charge of dance training in 1801. When Didelot arrived he assumed responsibility for the teaching of dancing, since Val'berkh was sent to Paris by Naryshkin, who had replaced Yusupov. Didelot soon began to attack the problems besetting the institution, but it took years to solve some of them—such as the retirement and replacement of former soldiers and impoverished widows who clung to their jobs on the staff. There were grave troubles with the building which housed the school. A memo from 1803 records that "due to the activities undertaken by the dancing master Didelot, everything will fall to the ground, making an enormous ruin, because the floor of the building is very badly damaged by damp." [53] As a result in 1805, the school was given better quarters on Yekaterinsky Canal.

Before long the conduct of some of the young pupils became a source of concern to their pious elders who felt they needed more religious training. It was therefore ordained that a church should be established near the theatrical school, because it was said, "Dancers may be dancers, but belief in God must not be shaken." The church was ready for their use by 1806, and the supervisors were relieved, for they said, "Now everyone can learn to dance and also pray to God." [54]

In the running of the school, Didelot had a competent helper named Yekaterina Alexandrovna Sazonova, whose married name was Bekker. Within three years of having been graduated from the school in 1803 she became a teacher in the ballet section. Sazonova guided the pupils through their first steps, producing adolescents who were well grounded in the essentials of the art. Didelot himself did the final polishing.

When Didelot became director of the school in 1804, the quiet two hours of Val'berkh's classes changed to four-hour and five-hour stormy sessions with the stern new master (*Fig. 21*). He immersed himself completely in the job of teaching, becoming fanatically devoted to the training of his students. After belaboring the young aspirants with years of arduous work, he was justifiably, unashamedly proud of them. In the forward to *Psyché et l'Amour* he talked of the merits of his numerous "children," declaring, "I beg forgiveness, but a father and teacher speaks—a teacher who sacrificed his own talent, his own pleasure to the tiresome obligation of educating a dance troupe." [55]

Under him, the schedule and system of teaching was exacting, severe, and uncompromising. On dark winter mornings, in a hall hardly lighted by dripping tallow candles, the students took their exercises from six o'clock to breakfast time. One pupil recalled that "at eleven o'clock the rattling of a carriage suddenly resounded. . . . 'Monsieur Didelot has come,' the population of the theatrical school cried out. The appearance of the Olympic Thunderer himself could have put no more fear of God in weak mortals. . . . The door opened noisily, and with a hat on the back of his head and an overcoat falling from his shoulder, the awesome balletmaster entered." [56] As he took up his pedagogical

Figure 21. Charles Didelot, a charcoal drawing by A. Orlovsky in the State Pushkin Museum in Moscow, from Pospelov's *Russkii portretnyi risunok nachala XIX veka*.

duties, the overcoat came off, revealing a short brown frock coat, unfastened, with no vest. A great white collar, almost reaching clear to his ears, was set off by a bright scarf around his neck.[57] While a violin played, an elm baton in his hand tapped the cadence as the students did their endless *battements* and *ronds des jambes*. One Russian explained that, "At lessons he always appeared with a thick stick, having correctly heard that you can't do anything with a Russian without a stick." [58] Anticipating this, many a student on the way to class or rehearsals made the Sign of the Cross and prayed to God to be spared blows either from his stick or from a hunting crop he sometimes used on their backs and legs.[59] With him as teacher one official, Philip Vigel, affirmed, "our Russian dancers learned by sweat and blood how the art of dancing was achieved." [60] Karatygin recalled Didelot's ballet lessons vividly, saying, "I know from experience how light was his foot and how heavy his hand. The more he found one capable, the more he turned his attention and generously gave signs of his inclination toward a student. Black and blue spots often served as signs of an outstanding future dancer." Even Karl, Didelot's own son, Karatygin explained, received "neither indulgence nor condescension, but was exposed to the same fate as all." [61]

Many students in the theatrical school who had no desire to become dancers feared Didelot and hated the lessons. Others, however, were fired with enthusiasm by his zeal. One observer remarked, "He wished by every means to convey his ideals. In view of this, he had no regard for pleas, tears, sweat nor choler, frequently resorting *ad argumenta lignea*." [62] Rafail Zotov confirmed the infectiousness of Didelot's enthusiasm. "People with genius have an innate ability to inspire people all around them. Didelot was not the least aimable with his pupils— however, they just the same obeyed him without contradiction, thinking only of how to please him. The character of Didelot was most ardent, often unbearable, however, all loved him, all worshipped him." [63]

Occasionally the intensity of the classes was broken by a lighter moment. Once Karatygin inched his way to the center of the room to escape the stick of the master. Didelot, swinging his baton to emphasize the beat, followed the would-be escapee. In the center of the room, Didelot's stick crashed into a crystal chandelier, unleashing a hail of crystal fragments which bruised and scratched the master's own bald pate. When Karatygin, shedding tears of remorse, besought pardon, Didelot only stroked his head, exhorting him to be more diligent, and above all, to stay out from under the chandeliers.[64]

In addition to his fanaticism for instilling proper ballet technique, Didelot worked equally hard to develop acting skills in his pupils. They took part not only in mass scenes of his ballets but also often played significant roles, such as that of Georg in *The Hungarian Hut*, Créon in *Raoul de Créquis*, and Bacchus in the opera *Télémaque dans l'Isle de Calypso*.[65]

Under his tutelage the school grew and produced creditable artists. By 1805 there were about sixty students of both sexes studying ballet. By 1806 a talented *premier danseur* of the serious genre was graduated, Yakov Liustikh, who later became a teacher and balletmaster himself. In 1809 one of Didelot's most ardent pupils, as well as his admirer, imitator, and unofficial press agent was graduated—Adam Glushkovsky, who achieved fame in Moscow and left one of the best accounts available of his master's activity. In the same year emerged Maria Ikonina and Anastasia Novitskaya, followed by the never-to-be-forgotten Maria Danilova in 1810.

Maria Nikolaevna Ikonina was noted for correct technique. "Anyone who does not believe that dance belongs to the fine arts should gaze at the majestic steps of Ikonina, the precision of her movements, her variety of position," [66] declared one critic. Her pantomime ability, however, was not as great as her technique. Another observer remarked, "What a marvelous figure, what an elevated chest, what method and grace! But, since there is no perfection in the world, the grace of Diana-Ikonina appeared to me somewhat chilly. There was no sort of response or life in her physiogonomy." [67] Unfortunately, Ikonina was also subject to fits of temperament which cost her frequent fines, and on one occasion, arrest. In a later stage of her career she declined much in beauty. Her figure became thin as a skeleton, and the rosiness faded from her cheeks. When this change occurred, a former admirer reported that her popularity fell, because he asked, "Who wants to watch the dance of a corpse?" [68]

Didelot's pupil Anastasia Novitskaya was both a talented dancer and pantomime actress. Karatygin declared that she was "incomparably more talented than Istomina," [69] the ballerina so praised by the poet Pushkin, while Zotov declared that she did not have to take second place even to Marie Taglioni in purity and finish of steps. She was able to combine tenderness and modesty, nobility and charm, with inexpressible lightness and purity.[70] In 1822 Didelot signified that the main role of a ballet should be danced by Novitskaya's rival, Yekaterina

Teleshova, while Novitskaya was to take an inferior part. When Novitskaya balked as being shoved aside Didelot appealed to Count Mikhail A. Miloradovich, governor-general of St. Petersburg and head of a special committee for the resolution of important theatrical questions, who was not above using his position to advance the interest of his favorites, Yekaterina Teleshova and Vera Zubova. Miloradovich, formerly a general who fought valiantly against Napoleon, was used to being obeyed. When Novitskaya resisted the general, Miloradovich ordered that she should end, for once and for all, her rivalry with Teleshova and threatened to have her committed to an insane asylum if it were not done. The shy, sensitive girl became seriously ill, and when the empress learned of the affair, she demanded that Miloradovich apologize to Novitskaya. She was so terrified when the count came to call on her for this purpose she died shortly after. A certain poetic justice seemed manifest in Miloradovich's life when he was shot by Decembrist revolutionaries in 1825.[71]

By universal agreement the supreme charmer among Didelot's pupils was Maria Danilova, styled, among dozens of beautiful epithets, "the eternal priestess of Terpsichore." "There was a time," one misty-eyed witness recalled, "when our theater had its own Russian Taglioni . . . when only the appearance of this enchantress brought rapture to the public. This Taglioni, like the former, was called Maria, but she was Russian, ours at heart and in origin. She grew up under our stern sky, on our cold shores, but with a soul of fire. Young, beautiful, and charming, she flashed in our theater like a poet's dream." [72] Another admirer confirmed the opinion, saying, "She was Diana, Juno, or Minerva . . . she was one of those beauties who appear once in a century. She had black hair, fiery eyes, correct facial lines—not Grecian, but rounded, carrying the imprint of Slavic nationality, with a heavenly smile. Of middle size, she had the form of Venus de Medici." [73]

Danilova was born in St. Petersburg in 1793 of noble but poor parents, named Perfil'ev, who, being unable to educate her, put her in theatrical school. According to the actress Alexandra Asenkova "she was strictly a mime artist, and danced no better than the others. However, she had the combination of talents which could make a fine dancer, but for some reason, Didelot scarcely gave any time to her training." [74] On stage she played the parts of little cupids and genies, always performing responsibly and intelligently. The lovely Yevgenia

Kolosova was especially attracted to the beautiful child and took upon herself the task of instructing Danilova in the art of mime. From this unrivaled mistress of the art Danilova learned to communicate by gesture all the ardor and passion of her young soul.

One of the most venerable Soviet ballet historians, Yuri Bakhrushin, asserts that through Danilova, Didelot first introduced *pointe* dancing— probably in *Zéphire et Flore* in 1808. Bakhrushin adds, however, that the practice then depended on the natural strength of the performer, whose feet were clad only in soft shoes or in sandals.[75]

There were many admirers at the theater who pursued Danilova, but neither their compliments nor wealth enticed her, for "she belonged entirely to her art and smiled at the passionate sighs of those who deified her." [76] However, when Louis Duport came to Russia in 1808 it was a different story (*Fig. 22*).

Duport arrived in Russia having blazed a trail of successes wherever he went. A Frenchman described him as "a fop, with a sauciness and feminine affectedness about him, a lewd smile and glistening eyes." [77] Observing that he was truly a master of technique, a German critic remarked: "His short, but completely proportioned physique had its own certain charm, softness, roundness, and femininity. He danced like a sylph, not a man." Actually, the German asserted that it was difficult for a woman, dancing near him, to distinguish herself by grace. Not only was masculinity impossible for him, but "anything heroic was unattainable for him." [78] However, no one ever denied that Duport *could* dance. Years later one of his viewers at St. Petersburg recalled, "It seems I behold him still. All of his bodily movements were performed pleasantly and quickly. Not very large, he was compact and lithe as a rubber ball. The floor on which his feet landed seemed to thrust him away on high. From the farthest depths of the stage he bounded across it in three leaps to appear in front of the spectators; his dances might better be called flights." [79] Other descriptions of him in Russia were just as enthusiastic. Bulgarin declared, "In all my life, I never saw such a dancer as Duport. . . . He was well built, adroit, picturesque, graceful in all his movements, and light as a bird." [80] In fact Bulgarin affirmed that he crossed the stage not in three, but in two leaps. Duport especially startled his new audience with dazzling pirouettes, done so quickly that the eyes of spectators could not follow him. Glushkovsky noted that he always made his pirouettes on his very toes and always finished them in a pleasant pose. Other dancers, he recalled, made endless pirouettes

Figure 22. Louis Duport, a charcoal drawing of 1809 by A. Orlovsky in the State Russian Museum in Leningrad, from Pospelov's *Russkii portretnyi risunok nachala XIX veka.*

gracelessly, turning on the toes, then sinking down on the heel. Duport, in his view, "was like a well built machine, whose activity was determined and always true." [81] Undoubtedly, another critic proposed, he was descended from some famed whirling dervish, inspired by Mohammed himself.[82] Mere technical ability, however, was not enough to satisfy the Russians, who liked "soul" in their ballets, and Duport soon became a thorn in Didelot's side. Being preoccupied only with demonstrating his own virtuosity, Duport demanded that Didelot create ballets which were adapted to his style. Didelot, with his own firm aesthetic creed emphasizing mime and the dramatic potential of dance, was little inclined to agree with Duport's views.

Duport had come to Russia with a famed tragic actress, Mademoiselle George (Marguerite-Joséphine Weimer). Considered to be political émigrés in Russia fleeing from the Napoleonic regime, they were shown much kindness by the Russian court and high society. For a dancing partner, he chose Maria Danilova, and began to supervise her training, using, it was believed, "more tender methods than the cruel Didelot." [83] Duport partnered her constantly: she was his Daphne, his Flora. Morning and evening he was with her, drilling her ceaselessly, and undermining the weak health of the fragile teen-ager. Danilova's flaming young soul, which had resisted the seduction of riches and flattery, responded with ardor to the Frenchman, her equal in talent and devotion to dance. Once Danilova was unreservedly his, however, Duport abandoned her for his former mistress, Mademoiselle George. To the young girl this was a shattering experience. In the romanticized version of the story "the inconstant Zéphyr soon took wing from his Flora; tortured by grief, she became ill and her light was extinguished." [84] Actually, the very real agony of her broken heart was compounded by consumption, the killer of scores of Russian dancers throughout decades of ballet history.

When Duport had begun to give Danilova so much attention, Didelot also began to work with her. In 1809 when he staged the ballet *Psyché et l'Amour* at the Hermitage, Didelot gave her the chief role. In one scene Danilova was lifted on high by machinery in order that her descent into the nether world might be portrayed. A group of devils stood waiting to catch her. Wearing a corset which attached her to the lifting device, she was being lowered almost to the stage floor when the machinery produced an unexpected jerk. Danilova screamed piercingly, and after she was let down, almost senseless, she suffered a hemorrhage and pains in the chest. Though ill, Danilova danced as long as she could, for she could not stand the thought that her roles would be given to other dancers. During her sickness the Parisian ballerina Saint-Clair made her debut in Danilova's role in *Psyché*. Kolosova came to visit her beloved student during the final days of her illness. Danilova suddenly started up in bed, saying, "So you know, little mother, why I don't want to die? Because Saint-Clair will get my roles. . . . How vexing this is." [85] She said she would give half her life if they would carry her bed into the theater so she could see Saint-Clair perform and learn from her.

The high born and rich of St. Petersburg came to call on Danilova. Emperor Alexander I even commissioned his own physician to care for her, but she died January 8, 1810, only seventeen years old. Many summers after her death garlands of fresh flowers adorned the modest monument on her grave. More than that her death called forth poetic laments from such currently popular *litterateurs* as Karamzin, M. V. Milonov, and N. I. Gnedich. In general, their poignant eulogies followed the tone of Gnedich's lines:

> From our vision you have hidden, like a star
> Which, fleeting through the heavens on a clear night
> Astounds with its radiance the watching wayfarer
> Then suddenly disappears into the gloom.[86]

For his part Didelot fully acknowledged the natural endowment of the young Danilova, admitting in the preface to the program for *Psyché et l'Amour* that "in the natural act of pantomime the master can only develop the talent of the pupil. If nature has not placed the seed in her soul . . . it is useless to bother; the master makes the mechanism of the art; he is able by a combination of movements to give grace, but nothing more." It is the soul, he affirmed, which truly makes the art. At the same time, Didelot resented the credit given to Duport for Danilova's training, and he complained about it in the same document, asking, "In five months, can one form a student who has danced and played the role of Psyché?" He answered his own question: "I declare . . . that not only she [Danilova], but all those in the school, who now compose the young *corps* at the theater have been formed by my endeavors, and that the principal subjects, those who have danced beside Mr. Duport, knew how to dance before he arrived." [87] Not only Danilova but Ikonina and Novitskaya had all previously danced with Didelot and could not possibly have learned everything from Louis Duport.

Actually, the preference given to foreign dancers had been a constant source of unhappiness to Russian artists, and in this respect, Didelot took up the cause of his Russian protégés fully, even though he himself was an outsider. Foreigners' salaries were completely out of proportion to those received by Russian artists. The esteemed Kolosova, for example, a *première danseuse*, received three thousand five hundred rubles a year, while the French dancer, Mademoiselle Batiste, on a lower rank than Kolosova, received seven thousand five hundred rubles. Russian performers in the same class as Batiste, such as Novitskaya, received one-fifth less than she. Significantly, the salary of Duport, sixty thousand rubles, was more than the cost of all the troupe of half a hundred performers.[88] Naturally, the Russians, as well as the government, were anxious to stop this munificence to foreigners.

By 1809 the ballet troupe of the Imperial Theater in St. Petersburg had grown to fifty-six, and it now included soloists and *coryphées*. Top positions were then occupied by Didelot's pupils. Finally, the *corps de ballet* had grown to forty-two members, with the number of females twice that of males. It was time, the government decided, to make a determined effort to replace foreign artists by natives and to eliminate the drain on the treasury to foreign talent. With this view clearly stated, in 1809, a new set of instructions governing the theatrical school were issued. According to the new plan up to their thirteenth year, the pupils in the theatrical school prepared for all aspects of theatrical work, and at the same time, studied French, Russian, arithmetic, music, the "laws of God," dancing, and drawing. At the age of thirteen general studies continued, but those gifted in a special field were to be put in classes of about twelve students where a master in the special art, such as Didelot in the field of ballet, would guide their growth. Russian ballet profited greatly from this reorganization. Each six months exams took place in the presence of officials and outstanding theatrical artists. The exact point for graduation was not designated, but if the aspirants had not acquired the necessary artistry by the age of twenty, they were dismissed as students. Humanely speaking, living conditions for theatrical students in Russia were better in many respects than in other capitals of Europe. Students were educated at the public expense and some unusual measures, for the day, were taken to insure their comfort and well-being. When leaving the school for performances during the dark, cold, northern winter evenings, they were bundled in warm clothing. Theatrical carriages, often long roofed wagons driven by four

horses and holding up to fifteen people, transported them to the
theaters—a service that continued throughout their performing careers.
If an ordinary citizen's carriage passed that of the emperor, the men
were obliged to step out, remove their hats, and bow; the ladies merely
bowed. Theatrical carriages were exempt from this annoying bit of
protocol. There were other fringe benefits for the students of ballet.
Each summer they spent some time at Pavlovsk or Gatchina, another
palace near St. Petersburg. There they walked freely in spacious
gardens forbidden to lesser mortals. At the end of his career, a faithful
performer received a pension of his full salary—in addition to any
recompense he might earn for teaching or other services after
retirement.

The sheltered walls of the theatrical school posed a continual
challenge for adventurous young Russians to penetrate. Once a clerk
named Kholopov wended his way into the school's washroom, disguised
as a tailor, where he somewhat clumsily helped sew the girls' costumes.
An officer of a lancer's regiment named A. I. Yakubovich penetrated
into the secluded corridors of the school posing as a soft drink vendor.
His ruse was discovered, however, because he made the mistake of
loading his canteen with fine chocolate and his bag with delectable
goodies no ordinary vendor would ever have had and then of giving
them all away.[89] His story does not end here, however, for before his
wild oats were all sown, the daring Yakubovich became involved in a
much more serious balletic scandal involving the dancer Istomina and
culminating in a duel. He gained notoriety as well for participating in
the Decembrist Revolt of 1825.

In the years that Didelot was constantly busy supervising the
training of a competent group of performers for his ballets, he also
managed to stage a few works. A warm reception was given to Zéphyr
and Flora when they finally cavorted about the stage of the Hermitage
in 1804. As everywhere the ballet was a great favorite, and in addition
to the Hermitage it became established in the repertoire of the Bolshoi
Kamenny Theater. For the Russian audience not the least of the
attractions of this ballet were the flights. In one scene, Zéphyr descends
from on high, and after dancing a bit with Flora, lifts and transports her
to the heights of the opposite side of the stage. In another scene, Flora
flies about the stage while around her a circle of cupids weave a
dance.[90] The ballet was warmly accepted by the discriminating
intelligentsia, including the great poet Derzhavin. Seeing it, he ex-

claimed, "The most flaming imagination of a poet could never beget the like." [91]

In 1806 Didelot had the opportunity again to show *Roland and Morgana, or The Destruction of the Enchanted Isle.* Though only one act, it was a fuller version than the 1803 production. One observer of the ballet left a comment in the German language magazine, *Ruthenia,* which speaks well for Russian ballet in general. In 1807 he reported to his countrymen, "In St. Petersburg there are three theaters which are visited most often, and are always filled with Russian, French and German spectators. Ballet is in the repertoire of each one, and as a rule, is given at the end of the performance. I have not seen any finer ballet than that of St. Petersburg. The superb music conforms unusually and exactly to the smallest movement of the actors. For the most part, the dancers are young, beautiful, and refined in their art. The decorations are superior, and their transformations proceed with astonishing swiftness. This happened in the ballet *Roland and Morgana,* where the stage was converted from a dark cave into a valley with a temple in sight, resting in clouds, while nymphs and spirits formed artistic groups in front of the backdrop." [92]

For the plot, Didelot borrowed characters from the poem *Orlando Furioso* of Ariosto. In Glushkovsky's opinion this ballet had appeal to all classes: the educated liked the subject and the gracious dances; the uneducated savored the combats of Roland against a giant, harpies, and a dragon.[93] Not all viewers agreed with Glushkovsky's enthusiastic appreciation of the production, however. Even though it was again expanded in 1821 to a five-act version, Zotov remarked, "It seems it was the only unsuccessful one in his [Didelot's] life.[94]

In 1806 Didelot enlivened two operas by François-Adrien Boieldieu, *Le Calife de Bagdad* and *Télémaque.* During the latter he had ample opportunity to show his ability to spark life into a production. In one scene Telemachus betrays Calypso and falls in love with one of her nymphs. His fellow traveller Mentor, who really is the persistent goddess Minerva in disguise, wants to drive Telemachus from the island in order to separate him from his new passion. In spite of his betrayal, Calypso wants to prevent Telemachus' departure, so she conjures a storm to prevent it.

In the ordinary portrayal of this scene Calypso simply waves her magic wand, and immediately theatrical thunder, lightning, and rain burst forth. Didelot, however, wanted to inject more dramatic action into the scene. He had Calypso therefore summon Aeolus, the god of the winds and entreat him to produce a storm at sea. Aeolus rolled away a huge stone from a cave in which the spirits of the winds were held captive; they burst forth with long hair streaming, with huge wings flapping, with cheeks swollen and lips protruding. Though chained, they rent asunder their bonds. Dividing themselves into groups some spirits were lifted into the air, producing wind by flapping their wings. Others furiously ran to the sea, stirring up waves; a third group clambered into the trees, making them sway from the winds, while a fourth group scaled the heights of cliffs, making the very clouds tremble amidst flashing lightning and rolling thunder. Finally, the last group sank into the depths of the earth, producing a frightful rumble as fires burst forth from several spots in the ground. In this unforgettable Dance of the Winds, all the storm activity was enacted by dancers, who effectively expressed the fury and rage of the elements by their very bodily movements.[95] Alexandra Asenkova later recalled that the effect of the beating of the winged winds was so traumatic that it sent shivers down the spines of the performers themselves.[96]

In the same ballet a scene which brought down the house's applause was enacted by a rosy-cheeked, rotund little girl who played the part of Bacchus. While admiringly watching the dance of the maenads, tiny Bacchus stole sips from a little golden goblet of wine, until, after graciously reeling about the stage for a time, the little god finally fell asleep in the arms of one of the maenads.

For the debut of his pupil Ikonina, Didelot revived Le Picq's version of *Medée et Jason* in 1807. By 1808 his years of preparation of dancers had borne sufficient fruit for him to launch forth upon a new burst of creativity, producing a part of the dances in a divertissement called *The Sea Pier* in February. In May in response to the request of a fellow French dancer, Jean Dutacq, Didelot staged for his benefit a two-act version of *Don Quixote*. Evidence points to the fact that he based his work on the Parisian ballet *Les Noces di Gamache*. In July he produced a divertissement entitled *Golden Wedding* for a court spectacle. In August for the debut of Louis Duport Didelot created a divertissement composed of four dances.

All these were only a prelude, however, to the presentation on January 8, 1809, of "an erotic ballet in five acts" called *Psyché et l'Amour*. Though Noverre, Gardel, and Dauberval had all produced versions of it, in the foreword to the libretto, Didelot declared that he tried as far as possible to depart from what was done previously by the great masters.[97] In this beautiful work Didelot had the collaboration of the composer Catarino Cavos, who was to provide scores for many future ballets of Didelot. The decorations were by Pietro Gonzago and Dominic Corsini, whose works were said to be "like Raphael and Rubens in their form." With costumes by Cherubino Babini and machines by Thibeault, Didelot finally had a combined artistic force capable of bringing to life his powerful creative urges.

Apparently either to secure the opportunity to produce the work or to obtain the material necessities to accomplish it, he "pulled strings." Through his wife, whose ballroom dancing lessons gave her regular access to important circles, Didelot could gain the ear of the widowed empress, Maria Feodorovna. Didelot dedicated his ballet to her, saying in the program, "It is the feeble tribute of homage and gratitude of an artist whose spouse, for a long while, has been showered with favors from Your Majesty, and who would be far from hoping for such favors for himself." Another circumstance also expedited the production of the work: the king of Prussia, Frederick-William III, and his spouse Queen Louise visited St. Petersburg in the winter of 1809, and those responsible for planning court entertainment decided that a ballet on this theme should be shown. Didelot alone was willing to shoulder the task, for production time was short. He himself declared that although Cavos had only eighteen days in which to write five acts of music, the composer displayed here, as always, rare talent and facility.

Didelot embarked on the task with a creative frenzy that mystified the onlooker. At the time of one rehearsal in the Hermitage, a member of the *corps de ballet* lacked a necessary lyre and vase. Didelot, in a dither, rushed out on Nevsky Prospect, the liveliest street in St. Petersburg, with a red shoe on one foot and a black one on the other. Lacking a hat, he wound about his head some kind of gauzy, rainbow-colored covering. In this costume he ran into the Maly Theater, took what was needed, and returned by the same route. He usually walked very fast but this time he almost ran. Naturally people thought he was insane and a crowd of spectators floocked after him.[98]

In spite of the short time for production Didelot sought collaboration with the Russian intelligentsia in this task. There is a letter preserved in the Saltykov-Shchedrin Library in Leningrad from Didelot to A. N. Olenin, the director of this library at the time, and the future head of the Russian Academy of Sciences. In it Didelot discussed even the scenic formulation and costumes with Olenin.[99] The rewards for his

diligent preparation were great, for the ballet was shown fourteen times
in two months, an unusual run in those days. But who would not want
to see a production with such extraordinary marvels as it contained?

There was one glorious scene depicting the flight of Venus into the
clouds on a chariot, which was propelled in its upward flight by fifty
living white doves. It is interesting to imagine the care that had to be
taken to harness each dove with its little corselet, which was then
attached to wires guiding the flight of each bird. Reminiscing years
later, Rafail Zotov declared that the Russian stage had fallen behind the
accomplishments of this earlier era, for in a scene in *Psyché et l'Amour*
depicting hell, "one demon flew from the very depths of the stage, from
the twelfth *coulisse* to the ramp, and there brandished a torch over the
spectators." He added, ruefully, "in our day, we don't have such flights
anymore. Now they fly only along the stage from one wing to the
opposite one; a flight from the depth of the stage to the ramp is
considered impossible." [100]

In addition to this scene of burning terror in hell, Corsini conceived
scenic decorations representing voluptuous gardens of love. Gonzago's
special contribution was a scene of Olympus, done in a new spiral form.
It seemed that the base of Olympus enveloped the globe, supporting
and lifting it up toward the empyrean. Didelot was tremendously proud
of these three scenes, affirming, "the best eulogy I can make of the two
artists is to thank my luck star which led my Psyché into these sites so
well made to embellish her.[101] Didelot revealed that he feared the
machines might become a stumbling block in the second and last acts,
but Thibeault's inventiveness had succeeded to his heart's content, and
he expressed gratitude to him for this.

Clearly Didelot reached a peak in the first phase of his Russian
career with this ballet, and his joy with the work was unashamedly
evident; however, like many of his life's triumphs it was to be
short-lived. First, his most precious Psyché died: the beautiful Danilova
—an unspeakable loss to him. On February 15, 1810, Didelot showed
his ballet to the public on the stage of the Bolshoi Kamenny Theater.
Soon after this the theater burned, and in the fire his expensive
decorations and costumes perished. It was then impossible to resurrect
the ballet; however, lovely memories of *Psyché* abided with the
directors and the public. Didelot's reputation was made.

Meanwhile, on August 30, 1809, at the Tavritsky Palace, he showed
a "one-act fairy heroic comic divertissement" entitled *Zélis et Alcindor*.

The plot left much to be desired, but Didelot liked it enough to stage the work again in England in 1812. Didelot's last new production in Russia for several years to come was given at the Hermitage on August 30, 1810. This was the three-act ballet *Laura and Henry, or The Defeat of the Moors*. Nine years later he would again bring the production to life in Russia.

It would seem that all was going well with Didelot's life by 1810. However, under the surface of his successes, trouble brewed. Soon after he arrived in Russia, the imperial government began to pay his salary not with silver, but with paper money—assignats. The difference was important, for the substitution involved a loss to the Didelots of about one-third of their salary. Although it had not been stated in the text of the contract that his salary should be paid in silver, this was precisely stipulated by inscription on the contract negotiated in the name of the director of the Imperial Theaters and Didelot. Didelot then turned to the authorities to intercede for payment in hard currency. He had only temporary victories in this respect. Further, when Rose Paul died the administration soon notified him that his salary was to be lowered from twelve thousand to seven thousand rubles at the same time that his obligations in the ballet were markedly increasing.

On October 9, 1810, his contract ran out. Usually a new contract would be negotiated long before the former was ended. Didelot was then faced with the news that the Russian theaters no longer needed his services.

Shattered by such ingratitude for his hard work, he took his case to the emperor himself. His appeal to Alexander I recalled that, although he came to Russia to be a dancer, he had formed a new troupe and fundamentally reorganized the system of choreographic formation. Here, he pointed to the fact that he had lost his talent as a result of injuries suffered while performing at the Hermitage. He angrily asserted that the authorities could not reproach him in the least, but in spite of it they fired him. As a result he felt his position was hopeless, and there was now not a court theater in Europe at which he could seek employment without attracting suspicion concerning his talent and honesty. He asked the emperor for a sign of mercy and clemency, a present which would allow him to dispel such suspicions. On October 18 Alexander I assented to giving the desired present to Didelot, but did not sweep aside the dismissal order as Didelot had hoped. At news of this decision Didelot again tried to save his position. He agreed obsequiously to accept his salary in assignats; he would not demand payment for special jobs, whether in teaching or directing ballets. His humility apparently softened the heart of the emperor, for on November 4, 1810, Naryshkin was advised of Alexander's new view by Prince Golitsyn, who wrote: "In regard to Your Excellency's letter to me from the second of the month, I had the happiness to report to the Sovereign Emperor about the balletmaster Didelot . . . who declared his wish to continue his service in the future for the same sum of assignats. . . . His Imperial Highness agreed: Balletmaster Didelot, according to his wish, may be retained in service and a contract may be concluded with him on the basis of a future salary of seven thousand rubles, paid in assignats." [102]

It seemed his case had quieted down as the New Year dawned in 1811. Didelot was returning to his Mikhailovsky apartment that night from a feast at which his students had performed in the home of Dmitri Naryshkin, when the sickening news rang through the streets that the Kamenny Theater was enveloped in flames. His spirit was utterly shattered as the theater burnt to the ground. There were other theaters in St. Petersburg where he could give ballets, but they lacked the type of machinery he needed for his special production. Finally a supreme humiliation came to the haughty, turbulent character on January 17. At that time, the director of the Imperial Theaters wrote to Didelot: "Quite often I notice, and His Imperial Highness notices likewise, that the *figurantes* constituting the *corps* do not zealously fulfill their duty—dancing quite negligently. With this in mind I recommend to you to keep unremitting watch so that their work may be performed with all possible care. . . . You are responsible. If, in the future, I notice any opposition, or anything is reported to me about you, I will deal with the matter in all strictness." [103] He could not stand opposition of this sort. Four months had not passed before Naryshkin received orders from above to dismiss Didelot and his wife from service, "because of his dangerous illness," giving them six thousand rubles upon their departure. Health probably had nothing to do with his leaving the imperial service on January 28, 1811. Didelot had simply made powerful enemies who saw fit to remove him from St. Petersburg. On March 5, 1811 he boarded the *Saint George* to sail again to Britain. With him went his wife and young son.

CHAPTER VII

The Uproar House

Even as Didelot fled from his Russian imbroglio, tragedy again stalked at his side. In his youth he had nearly perished in shipwreck while journeying from Stockholm to Paris. This time his voyage from St. Petersburg to Lübeck was cursed by a storm on the unfriendly Baltic. Though his life was saved, his art, the thing for which Didelot lived, suffered a sharp setback. He explained, "In my unfortunate voyage to England, all music, books, programs, manuscripts, dance compositions, drawings of my ballets—all perished in the shipwreck of the *St. George.* I lost everything." [1] The wreck augured ill for his final stay in London, and the years to come were replete with a sequence of such disappointments.

His creative work was retarded almost a year due to the loss of materials. Further, this time the London stage was not easily conquered, for new stars had captured the limelight while he had been in St. Petersburg. James D'Egville was not willing to share his new glory with this cantakerous companion who had monopolized the applause at Bordeaux, if he could help it. As for the second Rose Didelot's chances for adulation, they were less than her stately predecessor's, for the London public was now quite under the spell of a temperamental Italian charmer, Fortunata Angiolini. Added to that, the English musical theater was suffering, like the entire country, from the economic depression brought by the Continental blockade decreed against Britain by Napoleon Bonaparte. There was less capital for new productions, and Didelot's sumptuous works demanded much cash as well as ingenuity.

All in all, the burden of administration under such conditions weighed heavily on the shoulders of William Taylor, manager of King's Theatre. One day he was dining with friends when the subject of capital punishment came up. One member of the party advised abolition of it, while another asked, "What would you inflict, then on a criminal of the worst kind?" "By ———," said Taylor, starting up, "Make him manager of the Opera House. If he deserved a worse punishment, he must be a devil incarnate." [2] Though undated, the remark would certainly have been appropriate in the years 1812 and 1813, for Taylor was insolvent, in addition to his other miseries. After being involved in unsuccessful litigation, he lost the seat he held in Parliament in October 1812, spent some time in King's Bench Prison, and was at times unable to appear at the theater for fear of arrest. [3]

In spite of the general upset state of the theater and its personnel, by January 14, 1812, Didelot was ready to show his wares and *The Times* carried the announcement that King's Theatre would present "a new 'Ballet Féerie' entitled *Zélis, ou La Forêt aux aventures*, composed by Monsieur Didelot, Balletmaster and first dancer from the Opera of the Court of St. Petersburg." While Didelot was returning after an absence of eleven years, Madame Didelot would perform for the first time in this country. [4]

At first the press was gentle toward the new Rose. "She is an elegant figure, and dances with grace," [5] remarked *The Morning Chronicle*. *The Times* agreed that she "performs with sufficient ease, her movements are dignified and facile, and her figure . . . not unsuitable to the parts which she is intended to assume." [6]

The inane plot of his new ballet told of a young princess named Zélis who is under the protection of a sylph named Melissa. The sylph has promised to find an exalted match for her charge. Zélis happens to meet the prince of the country, played by Vestris, going a-hunting with his train. When Zélis sees him, she becomes enamoured, thus provoking the anger of Melissa, who has someone else in mind for her charge. Subsequently Melissa tries to woo the prince away from Zélis, but in the end, of course, love triumphs. [7]

The *Chronicle* warmly praised the new work.

M. Didelot is best displayed in the living pictures which his groups exhibit. . . . The painter on canvas is limited to one point of view, and to the delineation of one instant of action. Yet we know what power he can by this exert over the soul of the spectator. The artist who has to paint with living colours, who to the contour of the anatomy can add the influence of muscular exertion, the force of gesture, and the workings of emotion, may produce a still greater, though a less permanent, impression on our sympathies. Didelot possesses this talent in an eminent degree, and we are persuaded that if he had competent materials with which to display his art, he would be as much esteemed in the quality of a composer, as he was in that of a dancer.[8]

In spite of a competent cast that included Armand Vestris, grandson of Gaetan, the production did have its clumsy scenes. As *The Times* described one of them: "The Prince [Vestris] advanced upon an actual charger, shewily caparisoned, and though not peculiarly animated, yet certainly alive." His accompanying horsemen, however, entered on wooden horses. The first of these wooden animals stopped in mid-stage, no doubt from some mechanical difficulty. Since, as *The Times* explained, "it was impossible to use the ordinary arguments for locomotion . . . after a few experiments, [the rider] flung himself off, leaving his charger steady, but with his leg lifted, and all imaginable promise of a determined trot." [9]

There were other scenic wonders in abundance: forests sprang up in the midst of cottage floors, palace walls advanced and receded from each other, and whole colonnades of verd antique and porphry rose, fell, and floated in the air. The press complained of more clumsiness in handling these fancy stage effects. Moreover, in order to portray a scene taking place in one of the character's imagination, Didelot used a fore curtain to try to produce a hazy effect. All that was apparent to the critic was the coarse, ribbed sail cloth of the curtain. The action behind it was almost completely obliterated, instead of being enhanced with the mystical quality Didelot desired.

Rose Didelot became ill in February, and because of some schedule complications necessitated by her illness, her spouse put together a new ballet in two days entitled *L'Epreuve, ou La Jambe de bois.*[10] In it a sailor, upon returning home, decides to try his lover by pretending to have lost a leg, an eye, and an arm. She perseveres in her affection for her mutilated mariner, and he rewards her fidelity by suddenly throwing off his wooden leg and bandages.[11] The public was not over impressed by this work. To twentieth-century sensibilities it seems a trifle gauche, presented as it was in a nation entangled in a war with France for nineteen years, in which many a tar had returned to his lover in a similar condition.

In April Didelot presented a new version of *Zéphyr*, this time under the title *Zéphyr inconstant puni et fixe, ou Les Noces de Flore*. The story was still of the inconstancy of Zéphyr, who after professing his passion for Flora, falls in love with every other nymph whom he meets. Received by some, repulsed by others, after numerous pursuits of his lovers on earth and a few perilous flights in the air, he is stripped of his wings and forced to repent. Amidst groups of hymens, sea-nymphs, and celestials, he has to forswear his infidelity and pledge his faith again to Flora.[12]

Zéphyr was indeed a success. The *Chronicle* agreed that "it is one of the most lively and captivating entertainments that we had had for several years,"[13] in spite of the fact that at this time, Didelot was crippled by a lack of trained artists at the King's Theatre. Some performers had been spirited away by the Pantheon Theatre, and the Napoleonic Wars made it difficult to replace these losses by imports from abroad.[14]

The music for the production was a problem, since Didelot had lost his other score to *Zéphyr* in the shipwreck. Fortunately, he found a friend, Frédéric-Marc-Antoine Venua, a violinist and composer who had been employed at the Paris Opéra. In 1818 Didelot explained that since he wished to preserve some of the scenes already formulated, he hummed to Venua several of Cavos' beautiful motifs used in the St. Petersburg production. Venua partly imitated these and partly composed his own passages to provide a new score for *Zéphyr inconstant*.[15]

The Times had a serious complaint against the ballet in line with the humanitarian outlook developing in the nineteenth century. The paper reported: "The sight of children and young girls lifted up thirty or forty feet from the ground by a cord, so slight as to be invisible from the pit, can only give feeling and rational people a sensation of terror. Some means of dispensing with this expedient ought to be found out immediately; stuffed figures might be used." While care was usually taken at the beginning of such projects, the newspaper predicted that eventually the machinery would be neglected and "the audience will have the horror of seeing some unfortunate creature shattered to pieces for their diversion. Then will there be a public execration of the whole process, and the art of flying will be laid by for a season; but the mischief will have been done."[16]

In the foreword to the program Didelot penned, according to *The Times*, "some not ill-written pages."[17] Unfortunately, we know the contents of this writing only from *The Times*'s second-hand version of it. Didelot said that "the graceful, the sportive, the pastoral, the faery, the anacreontic, and the mythological are the proper sources from which to make dancing paint and display elegance, pleasure, love and all the evanescent traits of human character." In a great pantomime of action, the dancing might be simply an adjunct, but in a ballet it constituted the leading feature and could depict a story of dalliance, of mirth, or of naïveté. Though *The Times* approved Didelot's ideas, it complained vehemently about the fact that Didelot's writings were geared too much toward the nobility. Speaking for the rising middle class, the paper averred that "taste and feeling, and wealth—the skill to judge, and the power to reward—are in this country to be found among the multitude, and those who in Russia . . . would have been slaves, or in France . . . helpless and starving, are by the free and noble privileges of England, among the most scientific, tasteful, and liberal patrons of the arts that polish the character of a people." [18]

On June 4 for his benefit, Didelot presented a new grand ballet in the Indian style, *La Reine de Golconde*. One mishap occured during the initial performance which could have been a terrible tragedy. While performing, Didelot was also giving stage directions. At one point in order to give the carpenters a cue to set fire to the royal palace of a vizier he called out, "Fire." He spoke loudly enough that momentary alarm gripped the audience, which no doubt mistook it for a warning to all. When Didelot perceived the error in communication "he came forward with an agitation that convulsed every artery of his frame" and the spectators understood the mistake.[19]

The ballet itself brought forth the most divergent responses. The story was taken from a popular and widespread tale by the Chevalier de Bouffleurs. Though no copy of Didelot's adaptation of Bouffleur's tale could be discovered, the original story revolved around the seduction of Aline, a milkmaid, by a Frenchman. After being cast out of her home for bearing his child, she becomes educated and poised, later marrying a marquis. Her former lover subsequently encounters her in various unlikely circumstances. Once, while travelling in the Far East, Aline is taken captive and enslaved in a harem. Meanwhile, her erstwhile lover is sent to India for military service. There again he finds Aline, who has worked her way up in the oriental harem to become Queen of Golconde. In spite of her position she is still willing to receive her faithless philanderer.[20] *The Times* was strongly opposed to the ballet, saying, "In this country, we are if not universally grave and moral, at least sensible of the value of public decency; and disposed to look with no favouring eye upon the work, or the man, who makes up parties to its violation." [21] In short, the work was "flat, stale, and unprofitable."

Others disagreed passionately. In the *Chronicle's* view, the British public had responded to "the new and superb ballet" with enthusiastic patronage, "a just tribute to the zeal, talent, and unparalleled assiduity which he [Didelot] has constantly exerted as Balletmaster, by which he has restored this part of the entertainment to its former splendor." [22] After the initial performance the ballet was withheld from the subscribers for nearly a month, being replaced sometimes by hackneyed productions, sometimes by the popular *Zéphyr*. On June 20 the audience took matters into its own hands when the curtain rose on *Zéphyr*, instead of the promised *Reine de Golconde*. The account of *The Times*, usually appalled by mob action, read:

> The hissing began on the rising of the curtains, and as the ballet went on "grew with its growth," until every semblance of dancing was stopped by a general clamour of pit, boxes, and gallery. The passions of the audience were then touched, and Angiolini came forward with all the attitudes of graceful supplication. She was hissed off. Madame Didelot next tried her powers, but she was too nearly allied to the great offender to meet with much consideration, and she was also hissed off. Vestris then glided forward as Zéphyr, but this looked so like a presumption of his favoritism, that the only distinction made between him and the females was a more immediate and universal roar of displeasure. He looked round him for a moment with a Frenchman's astonishment at the insensibility of *les bêtes Anglois*, writhed himself, and walked indignantly behind the scene. The cry was then for Didelot, but Didelot had seen enough of the fates of others, not to put his own on the hazard. The ballet now stopped for a considerable time, and the audience of course grew more clamorous. At length Monsieur Didelot appeared in person; but as all modes of pacification on level ground had failed already, he resolved . . . to make his experiment in the air. His descent from the clouds was for the moment smooth enough; but some unlucky hitch in the machinery was lying in wait to give the finishing blow to his misfortunes. The descent was stopped; and the unhappy ballet master was seen suspended between heaven and earth, slowly turning round before the audience . . . and saluted on all sides with a thunder of groaning, laughter, and hissing.[23]

In spite of the initial clamor to see it, after reconsideration, some judged *La Reine* to be a waste which has "cost the concern a vast sum of money . . . completely thrown away on a heavy and confused composition, equally devoid of simplicity, grace, and interest." [24] A totally different verdict was dealt to *Zéphyr*, however. In late July the *Chronicle* declared that "this ballet affords the most satisfactory answer to the malignant insinuations thrown out by a low cabal against M. Didelot." The paper strongly denounced "the insidious misrepresentations that have been published against him." [25] Clearly, Didelot, as usual, had made enemies determined to break him again.

The press highly praised Didelot's pedagogical efforts at this point, saying: "the excellence of the performance . . . depends on the pain which this master of his art has taken to instruct the young dancers of both sexes . . . and these young candidates for public favours who form the new *corps de ballet* are all English." The youngsters, the paper averred, had "derived from his instructions and his indefatigable perservance an eclat that nothing but an enthusiastic love of his art could have occasioned." [26]

The winter season of 1813 opened on January 19 with *Zélis*. At first, Rose especially was marked out for praise. "Nothing could be more graceful than the entree of Madame Didelot," said the *Chronicle* "and she was honored with the most lively marks of satisfaction." [27] *Zélis* itself was only a tolerable ballet, at times incoherent and heavy in the eyes of *The Times* reviewer. However, he remarked that the opening dance saved the piece: "The evolutions of the chorus, the variousness of the stile, and the singular grace of Madame Didelot, make it one of the most beautiful on the stage." [28] Such eulogies were not to endure long in the press during that season, for Rose Didelot became involved in squabbles with the formidable, fascinating performer who had gained a potent following at King's Theatre—Angiolini. Much of the trouble centered on the question of money. Not only was it difficult for Didelot to obtain enough to present new spectacles, but even the salaries of many of the performers were in arrears. Both Angiolini and Vestris refused to dance unless they received their back pay. Rose stepped into the gap left by her Italian rival, and Angiolini's fans resented it. Trouble was clearly afoot.

In the meantime Didelot produced *Le Pâtre et l'hamadryade*. Hamadryads were nymphs whose lives depended upon the oak trees under which they lived. They therefore guarded the trees well. In the ballet the north wind Boreas, falls in love with a hamadryad, who disdains him. In revenge he makes his winds tear up her sheltering oak by the roots. The hamadryad lies prostrate, but a little cupid petitions the god Jupiter to fling a thunderbolt at Boreas and revive the nymph and her oak. Cupid then causes a shepherd to fall in love with the nymph. Under Cupid's tutelage, the shepherd becomes an elegant Adonis, who wins the hamadryad, and the oak changes into an hymenal altar for the celebration of their marriage.

Opinions differed about this ballet also. The *Chronicle* extolled Didelot for his poetical fancy and graceful taste, adding:

> He embodies his ideas and combines them with a skill that is truly dramatic, for without language he conveys his story with perfect intelligence to the eye, and excites the most lively emotions by the living and moving pictures of which he exhibits. There is an enthusiasm in his own soul, which he communicates by the energy that he infuses into the actors, to the spectators, and it is impossible to view a production of this, especially on the first night, without participating in the sensibility of the author. He is all nerve, all anxiety, all emotion, and everyone sympathizes in the feelings of a composer who is himself so sensibly agitated by zeal in the service of his art.[29]

The *Chronicle* bemoaned the fact that Didelot was limited financially, and it was astonished that he could "produce so much *éclat* with so little auxiliary power." *The Times* had another view. This ballet might struggle on for awhile, their reviewer remarked, "because though it is dull, it is not decidedly offensive; but we had a right to expect something better from Mr. Didelot." Then *The Times*' critic made a little disquisition on ballet aesthetics: "A ballet is almost as capable of telling an interesting story as any other stage representation, and under the hands of an intelligent and clever man, might give delight to more than the mere vacant idlers at an opera. Every finer image of classic beauty,—every richer relique of early times,—every loftier tale that irresistibly brings us back to the memory of youthful studies,—might stand before us in the vigour of living quotation; and children come to that spot for knowledge, where their fathers came for the joy of remembrance. . . ." *The Times* complained, however, against the performers. "Madame Didelot," it was remarked, "is a good dancer, showy and intelligent, but her figure disqualifies her for the lighter character of the ballet. A sylph of Madame Didelot's circumference would be new to all our conceptions; and her Hamadryad . . . was of a startling and suspicious dimension for being half a celestial, and presumed to be but slightly acquainted with the advantages of matrimony." [30] The hint of Rose's pregnancy was also carried in the *Satirist,* which commented that she was "seen to some advantage in this piece, though evidently too corporeal for a disem-arbor-ed nymph. She looks grateful, however, and seems ready to return the compliment of delivery." [31] The subsequent course of the pregnancy is a mystery, for no record of a child being born has come to light.

By March 1 the patience of Angiolini's partisans had been exhausted. During the ensuing weeks she had been trying to drive a hard bargain with the management. Actually, in the opinion of some, money was not alone the cause of her reluctance to appear again on stage. "She has formed an engagement of another kind with Lord ———," explained the *Satirist,* "and has given up for the present the *pas seul.* She has been offered the payment of her arrears, and a renewed engagement at . . . 1000 per annum; but she refuses to cooperate; and asks the money down first, and then 'she will perhaps talk about a new engagement.' " [32] In the press Angiolini declared that nothing would satisfy her but a salary equal to the first female dancer, presumably Rose Didelot, who earned one hundred pounds more than she.[33]

On February 29, 1813, Angiolini's fans began to display a riotous mood during the performance. While the ballet proceeded, cries of "Angiolini" alternated with calls for "The Manager," and "Off." The noise was loud enough to drown out the music, so the ballet proceeded amidst the tumult without music. The *Chronicle* judged that while it would be grand to have such an exquisite comic dancer as Angiolini, if it meant purchasing her services at the cost of retiring Madame Didelot, "her allowed superior in every classical line of the art," [34] then it was too great a price. By mid-March Angiolini's demands included a contract that would "relieve her from so hazardous a situation as that of flying." [35]

Actually she wanted to be relieved of subservience to any balletmaster. The *Chronicle* had no sympathy for her at this point, declaring that there had never been at the head of a *corps de ballet* a man "more truly disinterested, just and generous in the promotion and display of talents than M. Didelot." In regard to the flying, the newspaper asserted that Angiolini was never called upon to "fly" without her consent, that substitutes were always prepared in case she should not volunteer it, and that performers on the Continent felt no reluctance in complying with the practice. The *Chronicle* concluded that "the truth cannot be concealed—Angiolini thought the theatre was in a situation (from the shutting up of Continental supplies) in which she might demand terms inconsistent both with economy and discipline, and she is vexed at finding herself disappointed." [36]

Other signs of public disgust with Angiolini were appearing in print. The *Satirist* fumed that "we are fostering a nest of insolent and rapacious foreigners who are daily guilty of offenses, the least of which, if a native performer committed, he would be pelted from the stage," and offered a suggestion:

> As Angiolini will not soar
> Nor be an angel any more
> Suppose to Taylor they apply
> He may perhaps consent to fly.[37]

While animosity seethed in the company during the spring of 1813 Didelot treated the British public to some East European flavored productions. In late April he presented a new heroic comic ballet, entitled *La Chaumière hongroise, ou Les Illustres Fugitifs*. The incidents were partly taken from a little opera by Claparede given at St. Petersburg. In the program to the work Didelot declared he intended to give a grand Russian Ballet, but the theater could not permit the expense involved in such a production.[38] *La Chaumière hongroise (The Hungarian Hut)* was a work in a new vein for the ballet stage, completely veering from the classic or the anacreontic, but continuing and augmenting the style of *La Fille mal gardée*. In the opening scene villagers are busy harvesting hay. Armand Vestris, who played the part of Frédéric, the superintendent of the workers, is searching for Mouska, played by a Miss Lupino, on whom he had fixed his attentions. When Mouska arrives with Frédéric's dinner, all eat and make merry. Frédéric, who had been reproached by Mouska's father for not having been a warrior, performs some military maneuvers during the fun. The mood changes when Count Ferenc Rakoczi and his wife, played by Didelot and Rose, are seen coming with their son —almost overcome by fatigue—from the woods. The count, a real Hungarian national hero who had risen up in 1703 against the domineering Hapsburgs, is trying to escape from pursuing imperial forces. When soldiers are heard in the distance, the child is hidden in a basket in the bushes just before the military detachment enters the stage. A scuffle ensues in which the soldiers are killed. Mouska then assists the child in creeping out of the bushes and leads all three Rakoczis to Frédéric's house. Amid general rejoicing there Didelot and Rose danced a *Pas hongrois*, which merited a warm ovation. When more pursuing soldiers arrive, they are induced to drink enough that the count could escape. In the end, the Hapsburg emperor not only pardons the count, but also returns all his former titles and possessions, whereupon, all the people joyfully celebrate the reconciliation.[39] In real life, Rakoczi died in exile.

Lacking the trained dancers that he needed for such scenes, Didelot recruited performers from unusual sources. The *Satirist* remarked that during the production, "seeing so many young exhibitors on the stage, we thought that the [ballet] school had been set up a-new, but we understand that these brats are the pupils of the various schools of drummers and fifers of the town barracks." [40]

During one performance of this ballet, Taylor had to face even more disasters. As if he did not have sufficient trouble with the Italian ballerina, Angiolini, in the same season he was beset with similar misfortunes stemming from the following of a popular Italian soprano, Madame Angelica Catalini. In May Catalini's fans rioted in a grand way on behalf of their heroine when the management tried to stage the opera *Enrico IV* without her. During the performance of the accompanying ballet, *The Hungarian Hut*, the first symptom of trouble came when on the right of the stage the scenery depicting a forest began to shake. Thereupon the Rakoczi child, who had been carefully sequestered in a basket of laurels, jumped out of his hiding place from fright. In *The Times*'s account this was the subsequent course of events:

> Immediately afterwards, there appeared to be some mighty tumult behind the same part of the scenery, which was pronounced to be a fight; and the personages of the ballet seemed quite appalled. A most violent invasion followed, and the stage was in a moment, nearly covered with Gentlemen. . . . The dancers instantly drew back, and ranged themselves on a platform at the back of the scene. The first invaders rushed on, some with two canes in their hands, and others with one. They tore the lower parts of the scene, and broke the child's basket into pieces. The curtain fell, some of the Gentlemen came before it, and strutted about, flourishing their canes, with the most infuriated gestures, and waving laurels. . . . The curtain, being now in imminent danger, was again raised, and the host from the pit and boxes became complete masters of the area; their force amounted to more than an hundred. . . .

When soldiers appeared on the stage, their arms were wrested from

them. *The Times* affirmed that "it was unquestionably in their power
. . . to have wounded severely, or destroyed the lives of many of the
young Gentlemen who inflicted on them this temporary disgrace. What
seems quite shocking and met with hisses and groans, was the conduct
of the victors, who, after seizing the muskets, drew out and flourished
the bayonets, and then, with the most marked disrespect and contempt,
threw the arms into the orchestra among the lamps and desks." The
military withdrew, the *figurantes* fled, and amidst the general uproar a
peacemaker came forward on the stage, an actor named Robert
"Romeo" Coates, well known for his own bizarre behavior. Coates
pleaded, "Ladies and Gentlemen, it is a great misfortune, we must
allow, to be deprived of the talents of Madame Catalini, but it is of no
use for us to go a-rioting!"

When peace seemed restored a certain young man began to walk
backwards and forwards on the stage.

> In contempt of remonstrances, with triumphant insolence, and
> twice or thrice, after uttering some unheard nonsense, [he] ex-
> pressed his contempt of opposition by turning his back on the
> audience in a certain vulgar but significant manner. The victors who
> had signalized their courage in the eyes of the ladies by wresting the
> arms from the soldiery, had too much of gallantry about them to
> suffer the character of their devotion to the sex to be compromised
> by this glaring breach of politeness. Thrice they dragged the
> struggling offender to the front of the proscenium, insisting on his
> apology upon his bended knee, or, on the alternative, of throwing
> him over into the orchestra, as they had thrown the arms of the
> Guards. On his knees they did force him but he shewed no relish for
> apologizing, even after his comrades almost strangled him.[41]

By May 4 the offending gentlemen had inserted a full apology in the
press for his impudent conduct, begging the public's indulgence
because he was in "a state of inebriety" and did not know of his
conduct until apprised to it by his friends the following day.[42] The
Satirist was cynical, saying that "though nearly strangled, he never bent
his knees and maintained a most singular stiffness of limb for a man who
pretended to be so drunk." [43]

The colonel of the Royal Horse Guards had a face-saving notice
inserted in the press. He declared that *The Times'* report was incorrect,
that only one very young soldier lost temporary possession of his arms,
and two lost their bayonets while unfixing them at the direction of their

own officers. The arms which were thrown into the pit were those taken from men hired by the theater to perform in the ballet.[44] In rebuttal *The Times* held its ground, replying "that in every essential particular we recorded that which really did occur," adding, "the facts are, we believe, too well known to meet a second contradiction." [45]

The riot did have happy results, though many British gentlemen subsequently denounced the action taken against such behavior as a breach of their rights as Englishmen. A decree was published by the lord chamberlain of His Majesty's Household commanding that "no person of what quality soever, do in the future presume to stand behind the scenes or come upon the stage, either before or during the acting of any opera or ballet in the King's Theatre." [46] No doubt the performers were rapturously happy.

Figure 23. The Uproar House!!!, a colored print of 1813 by W. H. Ekoorb [Brooke] depicting the riot at the King's Theatre in the Haymarket on May 1. Didelot, the winged man, looks down toward the stage, saying: "Ma Vife take great fly! Hey diddle!, high Didel-ot Vy not you take a fly? You vell paid for all." To which Angiolini replies: "No! I'll be dam if I take a fly!!! I'll be de Angelle no longer—nor any what oder ting till I are payed." *Courtesy of the British Museum, London.*

The *Satirist* produced a print commemorating in vivid colors the riotous events (*Fig. 23*). In it Didelot and his wife were shown suspended from on high on the stage. He beckoned toward a haughty dancer on the right, saying, "Ma Vife take great fly! Hey diddle! high Didel-ot, Vy not take a fly? You well paid for all." The dancer, Angiolini, answered, "No, I'll be dam if I take a fly! I'll be de Angelle no longer—nor any oder ting till I are payed." To her left stood a stately figure representing Angelica Catalini. She pointed toward a cage above saying: "De Taileur Bird in yondere caige confine to me sing de note of Sorrow." The chagrined bird (Mr. Taylor) said, "I am tired of perching on this Bench! I wish they'd let me fly too." Amid general mayhem, soldiers rushed in from the wings, while "Romeo" Coates pushed forward exclaiming, "Ladies and Gentlemen! Where's the use of our going a-rioting?" [47]

These were busy days for Didelot, for on May 13 he presented a new divertissement called *Les Amants péruviens*. The *Satirist* conceded that Didelot had effected a "masterly disposition of the dancing part." [48] In late May for the benefit of Rose and himself, Didelot composed a grand Russian divertissement, based on a Russian festive game, the Kacheli (the Swing). It was given "with entirely new snow-scenery, and the appropriate costume of several of the northern nations." In it Rose and Didelot did an original Russian Dance, while Rose and Armand Vestris did a Cossack Dance. Tartar, Polish, and Bohemian Gypsy Dances were done by lesser members of the company. [49]

On the same program Didelot presented an entirely new comic ballet called *L'Indorf et Rosalie, ou L'Heureuse ruse*. The title was switched later in the press to *Rosalie et Dozinval*. The work was taken from a French opera entitled *Une Folie*, produced also under the English title *Love Laughs at Locksmiths*. The press had no complaints about Didelot's creative talent, but they bemoaned the fact that both for this work and for his Russian opus, he was so limited in means. Further, the *Chronicle* was unhappy that Didelot's exertions had been shabbily rewarded by the public, and attendance was not at all what it should be at King's Theatre. [50]

Thus, the summer season of 1813 faded away on rather unpleasant notes. In July Armand Vestris presented *The Deserter*, which was indifferently received, the *Satirist* reported, because Madame Didelot had taken the part which should have been given to Miss Lupino, a regular member of the company. [51] No doubt British performers were being aided by the war-weariness of the English public against France. Didelot prepared dances for a private concert, ball, and supper for six

hundred guests given by the earl of Shrewsbury on June 30, 1813. This
is one of the first recorded instances of the performance by his own son,
Karl.[52] Along with the great actress Mrs. Siddons, Vestris, and Catalini,
the Didelot couple took part in a very successful benefit in July
patronized by the prince regent for Lock Hospital and Asylum.[53] As
July ended and the season closed no doubt the performers at King's
Theatre breathed a hope that things would begin looking upward for
them in 1814, both in regard to audience response and financial support
for their art.

There were repeated delays in opening the spring season of 1814 at
King's Theatre. On April 12 *The Times* finally announced that "this
theatre will positively open THIS EVENING," with the performance of
Didelot's divertissement *Thamaida et Alonzo, ou l'Isle savage*. Because
Didelot was not sufficiently recovered from a severe and protracted
indisposition, there would also be a three-act work composed by a
Monsieur Favier called *Aminte et Sylvie*. *Thamaida et Alonzo* produced
no great reaction, good or bad, but *Aminte et Sylvie* brought forth some
caustic comments. *The Times* dryly asserted, "Of the story, as we
understood nothing, we shall say nothing." It was merely a work
"probably meant to try how far the labours of Mr. Didelot's genius
might be occasionally relieved by the talents of Mr. Favier." [54]

The management did not want the restiveness of the public to erupt
again, and repeatedly assured the subscribers that "a new grand ballet,
composed by Monsieur Didelot, and other novelties, are in great
forwardness, and will be produced with all possible expedition." [55] The
novelty came forward on May 16, "a new Military Demi-Character
Ballet, entitled *Karl et Lisbeth, ou Le Déserteur malgré lui*." In the plot,
Karl, a soldier, is secretly the husband of Lisbeth, a Swiss peasant girl,
played by Angiolini. One of Karl's officers admires Lisbeth, whereupon
Karl defends his wife and wounds the officer. Karl then tries to desert
but is pursued and sentenced to die. In the last minute, the officer
rushes in, admits his own guilt, and Karl is restored to the arms of his
lover. Didelot played the part of Lisbeth's father Gesler. Though an
apology was made for the imperfect state of the machinery used in it,
the ballet was praised because it abounded in graceful incidents and
beautiful situations.[56] Though this ballet was truly successful, as far as
press reviews indicate, this was not a phenomenal season for the
Didelots. Rose appeared on stage, the press reported, even though she
was not entirely recovered from a long severe indisposition.[57]

The most sensational news in the British dance world that summer was the appearance of Maria Mercandotti, a Spanish girl, reported to be not thirteen years of age, who danced the cachucha with uncommon grace.[58] Spanish dancing definitely monopolized the stage of King's Theatre in the summer of 1814. Didelot composed a new Spanish divertissement in which Vestris and Angiolini danced a bolero,[59] while Rose danced in *Les Folies d'Espagne*.[60] As the season closed, quite understandably, Didelot's thoughts were once again centered not on London, but on the city which was his first love.

On March 31, 1814, troops allied against Napoleon Bonaparte entered and occupied Paris. Ironically, this invasion aided Didelot in fulfilling his long standing wish of displaying his artistry once again there. August Bournonville declared, "Didelot was undoubtedly the greatest choreographer after Noverre . . . but the French could draw on his rare talent very little. Only the invasion of the allies and the command of the Emperor Alexander aided him to mount his charming ballet *Zéphire et Flore* in the Opéra." [61] Pierre Gardel, still in power at the Opéra, had acquired the felicitious art of supplying his masters with what was agreeable to them. After Gardel staged fervent, mammoth, revolutionary pageants portraying the masses of French patriots striving for freedom and equality, upon the restoration of the Bourbon dynasty to power, his assistant Milon staged a new work called *L'Heureux retour*. Mundt affirms that it was the Grand Duke Constantine Pavlovich, brother of Emperor Alexander I, who aided Didelot in breaking through the Gardel stronghold.[62] Slonimsky proposes that friendly support may also have come from Didelot's friend Count Mikhail Miloradovich, a gallant fighter against Napoleon whose duties took him to occupied Paris. Later, he became military governor-general of St. Petersburg.[63] Whatever the method used, all possible means of barring Didelot were tried, since, in the view of the French historian Castil-Blaze, he was "all the more dangerous because he promised something new." [64] For the gigantic new production of *Zéphire et Flore* which he envisioned, Didelot needed ten thousand francs. When the management balked at such a sum, Didelot affirmed his willingness to shoulder the risk. In no uncertain terms, he wrote the following:

> To His Excellency Monsieur le Comte de Montesquieu
> Grand Chamberlain of His Imperial Majesty

Monseigneur:

In daring again to importune your excellency, this time I hope at least to be more fortunate than the preceding times.

Since the time of the communication made to Monsieur le Comte against me and against my debut, it becomes urgent finally to name a balletmaster of the second and even of the third class. Very well, Monseigneur, I submit myself, I entreat for that place which I beseech your excellency not to refuse me, because nothing would be sadder for me than to expatriate myself once again. . . .

I do not object at all to propose myself, above all at a time when the Imperial Academy of Music is not able to support the cost of a grand ballet of Mr. Gardel. The entry of an assistant balletmaster would seem favorable, and would not change or violate any rule; there would be not outlay, because he would pay the expenses voluntarily if it would be necessary, and it would be demanded even by his superiors. I dare to await and solicit the grace of a response from your excellency to this new demand. I am with respect, Monseigneur Your Excellency, the very humble and very obedient servant.

C. Didelot[65]

On such terms he did gain the right to mount *Zéphire et Flore*. His troubles really began during the final rehearsals of the work. Didelot had needed a new forest back cloth to hide the wires for the flights from the public.[66] Though Didelot had himself shouldered the bill for the new stage decor, this back cloth was used in an operetta shown before the performance of his ballet. Further, the first act of his ballet was rehearsed in such a way that Didelot did not recognize it. At the dress rehearsal Didelot ranted and complained against such indignities, but no one paid any attention to him. In despair he was ready to forsake the production entirely, but in Mundt's account, some friend placated him, saying, "Calm yourself. On the day of the performance everything will be fine, only for God's sake, be quiet now." [67] Accepting the advice, Didelot refrained from speaking during the rehearsal. When it was finished he wanted to say something, but the violence of his own emotions deprived him of his voice; cramps seized his chest, his fever rose, and these physical manifestations of his inner agitation endured for several hours.

On December 12, 1815, the première took place. Didelot wrote a brief history of the work in the preface to the program:

I have strongly desired on my return to France to mount a ballet at the Opéra not with the intention of displacing anyone, as that has very falsely been said, but as homage that I owe to the public which

deigned to encourage my first attempt. . . . I am forced in spite of
myself, to speak of the epoch in which my ballet was composed,
having learned that it has been given in its entirety in several places,
under another name than mine. An outline of it was made in 1795 in
Lyon; the work was given in 1796 in London, with additions; it was
shown before their Imperial Majesties at the Russian court in 1804,
and considerably augmented at that time. I put it on again in
London in 1812 (where the person who was there availed himself of
it since). I would with pleasure have shunned making these
observations; but, at the time of a debut, I can not do otherwise.[68]

Didelot was setting the record straight for history, since different cuts
from his ballets had appeared on the stages of Paris and Vienna,
performed by Duport.

Didelot explained in the program that he had chosen the Greek
genre, because it was a noble, elegant style—the happiest for the
beautiful poses of the dance.

The critic of the *Journal des débats* agreed with Didelot's choice,
remarking, "From what other source than mythology have all the arts
drawn for three thousand years? . . . Choreography has become more
than a simple accessory in our theatrical presentations. Has it not, by its
mute dramas, furnished their most seductive marvels?" Continuing his
eulogy, the critic remarked, "These types of works are not susceptible
to a rigorous analysis . . . the ballet is a series of tableaux, of
picturesque scenes, of elegant poses of lively, light voluptuous movements." Like all viewers he was astonished at the flights of Zéphire
toward the heavens:

> This picture, which one would conceive possible only in the
> imagination, was realized yesterday under the astonished eyes of
> the spectator. There have often been seen admirable flights at the
> Opéra. In *Psyché*, for example, another Zéphire conveys Psyché to
> the Palace of Love, and vanishes with her in the air. The machine is
> well arranged and produces great illusion, but one sees, or at least
> supposes one sees, the machine. But the *Zéphire* of M. Didelot is
> very marvelous in another way: alone, isolated, without any
> accompanying features to deceive the eyes, Zéphire elevates himself
> in the midst of the theater by his own force; he shoves away with a
> disdainful foot the earth that he abandons, soars for several minutes
> in space, caresses with the tips of his wings the verdant heights of
> the trees and at last majestically is lost in the azure vault.

par

Théophile Wagstaffe

Figure 24. A cartoon by William Makepeace Thackeray of a dancer dressed for the ballet *Flore et Zéphyr. Courtesy of the Victoria and Albert Museum, London.*

The public, like the critic, "was not able to master its delirium; the applause was prolonged into the *entr'acte* and it redoubled with furor when Zéphire, redescending by the same way as his ascent, remounted a second time, no longer alone, but carrying Flore in his arms. This marvel, more than the first, evoked the heights of enthusiasm from the audience, and this sentiment was manifested by the most fervent acclamations." [69] Another wonderful novelty connected with this ballet was the use of *pointes* by the ballerinas. *Pointe* work developed gradually and the exact date of its initial use is unknown; however, prints exist dated 1821 showing the celebrated Opéra dancer Fanny Bias as Flore, clearly *en pointe*.

The ballet stayed in the repertoire of the Opéra until March 8, 1826, with one hundred sixty-four presentations given to that date. After a four-year-rest, it was renewed again in 1831 for the debut of Marie Taglioni and Jules Perrot.[70] Taglioni, with her supremely lofty technique, was able to reveal the true artistic potentialities of *pointe* work in her rendition of Flore. One of the best indications of the ballet's popularity was the degree to which it was spoofed. The popular French author Eugène Scribe wrote a humorous parody of it. Entitled *Flore et Zéphyre*, his work was shown at the Théâtre du Vaudeville in Paris on February 8, 1816. In it Flore goes about pursuing a husband, being not adverse to an English one, declaring,

> "Pour epoux l'Anglais est aimable;
> Il parle peu, mais aime bien." [71]

Using the pseudonym Théophile Wagstaff, the British author William Makepeace Thackeray, drew a series of hysterically funny caricatures of it, entitled *Flore et Zephyr, Ballet Mythologique (Figs. 24 and 25)* [72]

During the eleventh performance, King Louis XVIII of France was so charmed that he called Didelot to his loge in full view of the public and declared his appreciation of the work. The queen ordered that he should be given two thousand francs as a reward. However his very success was a threat to Gardel, and when Didelot went to the cashier to claim his reward, he received one of the cruelest blows of his heart-breaking career. After accepting the queen's reward of two thousand francs, he was presented with a bill of two thousand four hundred francs for the machinery used in the work. According to Saint-Léon, Didelot only answered, *"C'est juste, c'est juste,"* and suffered the four hundred-franc loss for his spectacular production.[73] By

that time he was thoroughly sick of Parisian intrigues and had tied his
fate once more to the Russian court.

Figure 25. A cartoon by William Makepeace Thackeray showing a dancer in the
ballet *Flore et Zéphyr*: "In a *Pas Seul* he expresses his extreme despair."
Courtesy of the Victoria and Albert Museum, London.

CHAPTER VIII

Soulful Flights in Russia

WHEN Napoleon Bonaparte's Grand Armée marched into Russia in 1812, Ivan Val'berkh became the choreographer of the hour. Rafail Zotov commented that "1812 was a most successful time for ballet, because in that year all kinds of nonsense with a patriotic title brought much money." [1] Val'berkh was especially adept at producing works capable of stirring patriotism, such as *Love for the Fatherland*. When open animosity erupted between France and Russia many French performers actually left Russia, fearing the worst (*Fig. 26*). However, in the spring of 1812, while Napoleon yet amassed his troops for the invasion of Russia, Naryshkin contacted the Russian diplomat in Paris, Prince Alexander Borisovich Kurakin, asking him to explore the conditions under which the choreographer Louis-Jacques Milon might be induced to come to St. Petersburg as director of the dance section. [2] Since this negotiation did not succeed, Naryshkin turned elsewhere.

By December 20, 1812, after the Corsican's armies had invaded, plundered, and retreated from the Russian land, Naryshkin sent a letter to the Russian ambassador in London, Count Lieven, declaring:

"Balletmaster Didelot, located in London, being known to me on account of his extraordinary gifts, is necessary for the advanced training of dancers in the theatrical school." Lieven was asked to invite Didelot to return to Russia under the title of "chief balletmaster and teacher of the school." Naryshkin added that he hoped an invitation so flattering to his talent would compel Didelot to moderate his demands. The dowager empress Maria Feodorovna had especially expressed the wish that Didelot's wife would assume her former place of dancing mistress in the court.

Naryshkin then wrote to Didelot himself, saying: "The desires of your public, your pupils, and my own desire unite to urge you to return

Figure 26. A contemporary cartoon depicting the exit of French theatrical performers from Russia during the Napoleonic War of 1812, from Vsevolodsky's *Teatr v Rossii v epokhu otechestvennoi voiny.*

to Russia. Your school, so full of high hopes, can achieve its goals only if its teacher returns. They have informed me of their regret and of their ardent wish to see you again. You and your spouse will not only find here all benefits which you had earlier, but also all those which lie in my power. . . ."[3]

Didelot delayed almost two years before answering. After the financial loss in Paris from *Zéphire et Flore,* however, he was willing to negotiate—on his own terms this time. Two French actors named Mézières and Dalmas took charge of negotiations. Didelot demanded a yearly salary of sixteen thousand rubles with an immediate payment of three thousand rubles to defer the cost of his voyage to Russia, as well as a guarantee of the same amount for his departure expenses if he were forced to leave. He asked for the usual yearly benefit, and demanded that his former years in St. Petersburg be included in computing his pension rights. He was to be given free use of a carriage, an apartment, and fuel. Instead of the usual contract for three years he asked this time for six years, since only then would he have time to train new artists.[4]

Prince Pyotr I. Tufiakin, director of the Imperial Theaters, then gave a firm recommendation to the Theatrical Committee:

I find balletmaster Didelot very useful and needed for the Imperial Theaters, because almost all the best ballet personnel appearing on the stage, such as Novitskaya, Ikonina, Kolosova and others, are obliged to him for their formation and art; in the same measure that all the best ballets existing in the Imperial Theaters were mounted by Didelot. During the period of my rule as director, I noted that from the time of his departure, ballet has gone to ruin, and especially the education of the ballet troupe in the school has fallen into disorder. In order that it will not disappear altogether, I most obediently beg the committee to agree with the reception of Balletmaster Didelot in the Imperial Theatrical service on the above mentioned terms.[5]

On March 26, 1816, Didelot and Rose returned to St. Petersburg, launching forth upon such a productive phase of his career that his contemporaries began to call him the Shakespeare and the Byron of ballet. "The renaissance of ballet began again with the second coming of Didelot," [6] another observer recalled. In St. Petersburg Didelot was to encounter great problems, but they were at least of a different character. Though the Imperial Theaters of Russia did not allow the actual invasion of the stage by the younger generation in the London manner, at the Bolshoi Theater of St. Petersburg, which opened in 1818 in place of the former building destroyed by fire, there was a coterie of youthful military officers and state servants with *abonnements* in the first rows of the left side of the auditorium. This self-styled "left flank" had their chosen favorites whom they applauded soulfully and delighted in calling out for bows. Though the group included such literary lights as Pushkin and Griboyedov, the ringleader was a certain cavalry captain who even hired people in the gallery to applaud wildly for the goddess of the hour. One evening the gallery had been hired to give a rousing cheer for Vera Zubova. She was a quick, extremely graceful ballerina of medium size, models of whose small, strong feet had been cast at the order of Count Miloradovich and distributed to about one hundred of his high-born friends for use as paperweights.[7] On this occasion, just before Zubova's appearance, a dancer who was much less famous entered the limelight and the captain absent-mindedly withdrew his handkerchief from his pocket. The hired cadre in the gallery took this as a signal and gave their vociferous demonstration. The poor girl was so discombobulated by the overwhelming welcome that she hid in consternation behind the curtain.[8] As for Zubova herself, she was also famous for her explosive temperament and was once docked eight days' pay for not dressing in time to do her solo. Though she was described in

1840 as "a most charming demi-character dancer who would do honor to the first theater in Europe," she was dismissed that same year because of some discord with the management.[9]

Another officer and balletomane once bought a ticket to an evening performance of a grand ballet. During the morning rehearsal, with all the aplomb of the emperor himself, he strolled into the theater and took his place. When Prince Tufiakin noticed him, he sent word that no one was allowed at rehearsals. The officer then showed his ticket and adamantly refused to move. When the authorities insisted that the ticket was only for the evening, he answered, "So what, I came to St. Petersburg just for the ballet. I already finished dinner and am waiting here for the performance, because I'm not sure whether I'll be arrested by evening. In such a case I won't be at the theater, and my money will be lost." [10] Prince Tufiakin only shook his head; the officer was allowed to see the rehearsal. Irksome as such characters could be, they were an important element in the growth of the special Russian brand of balletomania. With tastes well developed through years of watching nightly performances, the Russian audience knew an artist of the dance when one appeared. Didelot was welcome here.

One golden youth who had been graduated from a naval school in 1802 became so intrigued with Didelot's productions that he started taking lessons himself from the master, who told him that if he truly dedicated himself to ballet, he could become a marvelous artist.[11] Later, as Count Fyodor P. Tolstoy, he became president of the Imperial Academy of Art, and has left to dance history a set of hauntingly beautiful ballet drawings now located in the Russian Museum of Leningrad. Though they do not portray actual ballets by Didelot, they capture the spirit of the ethereal loveliness that permeated Didelot's productions.

When Didelot arrived in Russia his productive ability suffered no such delays as he had experienced in England over his lost materials. He had hardly returned when Empress Maria Feodorovna asked him to organize a performance in honor of the triumphal return of Alexander I and the Russian army from Paris. Didelot's ballet, entitled *Return of the Heroes*, took place in the elegant Rose Pavilion of the imperial palace of Pavlovsk.[12] In accordance with the wish of the empress, swiss cheese was made at this estate both for her own table and for sale in St. Petersburg. In his production Didelot chose to emphasize the rustic atmosphere of Russia, saying to the empress, "Your Majesty, give me your cows, sheep, goats . . . the cheese will not be the worse for it. I need Russian peasants—men, women, young girls, children—all Holy Rus'. Let them all do their folk dances, let them play, sing, and be gay. Your guests have become enough like Parisians; let them again feel that they are Russians." [13] The occasion, enhanced by the Russian folk flavor, was considered a huge success. The empress was delighted with his production because it recalled to her the idyllic prerevolutionary rustic days of Marie Antoinette, who with her ladies-in-waiting played as milkmaids at Versailles. In like manner it reminded the empress of the recent return of the Bourbon royal family to power in France.

At one time during rehearsals for *Return of the Heroes*, Didelot was very hot, and asked for a drink of water. The courtier standing nearest him did not condescend to comply. Didelot then simply sat on the steps of the pavilion and refused to carry on the rehearsal. When Maria Feodorovna approached him and asked, "Why aren't they continuing the rehearsal?" Didelot replied, "I asked for a glass of water and couldn't get it." At that, the empress herself fetched it for him. [14]

It was customary to present a new ballet each year to celebrate the name-day of Alexander I, August 30. For this occasion in 1816, Didelot presented his version of *Acis et Galathée*. The ballet was dedicated to Prince Tufiakin, whom Didelot thanked for the sacrifices he made to produce the work. There were also notes of apology in the program, showing the balletmaster's unhappiness at the general situation which confronted him. During his first sojourn in Russia there had been a good theater in which to work, as well as a school full of beloved pupils, so well formed in his ways that they would understand even his *demi-mot*. Now, he said, the Maly Theater in which he was working would never be suitable for ballets. This problem was to be ameliorated with the opening of the Bolshoi Theater in 1818, but problems in personnel would take longer to solve. Didelot had assigned the role of Galatea to a promising young beauty, Avdot'ia Istomina, while that of Acis, a male part, was assigned to Anastasia Novitskaya, since the role was absolutely not the genre of Yakov Liustikh, "the only male dancer with beautiful execution that is now active."

Didelot made it plain that Prince Tufiakin had chosen this subject in spite of the fact the troupe had no male Acis. In view of this, he asked the indulgence of the public both for Istomina, who was making her debut, and for Novitskaya, who, in playing the part of Acis, "made with infinite grace the sacrifice of her sex." Uneasily, he added, "I solicit indulgence for all in general, except for Mr. Auguste, whose recognized talents have no need of it." For himself, he added "I hope that the public will be good enough to pardon this digression, since it is that of a father regarding his infants, and of an author who fears the expectations in his works will not be realized." [15]

His uneasiness was apparently in vain. Glushovsky recalled that Novitskaya was beautiful, in spite of the fact that she played a man's character. Further, he said that each grouping in the ballet had an idea behind it, and that all the action was closely linked with the subject.[16]

In the classic myth, Galatea's lover, the shepherd Acis, arouses the jealousy of the Cyclops Polyphemus. Attempts of the monster to kill Acis provide the substance of the ballet plot. The result, in Zotov's view, was marvelous. "The ballet was pure poetry," he said. "Only two acts and in them lies a whole epic. The spectators tremble each minute for the fate of the lovers." [17]

The action takes place on islands dividing a bay, represented on the stage. On one island, lindens, oaks, and acacias form an arch of green under which nymphs gather for bathing. Acis and Galatea join in general festivity and are united by their protector Cupid, when Polyphemus arrives. Since the giant is unable to capture Acis, he grasps Cupid. Galatea and all the nymphs are horrified, as Cupid is their patron, so they kneel in supplication to the giant to save him. Cupid pulls an arrow from his quiver and promises to use it to aid Cyclops in his amorous pursuit of Galatea. The simple giant agrees to the bargain. When Cupid is released, he warns Galatea to pretend to love the monster. Cyclops, thinking that she shows a glimmer of love for him, humbles himself before her while the nymphs bind garlands about him and give him a sleeping potion, which he drinks, thinking it only grape juice. Upon awakening, he is furious at the deception. Twice during the ballet he almost kills Acis. Once when Polyphemus corners his rival, he seizes him by the foot and tosses him like a feather across the stage. Acis would have been destroyed except for Cupid, who picks him up in flight and carries him on a cloud to a safe place. Zotov explained that this was done, of course, with a dummy dressed like Acis.[18] Later Polyphemus tears a huge fragment of rock from a mountain to hurl at the lovers. The rock flies toward them, but suddenly bursts open, with the helpful Cupid flying out.

To celebrate the wedding of Acis and Galatea, who seemingly triumph over Cyclops, Didelot summoned the entire Olympic Who's

Who: Mercury descended from a cloud, bringing a crown. Venus, too, arrived, accompanied by Tritons who sent forth fountains about her. Apollo descended from a chariot and Phaeton, too, joined the act. Nereids came forth from the depths of the sea with Neptune and Amphitrite. Proteus and Nereus, father of Galatea, were near Neptune, while Tritons and all the inhabitants of the waves lined the shores of the island. From their curved shells several Tritons sent forth brilliant fountains of water against Zephyrs, hovering over their heads, who, in turn, showered the Tritons with flowers.

The gaiety was interrupted when Polyphemus again appears, but this time Jupiter himself, amid thunder and lightning, warns the giant to leave the lovers alone. Perplexed, Cyclops finally retreats to his cave for good. As night approaches Diana lightens the horizon with her silver sphere. All the joyful revelers, exhausted by dancing and their general happiness, fall asleep, while Cupid, his work done, extinguishes his own torch and joins all the nymphs accompanying his mother Venus back to her home on the island of Cythera.

The novelty which impressed contemporaries most was a moving mountain. At a culminating point in the spectacle, on the right of the stage a mountain, occupying all the space and teeming from top to bottom with fauns, oreads, and nymphs, moved forward toward the proscenium. One critic raved that "Monsieur Didelot is not a ballet-master, but a painter. To the flaming image of a poet he combined the indefatigable patience of an artist, soulfully bound to his art. . . . A spectator, looking at the beautiful groups, at the dances of fauns, nymphs and satyrs, is carried in imagination to that legendary time of ancient Greece when each stream had its divinity, each little grove was populated by nymphs." [19]

Though the effect produced by the flights and other mechanical marvels was stupendous, actually the performance of them was dangerous. The actor Karatygin recalled that during the dress rehearsal of *Acis*, while he was playing the part of Mercury, the machinery lifting him on high for a flight suddenly began to squeak, then stuck with him suspended in mid-air "like a sheep for the sacrifice." Fate, however, was kind to Karatygin. As he remarked, "perhaps due to his mother's prayers," he was eventually safely lowered. Didelot's former pupil and one of Russia's first women writers, Avdot'ia Panayeva, recalled a similar incident, however, where the suspension ropes broke, with children being bruised and receiving broken limbs during the resulting fall.[20]

The change which took place in costume design during the long span of Didelot's career can be seen in the description of a costume worn earlier by Val'berkh in this ballet. He recalled in his notes, "In 1785 I danced Acis in white stockings, in black shoes with red heels, in jeweled buckles, with hair combed in light curls and powdered with yellow powder." [21] By 1816 it was fully accepted that Grecian gods and goddesses should dress in flowering Grecian drapery instead of eighteenth-century ruffles.

Acis was his only lengthy ballet for the year, but Didelot also produced a grand divertissement in September, entitled *Holiday in the Seraglio*. Didelot was responsible for the dances in the opera *Aline, Reine de Golconde*, which in ballet form had so shocked the London *Times*'s critic. Zotov rapturously praised the dancing of Novitskaya in the opera, saying, "Here is the playfulness, vivacity, and gaiety of the most beautiful Odalesque, the charm and aimableness of Grace, the passion, tenderness and impetuousity of the most attractive Bayaderka, in other words this is the Terpsichore of our theater." [22] During the remaining months of 1816 Didelot arranged the dances for Mozart's opera *Belmonte and Constanze (Abduction from the Seraglio)*, as well as for a historic drama entitled *Marguerite D'Anjou*.

In 1801 Didelot's first Rose had carried to Russia their baby boy from England. By 1817 young Karl had developed into a talented teen-ager, musically gifted. On January 11 his father presented him to the Russian public in a divertissement entitled *The Unexpected Return, or Evening in the Garden*. Didelot explained in the preface to the program that his son's youth and growth, as well as a three-year interruption of his dancing exercises made him rather weak, but the lack of dancers in the theater impelled him to use all means to please the public. He introduced him as "the son of Rose, my deceased spouse, one of the best dancers up to this time." In Didelot's eyes, his son's stature and style of dance recalled that of his mother, though only as "a weak shadow." [23] Later Karl played such roles as that of Léon in *Leon and Tamaida*, and Alonzo in *Cora and Alonzo*. He had to quit the stage early in his career, however, because of ill health.

Another of Didelot's prize young pupils—Nikolai Diur—enraptured the St. Petersburg audience with his artistry in the ballet *The*

Unexpected Return. Diur danced the part of an unnamed boy with a canary in his hand. Diur was truly the teacher's pet. While the master had to strain with all his might to train many other aspiring dancers, for Diur, a light remark, a short explanation would suffice. Under Didelot's special tutelage, he grew to be a performer with great aplomb, surely fated to be one of the first soloists. To those who observed the relationship of master and pupil it seemed that Didelot doted on Diur's talent with all his heart, that all his hopes centered on the lad. Once, while Didelot watched from the wings, Diur changed a step, botching a pirouette. Tearing his hair and shaking his stick ferociously, Didelot showered oaths in three languages, calling down upon the boy all heavenly thunder. Then just as suddenly Didelot's fierce visage began to exude sweetness, light, and smiles; Diur had begun to improvise soulfully and gracefully. His grim master, ready the second before to thrash his pupil, embraced him with tears in his eyes when he emerged from the stage, and with touching tenderness hastily slipped a silver ruble into the boy's hand.[24] Diur tired of ballet, however, and with the administration's consent, when he finally summoned sufficient courage to manifest his wish to be an actor, it was said that an enemy bomb could not have produced a greater explosion than Didelot's wrath. For his debut as an actor, Diur was given a leading role in *Phoenix,* a musical comedy in which he utilized his dance training by performing a *pas de deux* with Vera Zubova.

On April 10, 1817 Didelot presented a one-act ballet entitled *The Young Milkmaid, or Nicette and Luke.* The story deals with a peasant, Luke, who is in love with Nicette, the milkmaid, in spite of the disapproval of Nicette's old grandmother. When Luke climbs into the window of Nicette's hut for a rendezvous, the grandmother is ready to beat her grandchild until a wedding agreement is reached. The landlord of the serf village happens along during a hunting trip just at the appropriate time to sign the marriage contract. All the villagers then make merry to amuse him. "It was a trifle," the press declared, "but a trifle composed by Didelot"—and that made all the difference in the world.[25]

For Val'berkh's benefit on August 19, Didelot fashioned a new divertissement entitled *Apollo and the Muses.* This was soon followed by a three-act ballet, *Don Carlos and Rosalba,* adopted from the French opera, *Une Folie* by Etienne-Nicolas Méhul. Didelot was pleased with the results, describing it as "one of the most pleasant presentations of all those I have had the honor to mount." The public apparently agreed for the ballet was shown often. The leading lady, Rosalba, was danced by Novitskaya. Didelot declared in the program that by assigning the role to her, he hoped to stifle one of those slanderous aspersions which were habitually showered upon him. This time it appeared that a rumor was afoot that he wanted to humble Novitskaya and prevent her appearing before the public. He affirmed that "in all possible situations I always will be just to my pupils; I will be their friend, their father. Indeed," he added, "is it possible not to love those whom one educates; especially when worthy conduct, courtesy and talent are combined—as in Novitskaya?" [26]

An important production took place in November of 1817: *Theseus and Ariadne, or The Defeat of the Minotaur*. Didelot said he would have preferred to call the work a pantomime embellished with dances and not a ballet. He used the ancient myth about King Minos of Crete, who each year required the Athenians to send seven youths and maidens as tribute. These were used to satisfy the appetite of the Minotaur, a monster with a bull's body and a human head who lived in an underground labyrinth. In the story the Athenian youth Theseus takes upon himself the task of annihilating the monster. The daughters of Minos, Ariadne and Phaedra, both love Theseus. Victorious Theseus sails away from Crete with both daughters, and since Ariadne had given him some magic thread to save him from perishing in his labyrinthine adventures, Theseus feels obliged to love her although he really loves Phaedra. When a chance arises at night, Theseus and Phaedra abandon Ariadne. Her grief is assuaged by the god Bacchus who takes her for a wife. Didelot deliberately inserted special detailed mimed scenes to heighten the drama of the conflict between the two women.

He took other liberties with the myth, less excusable. With no knowledge of the importance of the bull in Cretan art and religion, Didelot converted the Minotaur into a centaur, for he felt the appearance of a horse was more handsome and aristocratic than that of an ox. Rationalizing his action, he said, "On the stage nature must often be subservient to art." [27] In spite of Didelot's long explanation, one critic complained strongly against his substitution, relating how in the death struggle between Theseus and the centaur the jumpy stomping of the horse's heels provoked laughter in the audience. Yet, in spite of his disdain for such liberties, the critic did affirm that "the flow of the ballet pointed out that Didelot was a true historian[!], a rare painter, gifted with a rich and true imagination, and a great poet, observing the very smallest shades of human passion." [28] A chief complaint of another critic was that he felt the ballet should not have been called a tragedy, because no one was sorry to see the centaur die.[29]

The final scene of *Theseus and Ariadne* was a festival dedicated to the god Bacchus. There is evidence to support the thesis that this ballet directly influenced the great poet Alexander Pushkin in his writing in 1818 the poem entitled *Festival of Bacchus*, for at this point in his life Pushkin attended every ballet produced in St. Petersburg and probably discussed this one with members of a literary-critical circle to which he belonged, the Green Lamp.[30]

Didelot's last major production in 1817 was the same work he had first presented in London in 1813, *The Hungarian Hut*. Whereas formerly it had only two acts, the new Russian version had four. Certainly in Russia the work was even more successful than in Britain, due in great part to the superb talent of Kolosova. In the program Didelot said that Kolosova had wanted him to mount the work, and though it was a mimed work, he did so without contradiction, knowing that her mighty talents would embellish it. Since, at this time, Kolosova limited herself to pantomime, he had even shortened some of the dances. In this ballet, as in his whole artistic career, Didelot showed that his chief interest was in the mimed drama. Dancing in itself somewhat bored him. In the forward to *The Hungarian Hut*, he revealed that in the third part, he had yielded to his friend Auguste Poirot the task of choreographing the dances, and he would have asked him to do them in the first act if they had not been so closely bound to the action.[31]

Glushkovsky singled this ballet out as one of Didelot's most remarkable productions. He reported that during its scenes of high tragedy unwillingly many spectators burst into tears. In the wake of the sad scenes, however, the spectators likewise laughed to the limit at the ballet's amusing gestures.[32] The press agreed completely with Gluskovsky. One critic averred, "Everything that rare genius of art, consciousness of the heart and human passions, as well as the gift of sensitivity might produce and unite—all these gave birth to this ballet . . . there was not one superfluous role in it, not one minute in which the spectator did not see something entertaining." [33]

After the first presentation on November 17, 1817, for the benefit of Kolosova, it was repeatedly performed. In 1819 Glushkovsky staged the ballet in Moscow, and fifteen years after Didelot's death, on February 22, 1852, it was renewed for the benefit of Yelena Andreanova, with Carlotta Grisi and Jules Perrot taking parts.[34]

A most beloved pupil of Didelot, Anastasia Likhutina, gained special praise for her role as "the frisky Mouska" [35] in *The Hungarian Hut*. One observer declared, "Likhutina is captivating in good natured, guileless, keen witted roles. As her trainer Didelot bestowed on the public a charming gift. It seems one could never find another Mouska." [36] Even before the end of her schooling in 1817 she had made her debut at the age of fifteen as Galatea. In a draft of his poem *Eugene Onegin*, Pushkin once penned the line, "Alone Likhutina is sweet." [37] Beside straight ballet roles she also performed in pantomime melodramas with such compelling titles as *The Murderess and the Orphan* and *The Dog of Aubri*. In 1826 Didelot made her a teacher at the theatrical institute.

After Didelot had left Paris, his beloved work *Zéphire et Flore* won Continental fame. In 1814 it was presented for the participants of the Congress of Vienna,[38] no doubt to lighten their burden of rearranging the map of Europe after the defeat of Napoleon.

On January 26, 1818, Didelot again staged *Zéphire et Flore* at the Hermitage. Later, when the newly rebuilt St. Petersburg Bolshoi Theater opened, *Zéphire* played there to the delight of the spectators. At a summer performance of the work in which Antonin, a worthy French import, and Istomina took the leads, the emperor himself deigned to express his pleasure to the directors.[39] In order to present his two-act Parisian version of the work, Didelot had to utilize the score compiled in London, partly made up of strains he had hummed to Venua from Cavos' music, written earlier in Russia, but lost in the shipwreck of the *St. George*. In the new program Didelot explained his dilemma and acknowledged that "not the composer [Venua], but I, am guilty in this, and I am sure that M. Cavos, so well known for his beautiful compositions, will not be vexed by the small theft made from him." [40] It would be interesting to know if Cavos completely accepted this small theft without vexation. Didelot had few scruples about such filching of music for his ballets. From the operas of Mozart, Cherubini, Méhul, or Grétry, Didelot took what was necessary to complete his plans.[41] However, in the production of new works, Didelot made it a practice to work closely with the composer. Glushkovsky recalled that while Kapelmeister Cavos sat behind his piano, Didelot performed the pantomime of several scenes, explaining that a certain number of beats, a certain tempo, or special musical sounds were needed to support his action. Sometimes, tired from hard work at rehearsals, Didelot sang in a hoarse voice motifs of the music, which Cavos then recorded and harmonized.[42] In a final session the composer was at times obliged to cut his work at Didelot's insistence. Both Cavos and Ferdinando Antonolini, who also worked with Didelot, revolted against his dictatorial policies, but in vain. However, the Soviet musicologist Rabinovich, who has thoroughly studied Cavos' ballets and operas, concluded that his ballets were much better than his operas, perhaps because Didelot presented to him a united dramatic design for the works in which they collaborated.[43]

Didelot was so anxious to make sure the tempo was correct for his dancers that even during the most engrossing part of a ballet, he sometimes emerged out of the wings in a state of *déshabillé* to beat time or make signs to the orchestra to slow down or quicken the pace. In answer to a complaint written in the magazine *Son of the Fatherland* in 1817 against such conduct during *Theseus and Adriadne*, Didelot replied: "Our conductor is still young, and although he is a gifted person, he does not yet have sufficient experience . . . a dancer loses all his support if the beat of the dance slows down, and he is in no condition to bring pleasure to the public . . . [likewise] pantomime, accelerated by the music, may not express the movement of the soul in all forcefulness." [44] Such was his rationale for dashing out on stage to correct the tempo—a reasonable position, assuredly, but with results scarcely aesthetically pleasing.

Barely a month after staging *Zéphire et Flore*, on February 14, 1818, he presented a work entitled *The Young Island Girl, or Leon and Tamaida*. In this ballet the dancer Osipova represented the reflection in a mirror of the leading dancer, Likhutina, who played the part of Tamaida.[45] The public loved it. In August Didelot brought forth a two-act version of *The Caliph of Bagadad, or The Youthful Adventures of Harun al-Rashid*. The music of *Caliph* belonged in greater part to Antonolini, but in it were included large musical sections from the opera of that name by Boieldieu. Didelot had the task of conveying by mimed action alone various scenes of the opera in which words had been the means of communication with the audience. In the opera, for example, the Caliph appears on the stage in the costume of a Bedouin, and simply a word spoken by him explains that he is the Caliph. To convey this in ballet, in an opening scene, Didelot showed the Caliph actually changing from his rich garments into those of a Bedouin, while during the change, one of his minsters brought him a state paper to be signed. Having changed, the Caliph then pointed out to the minister a ring which was the sign by which he was to be recognized in his new guise.[46]

Didelot finished the year 1818 with a three-act production, entitled *A Hunting Adventure*. This work was inspired by a picture in the Hermitage by the Flemish artist David Teniers. In between these major ballets, he staged the dances for eight operas and comedies. Quantitatively, but scarcely qualitatively, in 1819 he slowed down a bit, staging only twelve works instead of the thirteen done in 1818.

Didelot's staggering record of productivity was possible because all his thoughts and energy were channelled in one direction. He was ruthless with his performers in making them measure up to his standards. Panayeva left a graphic description of the methods by which he prodded his performers, young or old. She recalled: "Didelot was horribly funny when he stood in the wings and followed the dancers on the stage. He twisted, smiled and pointed his feet, suddenly bad-temperedly beginning to beat time with his toes. When the little pupils danced he shook his fist at them, and if they missed the figures, he made their lives a misery. He pounced on them behind the curtain like a vulture, pulled their hair or ears, and if any ran away he gave them a kick which sent them flying." [47] Even soloists did not escape his wrath. While the audience applauded, as a dancer ran behind the scenes, Didelot might seize her by the shoulders, shake her, shower abuses upon her, and after giving her a punch in the back, push her on to the stage to receive more applause.

While being harsh to others, however, he was relentlessly despotic with himself. Karatygin described his perpetual restlessness:

> He was constantly engaged in some sort of unnatural movement, as if in his veins flowed quicksilver, instead of blood. His head was constantly occupied with the composition of some dance or the subject of a new ballet, and for that reason, his mobile features incessantly changed and his entire figure every now and then twitched; his feet were usually turned out, and he had the amusing habit of lifting one each minute and then turning it to the side. This he did even while walking on the street, as if he suffered from St. Vitus Dance. Anyone who saw him for the first time might, of course, take him for a madman, to such an extent were his movements strange, wild, and awkward.[48]

Since to Didelot ballet was no shallow setting for the display of virtuousity, he studied voraciously and discussed his plans with men of the intelligentsia. Didelot affirmed that

> in order to be a good balletmaster, it is necessary to employ a great deal of time in reading historical books to draw from them subjects for future creations, and to join to this all possible endeavors of his pupils, so that they might embellish his creations by their talents. A balletmaster must also have a knowledge of the morals and customs of different nations, and study their national inclinations and costumes. He must have a poetic gift in order to express his thought pleasantly in the programs. He must know painting and mechanics, in order to be able to arrange picturesque groups, and more suitably discuss plans with the decorator and machinist. The balletmaster's knowledge of music is a most necessary thing, both for assisting the composer and the orchestra director.[49]

Glushkovsky assured readers of his biography that by living a Spartan existence his master Didelot had indeed acquired all this knowledge in an eminent degree. "Didelot rose early," he recalled, "and spent some time reading historical books in order to draw subjects for ballets from them. Being good at drawing he drew groups for his ballets, then set out for the theatrical school where he gave dancing lessons. From there he went to the theater where he rehearsed ballets or mounted them. After dinner he set out again either to the theatrical school or to the theater where his ballets were performed. In such a way he passed all the days of the week, except Sunday. That day he fully dedicated to relaxation." [50]

Some of Didelot's drawings are still in existence to prove his talent in that field (*Fig. 27*). He was a good friend of the Russian artist Alexander Orlovsky, who often visited his home and taught him a few tricks of the artist's trade. Orlovsky also used his art to quiet Didelot's wrath. Once Orlovsky returned home late with the master after some theatrical unpleasantness had greatly ired him. To top it all Didelot's supper was not waiting him, and in anger he toppled over a large ink pot on an oak table. Without comment, using the spilled ink, Orlovsky's skillful fingers traced a porcupine, whose face depicted all the wrath then present in that of Didelot. The balletmaster enjoyed the gentle rebuke so much that he had the drawing framed the next day.[51]

Didelot's study of history and mythology bore an extra rich harvest of works in 1819. His artistic year began on January 9 with the mere

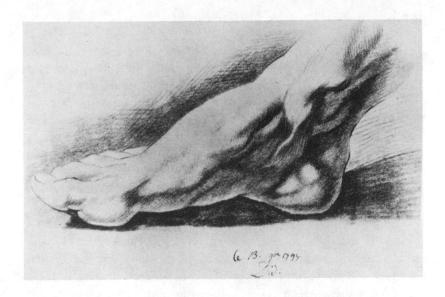

Figure 27. Drawings of a foot and the head of a young girl made by Didelot about 1794, from Slonimsky's *Didlo*.

formulation of the dances for a revival of Noverre's grand tragic drama *Medée et Jason*. Though he was distracted by the production of a divertissement for the opera *La Vestale* in April, the full flowering of four months' work appeared on May 5 in the production of "a great pantomime ballet in five acts," *Raoul de Créquis*. The story had been used in an opera by Nicolas Dalayrac, which was produced in Paris in 1789. Although he imitated at least one scene of the opera, Didelot had a different plan for the new work. His action was probably based more on Salvatore Viganò's ballet of the same name, shown in Vienna and in various Italian cities.[52]

The plot centered around the deeds of Raoul de Créquis, a feudal count who took part in a crusade to Jerusalem. In his absence, the neighboring lord, Baudouin, seizes his castle, his lands, and his wife, the Countess Adelaide. On his return de Créquis suffers shipwreck near his home, but manages to survive on a fragment of the ship. The action of the ballet developed by means of a series of scenes in a highly romantic style. As the curtain opens, a violent storm at sea is seen shattering the boat on which de Créquis is returning from the crusade. When cast on the rocky shore of his own property, the count learns from fishermen about the treachery of Baudouin. Begging help from a friendly neighbor, Raoul dons the clothes of a pilgrim and begs hospitality in the castle where his wife is held. Baudouin is then giving a lavish festival to honor Adelaide and to win her heart. During the course of it he orders his henchmen to inform her that de Créquis has died in a battle with the Saracens. Upon the order of Baudouin, even the false pilgrim assures her that he had been a witness to the death. When Adelaide almost loses her senses from grief over the news, Baudouin instructs the pilgrims to entertain her with music. This diversion affords de Créquis an opportunity to reveal his identity to his wife. Earlier, in her own quarters, distraught at her fate, Adelaide had played on her harp a song which Raoul had once composed for her. When ordered to sing, the false pilgrim played the very same song. His wife not only recognizes him, but his enemies perceive the light of recognition in her eyes, and a battle ensues in which de Créquis is delivered over to Baudouin for imprisonment and torture.

The third act shows the prison in which Adelaide and her small son are then kept. With the aid of friends, who shoot messages by arrows in through the windows, she manages to escape, after a fierce struggle in which the gentle woman runs a spear through the guard. In the fourth act the stage was divided into two sections: one showing de Créquis' cell and the other showing the adjoining room of the warder, with a door in between the two. Aided by loyal subjects the count also escapes in the last scene of the ballet, with a subsequent final struggle taking place between Raoul and Baudouin in which de Créquis conquers his adversary.[53]

Though the ballet was truly melodramatic, it was effective. Adam Glushkovsky has left a vivid, detailed account of the mimed action of several scenes (*Fig. 28*). In merely reading his description of the touching details, the reader can become involved. Further, the music was designed especially to heighten this emotional impact. De Créquis' cohorts help him to escape by filling his jailer with wine to the point of stupefaction. As his liberators open the door to the count's cell, they strive earnestly not to wake the sleeping captor. The music of muted violins became very soft, while special machinery, imitating the sound of bolts creaking in the door, produced a most realistic effect. As a result of Didelot's attention to such fine points, the spectators were so enthralled that a deep quiet pervaded the theater, as if the viewers too strove to keep from waking the captor.[54]

The carefully composed music was credited in the *affiches* to the composer Cavos and his pupil Timofei Zhuchkovsky. Actually the ballet was said to be the work of several authors.[55] One of the tender melodies from the ballet endures today as the well known Russian lullaby, "Spi mladenets, baiuski baiu."

Zotov, commenting on the work, affirmed that during Didelot's time relatively little attention was given to pure dancing. The public then wanted interesting content in ballets; in fact, they wanted a play. He recalled, "*Raoul de Créquis* was almost all pantomime scenes—but the extremely engaging quality of the subject, and the outstanding gifts of Kolosova and Auguste replaced all dances." [56] A second critic confirmed Zotov's impression, exclaiming, "This ballet is just about the best of Didelot's ballets. . . . In ballet, pantomime is most important of all, and in this, no one we have can compare with Kolosova. . . . Looking on her, one forgets that he is sitting in a theater, and involuntarily shares her feelings. . . . Ah, if only she were a Frenchwoman." [57]

Actually, though dancing was secondary to plot, it was not entirely replaced. There were colorful scenes with enchanting dances. The second act, in which Baudouin entertains the countess, afforded a chance for much colorful movement and pageantry. In it a knight's

Figure 28. Adam Glushkovsky in *Raoul de Créquis*, from a lithograph by Vilgelm in Vsevolodsky's *Teatr v Rossii v epokhu otechestvennoi voiny.*

tournament took place, accompanied by all the excitement of crashing armor. Special shields and spears were actually mechanically constructed for this, so that under the pressure of springs they resoundingly fell apart at the right moment. After the tournament, the knights' ladies stood in oblique lines, danced, and threw laurel wreaths to their gentlemen. The victorious warriors skillfully caught each wreath on their spears. Then the two lines of damsels threw wreaths to each other so that for some time a great roofed alley of wreaths was formed in the air. The knights then moved in between the lines of women, assumed militant poses, and while still dancing, looped the wreaths from the air on their spears. The scene was rehearsed so often that the warriors seldom missed, but in case they did, little pages dancing and playing lyres near them would unobtrusively pick up the fallen wreaths. Next, the girls formed another triumphal arch by tying their multicolored veils to palm branches carried by the victorious vassals.[58]

When this ballet was given for the first time, the spectators shook the vaults of the theater with applause and cries of "Bravo." After the second and third acts, Didelot was summoned to the stage by the whole audience, and many of the viewers from the expensive sections of the theater came to see him in the dressing room to congratulate him. Among these were his friend, the painter Orlovsky, who was noted especially for his portrayal of military figures and horses. Turning to Didelot, Orlovsky said graciously, "Permit me to pronounce my judgment. I have seen many pictures with beautiful subjects; you surpass all I have seen of this kind. No master's canvas can paint them as you do in your ballets, because there they are alive and animated by rich ideas." [59]

"This ballet was a crown of glory for Didelot," Glushkovsky recalled. "Never yet had there been so much interest in the subject of a ballet." [60] Yet it was relatively inexpensive, costing only five thousand rubles, because it was first produced as a benefit for Didelot's friend Auguste, and theatrical regulations did not allow great expenses for benefits. The ballet ran more than one hundred times, was chosen eighteen times as a benefice, and brought the directorate more than two hundred fifty thousand rubles in return. Recalling works of this calibre which he had witnessed, Glushkovsky affirmed that "Didelot was one of those balletmasters of which nature is niggardly, which she gives to the theater only from century to century." [61]

After staging dances for two operas and two divertissements,

Didelot treated the St. Petersburg public on August 30, 1819, to a bit of chinoiserie—*Ken-si and Tao, or Beauty and the Beast*. He adopted the tale of Le Prince de Beaumont, *La Belle et la bête*, as well as Marmontel's story, *Zémire et Azor*, used previously in Grétry's opera of that name. While the setting in Grétry's opera had an Iranian flavor, Didelot declared that he changed this in order to give the audience more variety. Actually the only resemblance between St. Petersburg and London versions of Didelot's *Ken-si* seemed to be in the stylized Chinese flavor of the costumes and setting. In contrast to the relatively austere budget of *Raoul de Créquis*, this production cost about twenty thousand assignat rubles, with special machinery and seven new pieces of scenery painted especially for it.[62] Charming Chinese character dances were enhanced by the customary umbrellas, bells, and multicolored lanterns. Glushkovsky explained that there were not so many fiery lanterns in *Ken-si* as there were in later Russian-produced Chinese-type ballets, but that in Didelot's work, there was more fire in the pantomime and dances than in later works, and his production was further enlightened by a sound idea.[63] As in many of Didelot's ballets, the story did have a lesson to preach.

In the ballet a cruel and arbitrary despot named Tao rules in a Chinese kingdom. He is served by a gentle maid named Ken-si who loves her own father dearly and is loved by him in return. When Tao wants Ken-si to become his concubine, she resolutely refuses. Not fearing the monarch's wrath, her father supports his daughter. Tao then orders Ken-si to be taken to his harem and her father escorted to the execution block. But at the moment the axe is raised over the father's head, an enchantress curses Tao, changing him into a beast. Thus the first act ends with the lesson that because Tao had lived as a beast, he was turned into one. As the ballet progressed, mild Ken-si achieves a transformation in the soul of Tao by her sacrificial love. Only after the completion of his interior conversion was the beast restored to human form.[64] When *Ken-si and Tao* was given for the first time in St. Petersburg, it was a complete disaster, in spite of the great expenditure. The fault rested completely with Didelot. Not only did he have charge of the actual dancing, but Didelot had also arranged with the machinist that changes of scenery should be made at his signal of two whistles— the first for preparing the machinist to act, and the second for the actual operation itself. In confusion Didelot once forgot that he had already given the preparatory whistle and gave it a second time, which the machinist naturally took as his signal to change the scenery. Antonin, who was still performing, very angrily went on dancing, though the setting for his *pas* suddenly changed from a chamber to a forest. The dancers who used the change of scenery as their entrance cue then ran out on the stage. Didelot, forgetting that he was in front of the public, ran out himself on the stage yelling that it was all a mistake. In vexation he gave another whistle, and again all the decorations were changed. While carpenters, lamp-tenders, and other stage hands ran about, the audience clapped and laughed. Thus the production ended in utter disaster. Both Prince Tufiakin and Didelot were in a frenzy; the first because he had spent so much of his budget on the disastrous production, and the second because of the failure of his brain child. *Ken-si and Tao*, however, was a story of redemption, and that is exactly what happened. The public blamed the machinist, not their favorite Didelot, and came back even a third and fourth time to see it.[65] *Ken-si* was subject to more mechanical difficulties, however. In one performance Likhutina was supposed to pirouette and then disappear. The machinist started moving the floor mechanism to accomplish her disappearance too soon, then recollecting himself, moved it back. In the meantime Likhutina was already submerging under the floor. As the floor moved back she was squeezed and began to cry out "like a goat." [66]

With all the vicissitudes, however, in the words of Zotov, "the ballet enjoyed huge success, it was repeated a multitude of times, brought great returns, and the glory of Didelot rose even higher." [67] At this point in his career, Didelot could scarcely wish for a better press. "In general," it was reported, "our ballets are now in a most shining state, for which we are obliged to the most incessant efforts of Didelot, whose name and talents are known in all European capitals." [68]

One of Didelot's oft-used themes, that of *Laura and Henry*, again became the subject of a three-act production in November of 1819. This time it had a new score by Cavos. In July of 1820 Russians saw a five-act ballet which Didelot had previously first worked out in England: *Karl et Lisbeth, ou Le Déserteur malgré lui*, described as "a demi-character and military ballet." After less than two months, for the customary August 30 extravaganza, Didelot brought forth the spectacular *Cora and Alonzo, or The Virgin of the Sun*. In its display of unusual effects, this ballet has hardly been surpassed in any age. Didelot declared that he wavered between the stories of Pizarro and Cortes but finally settled on

Marmontel's tale *Les Incas, ou La Destruction de l'Empire du Perou* as the basis of his work.

On the right side of the stage there was a temple to the sun, with a beautiful stairway leading from its portico. In the front of the temple stood a sacred garden. A column especially dedicated to the sun god stood in the midst of the stage. In the distance a lake could be seen from which a cascade fell; on the left side of the stage were fiery mountains. In the first act, a Spanish conquistador, Alonzo, is invited by the ruler of the Peruvian Incas, Ataliba, to attend a holiday in which a virgin would be dedicated to the sun. The maiden Cora is chosen against her will. During the rite in which she pronounces vows, her eyes meet Alonzo's and they fall in love.

In the second act, as Alonzo wanders about the temple, his eyes again meet Cora's while she prays to the sun to expel from her heart thoughts of her beloved. As the couple gaze at each other in mutual love, a clap of thunder sounds, the earth begins to tremble frighteningly, and the volcanic mountains begin to spout sparks and torrents of flames and lava. While the temple trembles, the earth is rent by cracks from which flames and smoke come forth, and the sun column is shattered into pieces. High priests and temple servants scurry about in terror among weeping children and women. Flocks of birds thrash about in the air to heighten the effect of terror, and the very fiercest beasts forget their bloodthirsty proclivities and mix with the crowd of terrified Peruvians. Glushkovsky compared the scene to Bruillov's painting, *The Last Days of Pompeii*.

In order to placate the god of the sun, the high priests decree that Cora is to be sacrificed. While Cora beseeches the priest to spare her life, the sacrificial fire is prepared. Alonzo then runs to rescue his beloved, and at that moment, the sun turns pale and then darkens, again terrorizing the people. Alonzo, taking advantage of the awed mood of the people, makes a mimed "speech." In effect, this noble Castilian tells the Incas that they should forsake their god with his terrible laws and turn to the worship of his God who is one, true, and everlasting. As he "speaks" the sun returns to its former clarity, and the people, thinking him a divine ambassador, kneel before Alonzo. The Spaniard refuses to permit them, pointing out that they should worship his God, not himself. Glushkovsky, who described the ballet in detail, recalled that "the last scene was solemn and touching. It left a most pleasant impression with the spectator." [69]

As usual, the dances were secondary in the production, but Didelot did choreograph a special sacrificial dance for Cora "as the most suitable means of presenting her to the eyes of Alonzo and of lighting the fire of love in his eyes." [70] If the plot seems a bit simplistic to a twentieth-century reader, Didelot also had some fears that it might appear so to his nineteenth-century viewers, for he explained in the program: "For a denouement, the ballet demanded simplicity and greatness, and I thought it best of all to end the activity by the annihilation of barbarous laws and the enlightenment of the whole nation of idolators, by acknowledging the true Creator of the world. If success does not correspond to the enthusiasm of my heart, then may the public forgive me the defectiveness of the action for a good idea." [71] Though the ballet could scarcely have been other than costly, Arapov recorded that it brought great returns. In 1822, Didelot chose this work for his own benefit, with his son playing the part of Alonzo.[72]

On December 8, 1820, the theme of the sacrificial virgin entered into another production, originally formulated by Noverre—*Euthyme et Eucharis*. The action this time took place in the city of Themis where the citizens are obliged to sacrifice a young girl in order to please the Shade of Libas, who terrorized them. As the ballet begins, an assembly of maidens are advancing toward an urn full of lots to determine the victim. When Eucharis draws the unlucky lot, her mother wants to substitute herself for her daughter, but is not allowed, so Eucharis is decorated with flowers for the ceremony. Just as the townspeople are ready to kill her, shouts are heard, indicating that her lover Euthyme has just returned. He is crowned with the laurel branches of a victor of the Pythian games. Euthyme vows not to allow his beloved to be sacrificed, drives off the priests, overturns their altar, breaks the urn full of lots, and summons the very Shade of Libas himself to battle. At that the earth trembles and the terrible Shade, clad in a white veil, emerges from his grave. The veil falls from him, revealing a ghastly moving skeleton wearing a helmet. When the Shade demands his sacrifice, Euthyme begins a titanic struggle with him, ultimately driving the Shade into the nearby sea, where he disappears in the waves. In the next scene the gods fête the hero. Cupid and Hymen unite the lovers, and Jupiter sends them ambrosia and a crown of immortality. Terpsichore and Flora gambol with Zephyr, while Mars, Apollo, the Muses, Bellona, and other deities congratulate Euthyme, all showing their joy by appropriate dances.[73] The production possibly evoked shades of nostalgia for the aging Didelot who had once danced the part of Mars in his youthful, more agile days.[74]

His first new ballet of 1821 was *Alcestis, or The Descent of Hercules into the Underworld*. The ballet portrays the classical tale of Alcestis, who offered her life to save that of her husband, and was confined to Hades as a result. The fourth act depicted Hades with all its mythical crew: at the entrance stands guard the three-headed dog Cerberus. Pluto, god of the underworld, sits upon his throne. While the three judges, Minos, Rhadamanthys, and Aecus, look in a book containing the sentences of the culprits in hell, the three Fates, Clotho, Lachesis, and Atropos, spin the thread of life. In the background Charon guides his boat across the River Styx, beating off with his paddle those who try to swim. In various places on the stage furies stir firebrands, forge chains, knives, and arrows on anvils, while others squeeze poison into a cup and nourish snakes, which crawl along the ground.

At the end of the action appears Hercules, who with the aid of Mercury frees Alcestis from hell by raising her upwards onto a cloud. In front of them flies Mercury, directing their way with his wand. To thwart their escape, however, Pluto orders the Furies to fly after them, but Hercules struggles with his pursuers in the air and defeats them. Glushkovsky, as well as the average Russian spectator, found such scenes highly edifying. He commented: "So much thought, variety, and grace was in all these pictures. Over and above the activity, the image itself was bound strongly to move the soul of the spectator. And in this the ballets of Didelot were outstanding." [75] No doubt aided by the presence of Kolosova as Alcestis, the ballet brought great returns to the directors and was repeated often.

Gradually, however, another rising star began to replace the aging Kolosova in Didelot's esteem—Avdot'ia Istomina, who had played the part of tender Eucharis (*Fig. 29*). This talented dancer had made her debut on August 30, 1816 as Galathea. She ended her stage career in 1836, marrying an actor named Pavel S. Ekunin. In old age, as Istomina became stout and unsightly, she tried to hide with thick, caked make-up the fading glory of her once lovely face. She died of cholera in 1848;[76] however, in her prime Istomina was the type of beauty for which men competed and died. Several painters tried to capture the charm of the woman on canvas. The results were very different, and we can only guess which portrait represents the true Istomina. One thing is certain, however: all who had anything to say about her raved over her

Figure 29. Avdotia Istomina. *Courtesy of the Glinka Central Museum of Musical Culture, Moscow.*

unique beauty. Pimen' Arapov, a theater critic and historian, noted that "she was of medium build, brunette, with a beautiful appearance and was very well-shaped. She had black, fiery eyes veiled by long eyelashes which gave a very special character to her physiognomy. She had great strength in her feet, aplomb on the stage, and together with that, grace, lightness, and speed in movements; her pirouettes and her elevation were astounding. . . . For a long time, Istomina had no equal in ballet." [77] Vivacity and dexterity in dance were combined with an acting ability that allowed her to fill such diverse roles as Liza in *La Fille mal gardée*, Alonzo's Cora, and finally the Circassian girl in *The Prisoner of the Caucasus*. A theatrical yearbook for 1825 entitled *The Russian Thalia* confirmed reports of her acting ability, saying, "Without doubt the portrayal of passion and soulful movements by gestures, and the play of physiogonomy demand great talent. Istomina has this." [78] Eventually, she also played vaudeville roles successfully, for her diction was true, her voice pleasant, her glance quick, and very coquettish. The viewers heard her "swan-like voice" for the first time in a vaudeville production by Shakhovskoi in 1821 entitled *Phoenix, or The Morning of the Journalist,* in which she played the part of Zefireta, a dancer.[79] Prince Shakhovskoi also presented for her benefit "a romantic-comedy ballet" on January 8, 1823, entitled *Lily of Narbonne, or The Knight's Vow.* Though the production included, amidst splendid surroundings, a duel, a knighting ceremony, and a pantomime divertissement by Didelot, the comedy was not successful. On the eve of her 1824 benefit she received several beautiful presents, including an emerald bracelet wrapped up in the *affiche* advertising the program.[80]

Istomina's "pure Russian" beauty provoked one of the most dramatic theatrical scandals of the era in St. Petersburg. The happy possessor of the heart of the dark-eyed enchantress was a captain of the cavalry named Vasily A. Sheremetev, with whom Istomina lived. It so happened that a certain Count Alexander P. Zavadovsky was also passionately captivated by the same dark eyes. Zavadovsky shared his dwelling with a government official named Alexander Griboyedov, who once invited Istomina home to drink tea after the evening performance. The dancer submitted, but in order to avoid arousing the suspicion of Sheremetev, she made a special point of transferring from the theatrical carriage into Griboyedov's sled at a place where she thought she could escape surveillance. Sheremetev, however, followed the carriage, suspecting that Istomina might be heading for Zavadovsky's quarters.

Incited by his friend, the celebrated daredevil officer Alexander I. Yakubovich, Sheremetev challenged Griboyedov to a duel. Yakubovich himself promised to fight with Zavadovsky. Griboyedov accepted the challenge, but declared that he wished to duel with Yakubovich, leaving Sheremetev and Zavadovsky to settle their accounts.

The contest between Zavadovsky and Sheremetev took place on November 12, 1817. At three in the afternoon they entered the appointed place, Volkov Field, and after the fateful counting of eighteen steps, Sheremetev shot first, piercing the collar of Zavadovsky's caftan. Zavadovsky then advanced and shot from six paces, piercing the chest of Sheremetev, who plunged to the ground and flapped in agony on the snow like a large fish. After twenty-six hours Sheremetev expired in his apartment. When the police questioned Yakubovich he refused to reveal the provocation, since he had given his word of honor to his friend Sheremetev not to reveal it. When Istomina was summoned for investigation, she revealed that she had been living with Sheremetev, but on November 3, he had treated her badly, they had quarreled, and she had walked out on him. On November 5 when Griboyedov invited her to drink tea, she accepted, but later made up with Sheremetev and returned to his lodgings.

Because of the death of Sheremetev the next episode of the duel was delayed. Meanwhile, in 1818 Griboyedov was sent to Persia on diplomatic duty. Though Yakubovich had apologized to Griboyedov, begging him to defer, their duel finally took place in Georgia, in Tiflis, in 1819. Knowing his adversary enjoyed playing the piano, the crack marksman Yakubovich shot Griboyedov through the palm of the left hand.[81] In 1828, after the war between Russia and Persia, Griboyedov, then Russian minister at Teheran, negotiated a peace treaty which infuriated the Persians, for one thing, because it contained a clause demanding the return of Christian women held prisoners in Moslem harems. When an angry mob of Persians invaded the Russian legation, Griboyedov perished in the fighting; his body, stripped and hacked to pieces by the rioters, was identified chiefly by the mutilated hand he had received in the duel over Istomina. The stormy Griboyedov is now known chiefly to literary history as the author of a celebrated Russian comedy entitled *Woe from Wit*.[82]

The romantic duels naturally had St. Petersburg agog. The poet Pushkin mulled over the idea of writing a novel about the incident with the title *Russian Pelham (Fig. 30)*. Griboyedov, Istomina, Shakhovskoi,

Figure 30. Alexander Pushkin, by E. Geitman, from *Russkaia starina* (April, 1879).

and Zavadovsky were to be the leading characters. Pushkin's notes reveal that he also envisioned a work called *Les Deux Danseuses,* involving, according to the sketchy plan left to history, a ballet of Didelot's given in 1819, Zavadovsky, Istomina, and a duel.[83] Whether this work was to be part of the proposed novel, it seems only Pushkin knows. Certainly the story provided drama worthy of the artistry with which Pushkin could have told it.

In his famous poem *Eugene Onegin* Pushkin did leave in verse a poignant record of the type of life the wealthy, bored youth of St. Petersburg lived in Didelot's time. After a day of accomplishing little the young socialites began their evening entertainment:

> Glass after glass is drained in drenching
> The hot, fat cutlets; you would say
> They've raised a thirst there is no quenching.
> But now it's time for the ballet.[84]

A short ride in his sleigh or drozhky took him to the theater, where he had a subscription seat:

> Onegin flies to taste the blisses
> And breathe the free air of the stage
> To praise the dancer now the rage
> Or greet a luckless Phaedre with hisses
> Or call the actress he preferred
> Just for the sake of being heard.
> . . .
>
> Where Shakhovskoi brought noisy laughter
> With his sardonic comedies;
> Didelot enjoyed his victories
> Upon those very boards thereafter.

Pushkin described in prose the conduct common in his circle: "Before the beginning of the opera, tragedy, or ballet," he recalled, "a young man walks along all the first ten rows of seats, walks on everyone's feet, and inquires both from those he knows and those he doesn't know, 'Where did you just come from?' 'From Semyonova's, from Sosnitskaya's, from Kolosova's, from Istomina's!' [The answer would be] 'Boy you're lucky. Today she sings—she plays, she dances. Let's clap for her, let's call her out.' 'She's a dear! Such eyes! What tiny feet she has, such talent!' The curtain lifts, the young chap, his friends moving from place to place, express their delight and clap." [85]

The thoughtless conduct was, it seems, their method of rebelling against "the system," for with all the surface glamor of their lives, these young men were sometimes bored to the point of despair, like Onegin:

> The house rocks with applause; undaunted,
> And treading toes, between the chairs
> Onegin presses; with his vaunted
> Aplomb, he lifts his eye-glass, stares
> . . . . his mocking
> Slow eyes come last to rest upon
> The lighted stage, and with a yawn
> He sighs: "They're past the age—it's shocking!
> I've haunted the ballet—what for?
> Even Didelot becomes a bore." [86]

The point when "Didelot becomes a bore" was indeed the very nadir of ennui. Commenting on his own phrase, Pushkin noted, "[These are] the chilly feelings of a devil, worthy of a Childe Harold. The ballets of Didelot are performed with vivacious imagination and unusual charm. One of our romantic writers finds in them far more poetry than in all French literature." [87] For the average viewer Didelot's productions and his dancers were considered sheer magic. For all the ages Pushkin preserved the excitement brought by a performance of Istomina:

> The curtain rustles as it soars:
> A fairy light about her playing.
> The magic of the bow obeying,
> A crowd of nymphs round her—lo!
> Istomina on lifted toe.
> One foot upon the floor is planted,
> The other slowly circles, thus,
> Then wafted as by Eolus
> She flies, a thing of down, enchanted;
> Now serpentine she twists and wheels,
> And now she leaps and claps her heels. [88]

Glushkovsky declared that Pushkin wrote this passage in praise of Istomina's role in *Acis et Galathée*. [89] Whatever the role, Pushkin left a description of the technical feats accomplished in Istomina's day: the *rond de jambe, jeté, renversé,* and *cabriole*. In other lines Onegin's musings upon the performance of Istomina described the very spirit pervading Russian ballet (*Fig. 31*):

Figure 31. Terpsichore, a print of 1779 after Cipriani. *Courtesy of the British Museum, London.*

Figure 32. Doodlings by Pushkin about 1825, reproduced from *Avtografy A. S. Pushkina.*

My goddess! How shall I trace you?
I sadly call on each sweet name.
Can others ever quite replace you?
And you, can you remain the same?
Oh, once again will you be singing
For me? Shall I yet see you winging
Your way in soulful flight and free
My fair Russian Terpsichore? [90]

The soulful flight—the union of performing virtuosity with deep sensitivity to the dramatic impact of the movement—was then, and still is, a fundamental æsthetic goal of the Russian performer, and Didelot was a prime force in instilling that special spirit, that happy combination of soulful expression with faultless technique in Russian ballet.

Strangely enough Pushkin himself was almost obsessed with women's feet; he seemed to notice them much more than a damsel's pretty face. Time after time his verses reveal this strange fascination, with lines such as:

Diana's breast, the face of Flora
Are charming, friends, but I would put
Them both aside and only for a
Glimpse of Terpsichore's sweet foot. [91]

He filled the margins of his notebooks with drawings of feet. Significantly one bit of this doodling shows feet which clearly seemed to be *sur les pointes* (Fig. 32). [92]

While it is hard to explain Pushkin's perfervid fascination for feet, it is easier to explain his powers of observation of dancers and his ability to record their complicated movements, for Pushkin himself had a dancing teacher who was to perform in Didelot's ballets. Facility in performing the intricate ballroom dances popular in their day was considered a most necessary part of the training of a gentlemen. In the special *lycée* which Pushkin attended, established in Tsarskoe Selo (The Czar's Village) for the training of future civil servants, one of the teachers was Ivan Eberhardt, a German dancer and soloist. He began teaching dancing to the pupils of the *lycée* in 1816. [93] Later Eberhardt appeared in ballets inspired by the fertile mind of his precocious pupil Pushkin, such as *The Prisoner of the Caucasus* and *Ruslan and Liudmila*. Eberhardt was rated as a very talented dancer-mime and a marvelous character dancer, noted especially for the deft turn he gave to a mazurka. In general he was considered indispensable in Didelot's ballets.[94]

As Didelot's fruitful career reached its climax, not the least of his accomplishments was his good judgment in appreciating the balletic possibilities of Pushkin's works. Glushkovsky was a bit ahead of his master in being the very first to choreograph a Pushkin poem, for he showed *Ruslan and Liudmila* to the Moscow public on May 15, 1821. However it was Didelot who first used Pushkin's *The Prisoner of the Caucasus.*

Pushkin finished this work in February of 1821. Though it went on sale only in September of 1822, Didelot's ballet, based upon the poem, emerged on January 5, 1823. The balletmaster, who had friends in several popular literary circles, undoubtedly knew of the poem before its publication. In the preface to the ballet program he explained: "All *litterateurs* praise this outstanding production of Russian poetry. I asked for a short extract of it to be translated, and found the content very interesting. Of course it would have been far better if I could have read through the original in order to feel the meter and the richness of ideas in it, but unfortunately, not being able to read Russian, I had to be satisfied by a translated extract." [95] Since French was spoken everywhere in polite society in St. Petersburg at this time, Didelot had never been obliged to learn Russian.

In Pushkin's haunting poem a Russian officer, who has fled from some unnamed cause is captured by the Circassians, a Caucasian tribe. His escape is aided by a beautiful Circassian girl. Even though they can not communicate orally, they recognize their mutual love. When the officer manages to flee across a river to safety, however, he forsakes his beautiful deliverer. As he looks back, rings in the water leave him and the reader to conjecture that his beloved has taken her life in despair.

Didelot made some significant changes in Pushkin's tale. In Didelot's ballet the time was pushed back ten centuries to ancient Slavic days. The nameless freedom-loving officer became Rostislav, a young Slavic prince. This transference in time, in the explanation of one commentator, removed the possibility that the viewers, many of whom were intellectuals disenchanted with their government, might identify the personality of the officer-prisoner with that of the poet himself. Pushkin had been exiled to Bessarabia for writings that the government had considered to be dangerous, such as an *Ode on Liberty*.[96]

Didelot also changed the ending of the story. He explained in the program it was done partly because "it would be unpleasant to see in the ballet an ending such as the one in the poem, for the spectator would unwillingly sympathize with the fate of the tender, flaming Circassian." Therefore, his work had a happy ending, with a ceremony of bethrothal between Rostislav and the Circassian woman, and to crown the event, the Circassian khan accepted Russian citizenship! Though Didelot did research for his work in a book entitled *Diction-naire géographique-historique de l'Empire de Russie* by N. S. Vsevo-lozhsky, there were some rather glaring inconsistencies in regard to the history and customs of the people. Yet, it is significant that in line with the newly developing Byronic romanticism, Didelot did try to portray the mores of these wild, mountain tribesmen, and he did so eloquently in the eyes of his contemporaries. "Never was a poem set to a new form so fully, closely, and eloquently as Didelot set the marvelous verses of national poetry into the silent prose of pantomime," recalled Glush-kovsky. "He captured the locale, the morals, the wildness, and warlikeness of the people." [97] In one scene a soaring eagle carried off a baby to a high rock and placed it in its nest. In order to recapture her infant, the child's desperate mother crawled like a snake to the top of the rock where the nest lies. In a scene portraying village life Didelot deftly displayed touches of local color: a warrior, with a wild look on his face, sharpened his weapon on a rock, while on a nearby tree a cradle had been made by plunging a sword into the trunk, then hanging a wide saddle upon the hilt. Covered by a jackal's skin, a baby slept peacefully secure in its improvised shelter. Circassian games, fights, and shooting contests—all were incorporated into the action. The public was entranced with the ballet, for it was held in the repertoire in St. Petersburg for thirteen seasons.[98] Glushkovsky himself staged it in Moscow, where the critic from *The Women's Magazine* (*Damskii zhurnal*) hailed it for its charming costumes, its lively action, beautiful scenery and folk dances.[99]

It was a sore trial for the exiled Pushkin not to be able to see his work on the stage, with his heroine performed by Istomina, who in the critic's words, truly "breathed of the East." [100] The homesick poet pleaded from Bessarabia to his brother, "Write me about Didelot, about that Circassian girl Istomina, whom I once courted, like the Prisoner of the Caucasus." [101]

This work was to be a lasting triumph for Didelot, for the theme of the ballet retained its popularity even in the twentieth century.° In Didelot's time dance also began to be used in dramatic productions staged from Pushkin's works, such as Prince Shakhovskoi's production in 1824 of a three-act version of *The Fountain of Bakhchisarai*, with a chorus and ballet.†

In 1824 Didelot had more exciting plans. At least since 1796 when he staged *L'Heureux Naufrage*, he had been an avid fan of *Macbeth*. Utilizing the mature virtuosity of Kolosova as Lady Macbeth, he intended to present the great drama to delight St. Petersburg on August 30, 1824. This, however, was a forbidden theme in Russia at the time. The reason was that the ruling emperor, Alexander I, had come to power when the group of discontented officials in the palace had simply murdered his father Paul I. Thus, even an illusion to regicide was dangerous and inadmissable.

Apparently Didelot thought he could somehow cajole the censor into allowing him to choreograph the story, for he commissioned Cavos to work on the score. The successor of Prince Tufiakin, theatrical director A. A. Maikov, explained what happened in a letter, saying: "In the fall of last year, M. Didelot presented to me the plans for two ballets, from which I chose one for the August 30 production. In the middle of the summer he changed his plans and wished to mount *Macbeth*. I explained to him that this tragedy was forbidden by the censor, but he took the trouble to try to go past me and ask the permission of the censor. Cavos worked prematurely on the composition of the music. . . . Things turned out as I expected; the censor did not allow *Macbeth*, so he turned to the subject of Phaedra." [103]

Phaedra, however, did not appear for many more months. In the meantime Didelot turned from English drama to the bright treasure trove of Russian folklore in another of Pushkin's works, *Ruslan and Liudmila*.

° Using a new score by Boris Asaf'ev, Nikolai Volkov, Leonid Lavrovsky, and I. Eil'bershtein staged a version in 1938 at the Leningrad Maly Theater. In Moscow during the same year Volkov and Rostislav Zakharov used the same theme. Later they were followed by companies in numerous Soviet cities. The ballet was given in Paris in 1951 to the music of Khachaturian's *Gayane* and staged by Georges Skibine for Le Grand Ballet du Marquis de Cuevas.[102]

† In the Soviet period this poem became the basis of the most popular Pushkin ballet of all, being embellished with the powerful talent of Galina Ulanova and Maya Plisetskaya. Many other Pushkin works have been choreographed since Didelot's time, including the classic *Eugene Onegin*, which was skillfully staged in 1965 by John Cranko of The Stuttgart Ballet, earning heartwarming praise from the world press.

This poem of Pushkin's was published in August of 1820. After Glushkovsky staged it first in Moscow, Auguste, with the assistance of Didelot, presented it to the St. Petersburg audience on December 8, 1824. The score was composed by Friedrich Sholtz, a German composer who worked with Glushkovsky in Moscow. Sholtz attempted to portray local color by including lively Cossack dances; however, he scarcely achieved the depths of artistry found in the later opera of the same name by Glinka. The story dealt with the abduction and whisking away on a black cloud of Liudmila, the betrothed of a Kievan knight Ruslan, by a dwarf named Chernomor. The tale, full of fantastic devilish creatures, afforded great opportunities for the lavish stage effects ever popular on the Russian stage—such as a battle with a twelve headed snake, fireworks, and flights of enchantresses, furies, and cupids. The latter were never a part of authentic Russian folklore, but apparently the public in 1824 overlooked such faults, for the ballet stayed on the Moscow stage more than ten years. By 1831 the critic Fyodor Koni was quite bored with it and complained about its abiding presence in the repertoire. Admitting that it was good in its time, he complained, "Why have it now, when the public is no longer happy with fireworks and devilish revelries, but demands from art more æsthetic productions? . . . Spare us, God from similar witchcraft." [104] The St. Petersburg version of *Ruslan and Liudmila* was enriched with the talented performance of Didelot's famous pupil Yekaterina A. Teleshova, who being a relative of Prince Shakhovskoi and a close friend of Count Miloradovich, had abundant "pull" in the Imperial Theaters, which she often used to gain roles. Happily she also had talent to accompany it. In 1825 *The Russian Thalia* carried her portrait with the explanation, "This young disciple of Terpsichore is outstanding in the difficult art of pantomime. She performs all her roles with unusual pleasantness and rare success." [105] Another viewer agreed that "she had delightful talent in demi-character form, and as a pantomime subject, we have never seen the like since her time, and truly won't soon see it. . . . She captivated the most dispassionate spectators." [106]

Teleshova also captivated several artists, including the painter Bruillov, who included her in a work entitled *Italian by the Fountain*. Her best known likeness was painted by Orest A. Kiprensky in the role of Zélis. She also inspired some charming lines by Griboyedov, who noted:

> And suddenly, how like the wind her flight
> As a fleeting star lights the night

Then disappears; with her foot she beats the air
As if from on high with wings endowed.[107]

In *Ruslan and Liudmila* Teleshova played the part of a sorceress. The next year she played the part of Phaedra when Didelot produced this work. Having suffered so many setbacks in his career, Didelot approached this new task in a fatalistic frame of mind, saying in the program—his last words in print—"The lot is cast; the ship weighs anchor, in spite of many opposite opinions. Will not the hurricane lift? Flattered by so many happy sailings I decided to set out anew. If I fail, then I will fail like Phaeton. He wished to rule the chariot of the Sun; I was bold enough to treat a subject enlightened by the name of Racine, and to follow in the footsteps of that deathless author . . . Diligence, patience, hope." [108]

As usual Didelot's ballet seemed to emphasize the spectacular. Phaedra, the wife of the minotaur-slayer Theseus, fell in love with her husband's son Hippolyte. The father avenged his son by having the god Poseidon send a sea monster out of the water to prey on unsuspecting Hippolyte as he drove along the coast in his chariot. The swooping down of this monster and the subsequent wreck of the chariot was advertised as one of the great attractions of the ballet.[109] No doubt the work failed to achieve the glory of the Racine production, but it was praised for its beautiful, ravishing groups, its multitude of flights, and the wonderful talents who embellished it.

On October 29, 1825, Teleshova, along with another of Didelot's pupils, Nadezhda Azarevicheva, were honored by a benefit. For the occasion a new three-act ballet was presented, called *Satan with All His Devices, or The Lesson of the Sorcerer*. The divertissements in the first act, as well as a holiday celebration which terminated the ballet, were the work of Didelot.[110]

The year 1826 was creatively the bleakest year for Didelot since his return to Russia, but it was a hard year for all Russia. Discontent had fomented in Russian society in the years after Napoleon's invasion. Russian officers who pursued Napoleon's troops westward had their eyes opened. Having learned of some of the attractive features of constitutional government and of a free agricultural labor system, they were impatient to introduce these features into Russian life. For this reason members of the intelligentsia formed secret societies to discuss how a revolt could be effected. When Emperor Alexander I died in

1825 and a crisis of succession ensued, young officers attempted an abortive revolt on Senate Square in St. Petersburg on December 14. The staging of the revolt opened as an *opéra bouffe*—but proceeded to a denouement that sent five men to the gallows and many more to Siberia.

In the wake of the stifled coup, a general malaise, an air of frustration and helplessness, gripped Russian society. No doubt the mood of discontent was aggravated by the fact that, in keeping with the solemnities of mourning for the death of Alexander I, Russian theaters were closed for nine months afterward.

Didelot then produced only two divertissements and the dances for an opera in late 1826. The following year, he staged, among lesser works, Dauberval's classic *La Fille mal gardée* under the title of *Liza and Colin, or Vain Precautions*. During 1828 and 1829 such works as *Joy of the Moldavians, Dido, or The Destruction of Carthage, The Mad Woman, The New Heroine, or The Cossack Woman*, and *Piramo e Tisbe* were done in collaboration with Auguste.[111]

Didelot became involved in a ballet in 1828 which he was never able to complete. It could have been the type of production in which he revelled, and being forced to relinquish his part in it was a bitter experience. In that year there began the building of the Alexandrinsky Theater of St. Petersburg, which today is known as the Pushkin Theater of Drama. A member of the Theatrical Committee proposed that the grand opening should include a new ballet taken from a theme of Russian history, entitled *Sumbeka, or The Subjugation of the Kazan Kingdom*. The action centered around the conquest of the Mongol khanate of Kazan by Ivan the Terrible in 1552. It was a popular theme in Russian literature, used by the author Mikhail Kheraskov in an epic work entitled *Rossiada* in 1779. Didelot immediately launched into the project, arranging meetings between composer Cavos, machinist Natier, and the costumers. Didelot wrote enthusiastically to the Directorate of the Imperial Theaters on September 15, 1829:

> One never will find a production of a more noble genre, more suitable to the circumstances, a reconstitution of an epoch more glorious for Russia than the history of the taking of Kazan. It is worthy of the day in which it must be presented. . . . We ask that your excellency the chief director give the order for the production. May my comrade Auguste or I prepare it, or together do it?—he, the national dances, I, the rest, with M. Gomburov, under our direction,

doing the military part, the seiges, etc. May the music also be composed? Cavos has begun. [Signed] Didelot and Auguste.[112]

Indeed Cavos had already begun the music and Natier had already created models of the machinery to be used for the "flights." But before Didelot could see the work through to completion, his services with the Imperial Theaters were terminated. For the opening on August 31, 1832 of the Alexandrinsky Theater, a worthy new building for the very oldest of Russian dramatic troupes, the Directorate of the Imperial Theaters used a work entitled *Pozharsky, or The Liberation of Moscow,* first given in 1807.

The postponed ballet was finally produced with Istomina as Sumbeka on November 3, 1832. However, not Didelot but Alexis Blache was choreographer. In the words of one author, "Blache was a retired artillery officer, very much like Napoleon. He turned out to be worse than mediocre." [113] The name was certainly familiar to Didelot, for Blache was one of thirty-two children fathered by Jean-Baptiste Blache, a competent choreographer and musician who had followed Dauberval as balletmaster in Bordeaux.[114] Instead of the score begun by Cavos, Blache used one by Louis-Hippolite Sonné. Though the program credited the last three acts of *Sumbeka* to Blache, no one was credited with the first act. Undoubtedly it was the work of Didelot.[115] The reason the program remained silent about his part in it was probably because the administration feared that the public would give Didelot too great an ovation, since the popular balletmaster had been dismissed in a seemingly abrupt decision in 1829. Commenting in 1833 on the works of Blache and other foreign choreographers in St. Petersburg, a critic said, "These productions aggravate our regret over the loss of the incomparable Didelot." [116]

CHAPTER IX

The Master's Wing-Clipping

"In ballet a revolution occurred. Didelot, who for nearly thirty years despotically ruled the choreographic czardom, was suddenly dethroned, and not by indignant subjects, but by his rulers,"[1] reported a nineteenth-century chronicler. In retrospect, however, only the final dethronement was sudden. The causes of mutual animosity between the master and the directorate of the Imperial Theaters had been accumulating for years.

In 1824 Didelot asked that the directorate include in a new contract an unusual stipulation. It had been many years since he had been in Paris and he wanted to revisit the Opéra. Didelot had always surveyed others' creations to find ideas for his own. Now he wanted once again to renew his creative wellsprings. Therefore he asked that he and his son might have a vacation during the next year or two in Paris, to see new ballets that he might reproduce in the St. Petersburg theaters. He justified his request by saying that no one could have inborn knowledge of every art and skill, and why should the public be denied productions which they might enjoy, only because he was not their author? He also asked that his coworkers Dutacq and Kolosova might go with him at his own expense. Didelot then made a second request. Soon the Bolshoi Theater of Moscow would open, since their former building had also burned down. He asked that a group of St. Petersburg dancers be allowed to go to Moscow to take part in the opening of the theater. He was denied both requests.[2]

In 1826 new quarrels arose over contract terms. There had been preliminary negotiations made, to which both sides agreed. If Didelot had possessed eight legs, it would seem impossible for the aging man to do all the contract demanded. According to the new terms, he was obliged:

to discharge the duties of balletmaster and dance teacher of the theatrical school, teaching pantomime as well as ballet, character, and ballroom dancing;

to compose ballets—grand as well as demi-character, comic ones, and also divertissements;

to embellish operas and plays with suitable dances;

to be present when the ballets were given, whether in the St. Petersburg theaters or in outlying palaces;

to appear at the designated time unconditionally for try-outs and meetings of artists.[3]

Didelot refused to sign the contract. Overwhelming though the labor seems, it was not the volume of work which motivated his refusal. He had been performing all these duties for years. Further it probably was not a matter of salary. He had been offered, as artist, six thousand four hundred rubles; as balletmaster, one thousand six hundred rubles; and as teacher, eight thousand rubles, totaling sixteen thousand rubles.[4] While this far surpassed the normal salaries of Russian performers, at the same time the French dancers Antonin and Velange were making twenty-five thousand and twenty thousand assignat rubles, respectively. Didelot had other complaints, and he refused the contract this time because he wanted to bargain with the directorate over them.

On May 20, 1826 he sent a protest which revealed one of the issues which galled him. It had been a constant cross in his life that he would carefully nourish students through years of ballet training, only to have them whisked away from him to other theatrical work, noble or ignoble. This time it was the latter. There was a certain student named Seleznev who had studied ballet eight years, and in spite of Didelot's and Seleznev's protests, the directorate assigned him not as a dancer, but as a costumer. Didelot was furious. In a letter which was a prototype of many more which he sent to the directorate to defend his students, he declared:

> As a consequence of the system of constantly taking away from me my pupils, on which I have put many years of work—a system impoverishing and ruining the *corps de ballet*—they have once again, without even notifying me, taken a young man with superb physical gifts, who though he was scarcely an eagle in dancing, nevertheless was highly useful to me. And for what? To make him a costumer. As proof that I am not acting capriciously, and that this young man is really necessary to me, not long ago I yielded to the

directorate one of my pupils who had not the slightest ability for dancing. I object all the more to this, since Seleznev wants to continue to dance, and I beg the office to deign to take my just demands to the knowledge of the theatrical committee.[5]

Didelot's superiors paid no heed to his request. On May 23 the decision was made to explain to him that the distribution of the pupils of the theatrical school to different sections of the Imperial Theaters was their prerogative, and that the number of *figurants* already exceeded the stated number.

Didelot replied by refusing to sign the contract under consideration, and demanded to include new points in it. The authorities held their ground, complaining that "By the title of balletmaster . . . he confers upon himself complete ruling power. He wants to go past all lower officials and deal directly with the chief directorate, which is not in line with the established order. Above all, Didelot insists that never, under any pretence, may any pupil studying dance be removed. If Didelot gets his way, then all the theatrical school must be predestined for dance only, since all the youngsters begin their studies, among other subjects, with dance."[6] Actually, Didelot wanted only the right to distribute roles according to the ability of the artist, a practice then permitted the author of a drama, as well as the right to select in the school a stated number of students showing especial talent, who would not be assigned to any other job without a most serious casue.

There came a period of stalemate over the contract. On April 19, 1826, he received a life pension of four thousand rubles a year as reward for his zealous service. According to the stipulations, he was obliged to serve two more years in gratitude for the pension. After about a year of waiting, both sides made sufficient concessions that his contract was renewed in March of 1827, to March 1, 1830.[7] He was given the right to select each year in the theatrical school a stated number of students who would specialize in dance and would not be changed to another section without his permission. In the same contract the management agreed to intercede for him to get six months leave with salary.[8]

After reading about the cruel, heartless manner in which Didelot drove his students and performers, it is puzzling to read a passage by his biographer Mundt who asserts, "In private life Didelot was outstanding for gentleness, philanthropy, and unusual goodness of heart. He was bound as a father to his pupils, he aided them in their needs, looked after their future, and never in all his life did any kind of harm." [9] A number of letters preserved from his later life amply support Mundt's assertion, for a large amount of Didelot's time in these years was consumed in trying to alleviate the financial plight of his dancers. He strongly supported the needs of one of the best male dancers whom he produced—Nikolai Holtz. Holtz had been in theatrical school from 1806 to 1822, an unusually long period in his day. The theatrical directors liked to prolong the schooling of talented pupils because they could be used in performances without receiving performers' salaries. Further, Holtz's talent was so varied that all his teachers wanted him to specialize in their field, and he had received more than the normal amount of development in fields other than dance. His dramatic talent was so impressive and his voice so powerful that Shakhovskoi had insisted he become an actor, while his fencing was so superb that his teacher in this skill wanted him to become a fencing master. Since Holtz was also a talented musician who specialized in the violin, Didelot had to fight hard to keep him under his own wing, but Holtz emerged from theatrical school as a powerful dramatic dancer, the first male student of the school to graduate as a soloist.[10] Didelot valued his pupil's outstanding ability at mime so highly that upon graduation he let him make his debut in *The Prisoner of the Caucasus* in January of 1823. Soon afterward Didelot wrote to his superiors that Holtz's salary of one thousand two hundred rubles, plus four hundred rubles for an apartment and wardrobe, was so inadequate that he had to give private lessons to survive. As a result Holtz was fatigued, overstrained, and the Imperial Theaters risked losing his valuable talent. By constant intercession, Didelot and Auguste managed to persuade the management that Holtz deserved a twenty-five ruble payment for each performance. This, however, was not enough; again he started giving private lessons. Didelot pointed out that "this fatigued young man is like a beautiful flower which is beginning to bend on its stem; he will lose his dancing talent if they fail to grant him the means to refrain from giving private lessons . . . people far below him in talent and usefulness are paid a salary twice what he receives." [11]

In his first petition, Didelot had predicted, "If this young man is given the means for a comfortable existence, he will be of great help to the directorate, and the pride of the school—both by his exemplary conduct and his talent." Didelot's prediction was surely fulfilled, for Holtz served the Imperial Theaters for five decades, taking part in eighty different ballets. He was noted especially for roles in *Raoul de Créquis, Ruslan and Liudmila, Phaedra,* and *The Prisoner of the Caucasus.* In later years he was chosen as a partner by Marie Taglioni, with whom he performed more than two hundred times. He also played beside Fanny Elssler as Frollo in *Esmeralda.* Holtz was later judged to be unquestionably the first Russian male dancer who could compete with foreign stars on an equal basis, one in whom shone forth "the superb method of the school of Didelot—a deep study of mime and graciousness of poses." [12] Further, Holtz's teaching had a more far-reaching influence than Didelot could envision at the time, for one of Holtz's pupils in the mid-twenties was the future composer, Mikhail Glinka, whose operas were greatly enriched by their dance music. In 1842 Holtz choreographed a mazurka for *A Life for the Czar* at Glinka's request. [13]

Didelot wrote many more letters supporting the just demands of his dancers. Some are very revealing of the hard working conditions in the theaters of his day. In August of 1825 he and Auguste defended a certain Piotr Didier's request for more salary. Didier was earning six hundred rubles a year, plus a two-hundred-ruble apartment and one hundred fifty rubles in other aids. Didier never achieved great fame, but it was not because he failed to work for it. Didelot explained, "He occupies the rank of *coryphé* and dances character dances, plays roles in grand ballets, and at times fills several roles in the same production. . . . He composes quadrilles and rehearses character divertissements in case the balletmaster is absent. He compiles lists of costumes for the costumer; makes lists of accessories for the property man, and even makes the accessories. He appears in scenes of supers, directs them, takes part in staged battles, and keeps so busy that he has not a minute for himself, so that he might take private pupils." [14] Their efforts won for the industrious Didier a two hundred ruble increase. Before too long Didelot was again busy writing letters to gain an even better salary for him.

Didelot felt humiliated in 1827 when the directorate imported from Paris a new ballerina, Adèle Bertrand-Astruc, and her partner Alexis. Didelot was given instructions to give her the main parts in his ballets. This meant not only depriving Russian artists, such as Istomina, Ikonina, Novitskaya, and Teleshova of their roles; he was also obliged to stage new productions copying Parisian ballets in which Bertrand-Astruc could display her not overwhelming talent. Attempts to satisfy her petty demands no doubt consumed much of the energy of the balletmaster, who had never been oversupplied with tact and patience in handling such people. If she had been a brilliant performer, he could have accepted her caprices. However, she was only an ordinary soloist of the Paris Opéra—scarcely even a competitor with his most talented pupils. Yet she began to shower the directorate with complaints about his hostility. She wanted a part in *Acis et Galathée*. Didelot refused. In defense, he wrote, "I offered her three of my ballets. I will be silent about the tone in which she refused them." He asked that another balletmaster be imported to stage the works she wanted; negotiations were begun to this effect. In the meantime, she still demanded the role in *Acis*, and Didelot recalled, "Istomina then stood up for her rights. I supported her just demands. . . . In regard to my hostility, that is a very old method which many phony talents who came here long ago used at different times to damage me and enhance their reputation. Rather I can complain of the hostility to which my pupils are subjected, whom Astruc moved aside at the time of their debut—and for whose sake?" He affirmed that if competent artists were imported, his hostility would be turned into rapture, and he would gladly use them as examples to his students. He had been good friends with the Frenchman Antonin, for example, when he had been brought to Russia in 1817. "How I regretted when his shaken health prevented his remaining among us," Didelot commented and then concluded, "It is completely evident that hostility, intrigue, ingratitude and slander pursue me, and for my part I beseech Your Excellency not to forget it." [15]

After the Decembrist Revolt, new changes in personnel and administration were inaugurated which had a far-reaching influence not only in Didelot's life, but in all Russian artistic life of the mid-nineteenth century. On the day of the Decembrist uprising, Governor-general Miloradovich was fatally wounded by insurgents. His day had begun in a festive mood. Dressed in a parade uniform he paid an early visit to his favorite Teleshova, and was ready to breakfast with the dancer Azarevicheva and another friend when he was told of the rebels' assembly on Senate Square. Upon reaching the scene the governor-general was mortally shot. As he was taken away Miloradovich remarked wryly to a friend, "Eh bien, la comédie est finie." [16]

The end of the sad comedy brought a finish to the power of Shakhovskoi on the Theatrical Committee, for Miloradovich was replaced by Prince Vasily Dolgoruky who fired Shakhovskoi and installed in power Dolgoruky's brother-in-law, Prince Sergei Sergeevich Gagarin. Besides quarrels with the new directorate over money and privileges, Didelot became disenchanted because of the government's stifling of his creative plans. His own bad mood was very much in harmony with a general air of discontent pervading Russia after the abortive revolt. The new emperor, Nicholas I, established an administrative unit called the Ministry of the Court, which henceforth was in charge of managing everything connected with court life, including the Imperial Theaters. In order to ferret out future conspiracies, Nicholas also established a secret police apparatus called the Third Section, which began censorship activity in April of 1828. On July 24, 1828 even the art of ballet came under the scrutiny of the Third Section, when they ordered the directorate of the Imperial Theaters to submit programs of new ballets and divertissements for their approval before presenting them to the public. The following day the directorate passed the order to Didelot, who had to compile a detailed program of each work to refer to the censor's office. Only when the proposed program obtained the censor's approval could *affiches* for the new ballet be printed.[17]

By April of 1829 Gagarin's power had grown to the point where the last vestiges of collegiality disappeared in the Imperial Theaters, and sole authority fell into his hands. He was noted for his coarse manners and hot temper. Symtomatic of his whole attitude toward the staff was his manner of receiving them. "Never," he affirmed, "will I receive a subject otherwise than dressed and standing." [18] The history of Didelot's career boded ill for his relationship with such a man, and eventually the explosion occurred. As far as the balletmaster was concerned, the last straw came on October 28, 1829, when the management distributed the graduates of the theatrical school. At this time his beloved Nikolai Diur was allowed to escape from Didelot's hold into the drama theater. Didelot was crushed. Three days later he erupted.

"From the first, Prince Gagarin had looked unfavorably upon the choleric and independent balletmaster, who did not lower his spine sufficiently before His Excellency," [19] reported a Russian source. One evening Gagarin found something with which to needle Didelot when the *corps de ballet* seemed unusually slow in making a change of costumes. "Too long! Too long!" he exclaimed. "Everything is fine but too long. His Majesty is impatient." When Didelot paid no attention to his raging, Gagarin exclaimed, "Do you understand? Who is the master here?" Didelot only responded, "You, Monsieur le Prince," and went right on ignoring Gagarin's fury. At that, Gagarin yelled, "Arrest him!" [20]

The dispassionate official account of the incident related that "at the time of the performance on October 31 in the Bolshoi Theater of *Theseus and Ariadne,* on the stage before the ballet Didelot spoke with unforgivable impudence to His Excellency Monsieur the Director, who for that reason ordered him to be put under arrest, and this was done after the performance." [21]

Thus the giant fell. All St. Petersburg was shocked. "Didelot under arrest," one account declared, "Didelot on whom not only the *corps* and *figurants,* but even the soloists looked with fear and trembling, as on a demigod." [22] After being under arrest for a short time, the balletmaster went home. He then took the unprecedented, unthinkable step of declaring himself free from service to the Imperial Theaters. Gagarin, however, insisted that he should not be released until his last contract expired—March 1, 1830. Ignoring Didelot's pertinacity, the management continued to send the theatrical coach each day to his house to escort him to the theater. He was showered with notes calling him to the office of the directorate to receive his salary, but Didelot was adamant. He had ignored the summons of the king of Sweden in his youth. At sixty-two he was unwilling as ever to bow to the orders of the emperor of Russia. Didelot then put in a second resignation, which fell into Nicholas I's hands, and was accepted. Before Didelot's release, Gagarin gave orders to the music librarian, the wardrobe master, the shoemaker, the wigmaker, and the keeper of flowers and plumes to report any theatrical property which Didelot might have in his possession. Their reports, stowed away in imperial archives, reveal that Didelot indeed did have some music, a pair of silk brocade slippers, and a blackamoor's wig in his possession.[23]

The official dismissal of Didelot came on January 29, 1830. At that time the cantankerous balletmaster refused to sign the final dismissal papers formalizing the break with the Imperial Theaters. This caused more consternation in several offices of the bureaucracy. The bookkeeper complained because of money not claimed by the balletmaster, and Gagarin himself wanted desperately to end the affair with the troublesome old character.

Didelot held his ground, however. He wanted a chance to be

publicly vindicated of the insult that Gagarin had dealt him. According to his contract, he was entitled to two benefits per year—one for his service as balletmaster, and the other as teacher of the theatrical school. The first had been given on September 26, 1829, and the second was scheduled for January 27, 1830. Since his official dismissal came after that date, he demanded his benefit. Explaining his stand in a letter, he declared, "If, kind Sirs, there can not be a just decision of this affair, I prefer to lose the salary together with the benefit, rather than legalize by my signature such a scandalous breach of my contract." [24] He then carried on a war of nerves with the administration until the authorities finally consented in May of 1831 to the benefit; only then would he sign the dismissal documents. The benefit, however, did not take place until October 4, 1833. Perhaps the administration thought that by that time the public would have forgotten him. If this was the motive for the delay, they were sadly mistaken. The benefit was an unbounded triumph for the old master. As the curtain closed, the audience began to call out for Didelot. When an order was given backstage that none of the performers should accompany him onto the stage, the uproar was terrific. Dancers on pension led him out, and the old man, so weak from emotion, needed their support. From the orchestra his followers gave him two great wreaths and one small one. One of the soloists put the small wreath on Didelot's head. After the reading of an address by one of the young actors, all on the stage began to bid him farewell. They kissed Didelot, embraced him, and the young pupils kissed his hands. There was no end to the applause and calls, even from the high born ladies seated in the loges.[25]

On August 20, 1834, Didelot was given a written testimonial to the termination of his services, officially acknowledging his "outstanding talent, indefatigable zeal, and laudable conduct in the service of the Imperial Theaters." One chronicler remarked that "the power-loving Prince Gagarin was very happy to be delivered from the insubordinate subject, but the public lost in Didelot a balletmaster, the likes of which existed neither before nor after him." [26] The press began a series of sarcastic critiques of the post-Didelot ballet scene, noting in 1834, "As for our ballets, it is better not to speak of them. . . . They are feet without a head, language without speech, gestures without understanding. For them it suffices to have five thousand yards of silver lace, five hundred candles, fifty dressmakers, five scenic painters, and their success will be brilliant and sure." [27]

Occasionally his months of retirement in Russia were brightened by a bit of glory accorded him. In 1835 during the presentation of *The Prisoner of the Caucasus,* in answer to a curtain call, the first dancers embraced Didelot behind the curtain, covered him with kisses, and led him out to the public. All the members of the audience stood and clapped while the old man wept.[28] In this year the press again lengthily bemoaned his loss:

> Unforgettable Didelot! How many theatrical memories are in that name. Things are not the way they used to be. Now the balletmaster is not needed. Now the machinists are needed most of all. He is the true ballet genuis, the creator and executor of it, and then comes the scenic artist and costumer. The machinist gives the ballet trans-formations, demolitions, flights, magnificent palaces, picturesque tombs, raging oceans; the costumer gives the ballet bonnets, armor, little dresses, charming waists. No less important is the shoemaker. He shoes all these light little feet which support the heavy ballet. The honorable management does not spare expenses; it bestows all the means to stage these magnificent ballets—decorations, ma-chines, costumes—everything is superb, all is elegant. But where is the balletmaster? Where is his choreographic labor? He leads masses of people onto the stage, he leads in thousands of shapely waists, hundreds of shapely feet, but he is occupied only with these, forgetting that these little feet belong to a person for whom he does nothing for want of activity in the ballet. . . . In Didelot's time there were not such rich, abundant means, and for that reason he was not able to use such brilliant scenic, pompous effects. . . . Didelot based everything on the poem of the ballet. He produced it as one produces a drama, a tragedy. There was pantomime in his works; now there is none. Now there are dances, dances—still more dances!! For the ballets of Didelot, mime artists were needed; for the present ballets—only dancers. . . . The public still remembers the former balletmaster and with pleasure views his superb pro-ductions, all the more so, because they are given only rarely.[29]

The public continued to miss him three years later. Praising a production of *The Prisoner of the Caucasus,* the critic in *The Northern Bee* ruefully pointed out:

> Among the newest ballets, only *La Sylphide* can rival the productions of Didelot in fascination of conception and arrange-ment; in other ballets of the present school there are happy scenes,

picturesque groups, and charming dances, but they lack an idea, and consequently poetry, without which there is no ballet. In the newest ballets, dances and groups occupy the first place and the subject remains in the background of the picture. With Didelot, on the contrary, the drama and action occupy the first place, and the dances serve only as an aid and an adornment. The productions of Didelot deserve the name ballets in full measure—that is, a poetical idea, invested in pantomime and dances. Our present ballets are nothing more than brilliant divertissements. They display a series of beautiful dances and a series of beautiful decorations, but one must not demand more from them. *The Prisoner of the Caucasus* was performed with fire, with harmony, and precision. . . . The memory of the unforgettable Didelot inspired the artists, of whom the greater part were his students.[30]

In 1836 at the beginning of December in Moscow, Glushkovsky was surprised at nine one evening by his servant, who announced that a foreigner named Monsieur Cafarelli from St. Petersburg wished to see him. Not knowing any such person, but curious to see what the foreign visitor might want, he had the servant usher in the visitor. When the door opened, Monsieur Cafarelli turned out to be Didelot. After a warm embrace Glushkovsky learned that his master was going to pass the summer in sunny Kiev, since the doctor had urged him to choose a healthful climate. On the way he had come to Moscow to see all the historic churches and monuments.

Glushkovsky expected to serve as guide about the town, but when they visited the wonderful showplaces of the Kremlin, the Granovitaya Palace, the Bell Tower of Ivan the Great, and other monuments, Didelot again became the teacher. His study of history as background for ballet had given him an intimate knowledge of Ivan the Terrible, the False Dimitry, and other fabulous personages who had made Russian history more fascinating than any novel. Didelot was deeply touched by the fact that Glushkovsky had his portrait hanging on the wall of his home. It was a copy of a painting by Vasily Baranov, a former serf who became one of Russia's best portrait painters of this era (*Fig. 33*).[31]

Didelot often wrote to Glushkovsky from Kiev. Plainly, the old man was lonely. His own son Karl remained in St. Petersburg. After having left the theater because of ill health, Karl entered government service as a translator. From 1832 to 1838 he taught dancing at the artillery school in St. Petersburg. There he conducted class in his father's manner—

Figure 33. Charles Didelot, the oil painting by V. Baranov (1820), in the collection of I. S. Eilberstein of Moscow, reproduced from Slonimsky's *Didlo*.

sharply and rudely, being reproached once for saying a cadet's head lacked brains. In line with eighteenth-century traditions, by which cadets of the military academy had danced in Italian operas given at court, Karl tried once to put together a form of ballet, but was not encouraged in his efforts.[32]

While longing for his son, Didelot also missed the theater and was troubled by sheer boredom. He was full of ideas for ballets, and Glushkovsky believed that he was on the verge of offering his services to the Moscow Bolshoi Theater, but fate intervened. In early November of 1837 Glushkovsky received a letter saying that Didelot planned to come to Moscow on November 15 for several reasons. After a few days, however, he received another letter from Kiev in which Didelot's servant revealed that on November 7, 1837 (in the old-style Russian calendar, now November 19) the master died from a boil in the throat which asphyxiated him, although he was not ill more than a week from it. Apparently, Didelot's forced inactivity after such a strenuous life, combined with the emotional strain of fighting the administration had undermined his health. Didelot made the St. Petersburg theatrical school the residual legatee of his estate.[33] His second wife Rosa died in 1843.

One of Didelot's chief aims when he came to Russia was to create a troupe capable of rivalling that of Paris. As a result of his dogged pedagogy, he worked wonders. Tufiakin had remarked that though the school fell into complete decline during Didelot's first absence, after his return, his zeal made it once more blossom forth.

In the ten years after his return to Russia, seventy dancers were graduated from the school. Numerically his school came to surpass those of France and Italy. In quality the great Danish choreographer August Bournonville acknowledged that "Didelot created [in St. Petersburg] a ballet troupe in its entirety far superior to that of Paris." [34] It was then no longer necessary for the administration of the Imperial Theaters to rely on foreign dancers. From the *corps* to soloists, Russians could fill all parts well. A table[35] emphasizes his results in this line:

	1792	1822	1828
Soloists (Male)	11	10	12
Figurants (Male)	16	13	20
Soloists (Female)	6	21	27
Figurantes (Female)	19	39	39
Corps	52	83	98

Before Didelot St. Petersburg only had a troupe of soloists, chiefly foreigners. During his day he developed an ensemble troupe of native dancers who provided an adequate supporting background for native and foreign soloists. In short with Didelot at the helm, "Talent grew as in story books—not by days, but by hours." [36]

In Didelot's day Russia dance training for the Imperial Theaters took place in schools where all arts of the theater were taught. A dance student in such institutions would receive instruction in acting as a part of his training. Under such a system, it was easier to train a dancing actor than in schools whose aim was instilling knowledge of dance alone. Didelot, however, especially emphasized the combination of the two skills.

Qualitatively speaking Didelot's emphasis on mime in the training of his dancers had wide artistic consequences in Russian ballet. Though mid-twentieth-century balletomanes of Western Europe and America have come to value dance for the sake of dance, austerely devoid of mimed gestures or even facial expression, the tastes of Didelot's epoch were different. In 1741 Rémond de Saint-Mard in *Réflexions sur l'opéra* voiced the plaintive observation, "Our dances are almost all designed one like the other. No variety, no spirit. Would it be so difficult to put more fire and invention into them? I do not say that our dancers should become entirely pantomimists . . . but would there be any harm if they were a little?" [37]

Didelot managed to alter this situation more than a little. Summarizing his influence, a commentator in 1859 affirmed, "Didelot first began to stage ballets with dramatic content in which pantomime, the expressive language of gestures and play of the physiogonomy explained to the spectator the passions and sensations of the performers in various moments of the drama. Didelot produced a complete revolution in the art, and one might say, gave life to ballet." [38] Pantomime prevailed especially in productions of the second St. Petersburg period of his career, while in the first period, more attention was given to dance itself.

At the end of the eighteenth century Russian ballet dancers merely performed twenty or thirty steps learned from foreign masters.[39] The technique of the pirouette was undeveloped, in line with a general lack of development of the dancer's *pointes*. Early prints of Didelot's works show the dancers wearing Greek cothurns—quite in keeping with the popular mythological themes. As these gave way to satin slippers, the dancer stood *sur les pointes* only in certain fleeting movements, since their shoes did not have blocked toes. If Didelot did not *begin* the practice of *pointe* dancing, there is evidence both in Russia and in France indicating its use in his productions at a very early stage in the history of the technique. However, for Didelot, technical feats were chiefly useful for conveying dramatic content. If the character of his sportive Flora could best be revealed by a *danseuse* flitting about *en pointe*, then *voila!* on her toes she must appear. The same could be said of Didelot's astounding use of flights. When a naughty Cupid stole the wings of Zéphyr and gave them to Flora, the program of the 1796 production reveals that Flora donned the purloined wings on her snowy shoulders to "take a survey of the sky," leaving the wingless Zéphyr earthbound and disconsolate. It was a cardinal principle with Didelot that there should be *soulful flights,* literally or figuratively, in his works which either were part of the plot, or greatly enhanced the dramatic impact of it. When he had to work with a performer who strove to dazzle the audience with mechanical feats, such as Louis Duport, Didelot was frustrated, even bored. The soulful expression of an idea—this was the focus of his attention, and this tradition still abides in Russian dance. Twentieth-century viewers of such Russian-trained performers as Ulanova, Bessmertnova, or Nureyev still appreciate the meaning of "soulful flights."

In Didelot's day in Russia male dancing predominated, abounding in strong, high leaps and turns, on the floor and in the air. Female dancing was less complicated; it lacked the great leaps and was based primarily on the partner's movements. The male seldom supported the partner, lifting her in rare cases to the level of his chest, and never throwing her into the air. In duets both partners made the same uncomplicated steps, while all virtuoso dancing took place during the male's solo.[40] Glushkovsky believed that a female dancer, in aligning herself, should imitate a good picture or statue, because those, in their turn, imitated nature. A great accomplishment of Didelot was his ability to achieve a harmonious union of pantomime, *plastique*, and music. Reviewers constantly referred to the unusually beautiful groupings of dancers in his works.

Serious dances in his ballets were done to the accompaniment of an *adagio* with a martial strain. For the chief dancer Didelot always choreographed smooth dances with various attitudes. Very rarely did he insert an *entrechat* or light pirouette. Demi-character performers danced to *andante graziosi* strains, in a fashion more graceful and lively than the first dancer; such dances consisted of more little steps, quick pirouettes, and were accompanied by completely different positions of the body and arms. A comic dance would be performed to *allegro* music with the dancer performing various kinds of leaps, *tours en l'air*, and assuming completely different positions of the body and arms. Didelot carefully avoided those exterior effects which might impress an inexperienced spectator, but which did not satisfy the demands of true artistic taste. In all he displayed striking artistry in making the dance suitable to the character and mood of the epoch. Each dance answered the demands of refinement and beauty, while at the same time they fit the nationality and character of the persons portrayed.[41]

Didelot was never ashamed of borrowing from others. One author concluded, "He combined the pedantic and strict school of Noverre with the school of the adroit Vestris, and having developed character and comic ballet, brought them to the highest perfection . . . he was such an enthusiast, that he was almost at the point where genius crosses into madness." [42] He strove to overcome all his competitors in a manner that approached the maniacal. Glushkovsky believed that if Duport had not come to Russia, then Didelot would not have produced his own ballets so superbly, such as *Psyché et l'Amour*. When Didelot finally became the undisputed, unrivalled master in St. Petersburg, he competed with foreigners located thousands of miles away. When well known European travellers who were interested in ballet came to Russia, if Didelot heard of it, "he forgot everything in the world; there remained only one thought in his head—his ballet. He gave himself no rest, did without sleep, scheduled extra rehearsals, and tried to improve each trifle in the ballet. With such effort expended, good ballets were made superb. In all this competition ruled his life; he wanted to surpass all rivals so that the famous travellers and European artists, having seen his ballets, would return to their homeland and praise his talent." [43]

Didelot's contribution to ballet has been compared with that of Wagner to opera. Just as the composer was responsible for the mature development of musical drama, the balletmaster aided the development of the choreographic, mimed drama. Didelot indeed bridged the way to the romantic period of ballet. When he began his career, the gods of Olympus reigned on the ballet stage. Didelot produced supremely successful works in the classical or anacreontic, mythological idiom of the eighteenth century. However, along with his master Dauberval, Didelot became a chief rebel in overthrowing the choreographic czardom of the Grecian deities. Into his works came a crusader worthy of Sir Walter Scott, a Byronic Circassian maiden, and a revolutionary Hungarian national hero wresting the limelight from the Medeas, Phaedras, and Apollos. In Russia Didelot led ballet from stilted myths and pastorals to the heights of dramatic narrative, pervaded by a folk atmosphere based on ballads and fairy tales. Indeed, it would seem fitting to agree with the judgment that "the history of the development of choreographic art in Russia—and not alone in Russia—can be divided into two periods: before Didelot, and after Didelot." [44]

Chronological List of Dances and Pantomimes Staged by Charles-Louis Didelot

The following list was compiled from a list in Slonimskii's *Didlo*, corrected from my own newspaper research and compared with Ivor Guest's *The Romantic Ballet in England*. Since Slonimskii's titles were in Russian, I had to translate, or find the accepted translations—from musical scores and other sources—for Didelot's works. The Russian dates used here, as well as those in the body of the text dealing with his work in Russia, are from the Old Style Julian calendar used in prerevolutionary Russia. In the nineteenth century, such dates were twelve days behind what they were in the Gregorian calendar. Slonimskii affirms that previous lists of Didelot's works included works which were not attributable to him.

STOCKHOLM

1786   *Pas de Deux*

1787   *Frigga.* Opera in one act. Music: Åhlström; libretto: C. G. Leopold; dances by Didelot. May 31.

LONDON

1788   *La Bonté du Seigneur.* Ballet-divertissement. May 22.
       Richard Coeur-de-Lion. Grand ballet in five acts, pantomime tragedy. May 22.

1789   *New Divertissement.* January 10.
       L'Embarquement pour Cythère. January 10.

BORDEAUX

1790   *Chimène.* Opera. Music: Sacchini. Dances by Didelot. July 7.

LYON

1795   *La Métamorphose.* Anacreontic ballet in one act. November–December.

1796   *Pas de Deux.* Debut of Didelot couple. February 20.

  Pas de Deux and *Pas de Trois* in Onorati's *Le Bouquet.* Music: Mazzinghi. March 1.

  Pas de Deux (of a Polish character). March 8.

  Little Peggy's Love. Scotch ballet. Music: Bossi. April 21.

  Caravan at Rest. Indian divertissement. June 2.

  L'Amour Vengé, ou La Métamorphose. An episodical anacreontic ballet in two acts. June 2.

  Flore et Zéphire. Ballet-divertissement in one act. Music: Bossi; scenery and machines: Liparotti. July 7.

  L'Heureux Naufrage, ou Les Sorcières Ecossaises. Dramatic ballet in three acts. Music: Bossi; scenery: Liparotti; costumes: Sestini. July 7.

  Zémire et Azor. Opera by Grétry. Didelot composed "dances incidental to the opera." July 23.

1797   *Sappho et Phaon.* Grand ballet erotique in four acts. Music: Mazzinghi; scenery: Greenwood; costumes: Sestini. April 6.

  Acis et Galathée. Pastoral ballet in one act. Music: Bossi. June 15.

1800   *Laura et Lenza, ou Le Troubadour.* Grand ballet in two acts. Music: Bossi. June 8.

1801   *Alonzo the Brave and the Fair Imogene.* Grand ballet. Music: Bossi and Federici; scenery: Marinari and De Maria; costumes: Sestini. March 26.

  Ken-si and Tao. Grand Chinese ballet in three acts. May 14.

1802   *Apollo and Daphne.* Ballet in one act. Debut of Didelot couple at Hermitage Theater. April 4.

1803   *Roland and Morgana.* Ballet in one act. Music: Cavos. May 16.

  Le Pâtre et L'Hamadryade. Anacreontic ballet in one act. December 1.

1804   *Zéphyr et Flore.* Anacreontic ballet in one act. Hermitage Theater.

1806   *Le Calife de Bagdad.* Opera in one act. Music: Boieldieu; ballets: Didelot. April 16.

  Télémaque dans l'Isle de Calypso. Opera in three acts. Music: Boieldieu. ballets: Didelot. Hermitage Theater, December 16; Bolshoi Theater (St. Petersburg) December 19.

  Roland and Morgana. Ballet in one act. Music: Cavos; scenery: Corsini.

1807   *Medée et Jason.* Ballet in five acts by Le Picq. Renewed by Didelot. May 2.

1808   *The Sea Pier.* Divertissement. Some dances by Didelot. February 5 (?).
    Don Quixote. Ballet in two acts. May 27.
    Golden Wedding. Divertissement. July 9.
    Divertissement (four dances). August 21.

1809   *Psyché et L'Amour.* Erotic ballet in five acts. Scenery: Gonzago and
    Corsini; machines: Thibeault; costumes: Babini. Hermitage Thea-
    ter, January 8; Bolshoi Theater (St. Petersburg), February 15.
    Solange Rose. Anacreontic ballet in one act. July 1.
    Zélis et Alcindor, ou La Forêt aux Aventures. Fairy heroic comic
    divertissement in one act. Music: Cavos; scenery: Corsini. Tavritsky
    Palace. August 30.

1810   *Laura and Henry, or The Defeat of the Moors.* Ballet in three acts.
    Hermitage Theater, August 30; Bolshoi Theater (St. Petersburg),
    September 13
    Dove of Zélis. A variant of *Zélis et Alcindor* was presented by pupils of
    the ballet school. 1810?

LONDON

1812   *Zélis, ou La Forêt aux Aventures.* Fairy ballet in one act. Music: Venua.
    January 14.
    L'Epreuve, ou La Jambe De Bois. Ballet in one act. Music: Venua,
    scenery: Grieve. February 8.
    Zéphyr Inconstant Puni et Fixe, ou Les Noces de Flore. Ballet in one act.
    Music: Venua. April 7
    La Reine de Golconde. Ballet in five acts in the Indian style. June 4.
    Le Bal Champêtre. Divertissement in which there was a Russian Dance
    by Didelot couple. Music: Venua. June 4.

1813   *Le Pâtre et l'Hamadryade.* Ballet in one act. Music: Venua; scenery:
    Grieve; machines: Paulinson. February 9.
    Une Soirée d'Été. Divertissement. February 23.
    La Chaumière Hongroise, ou Les Illustres Fugitifs (The Hungarian Hut).
    Ballet in two acts. Music: Venua; scenery: Grieve. April 20.
    Les Amants Péruviens. Divertissement. May 13.
    Kacheli. Russian divertissement. Music: Fiorillo. May 27.
    L'Indorf et Rosalie, ou L'Heureuse Ruse (Rosalie et Dozinval). Comic
    ballet. Music: Mortellari; scenery: Grieve. May 27.
    Le Troubadour. Divertissement from ballet *Laura et Lenza.* June 10.

1814   *Thamaida et Alonzo, ou L'Isle Sauvage.* Divertissement. Music: Jouve.
    April 12.
    Karl et Lisbeth, ou Le Déserteur Malgré Lui. Military demi-character
    ballet. Music: Horn. May 18.
    New Divertissement. June 14.
    Le Bazzard D'Algier, ou Le Retour Du Corsair. June 27.

1815 *Zéphire et Flore.* Anacreontic ballet in two acts. Music: Venua, with added airs of Hus-Desforges and Lefèvre; scenery: Ciceri; machines: Boutron; costumes: Marches. L'Académie Royale de Musique. December 12.

1816 *Return of the Heroes.* Pavlovsk.

Acis et Galathée. Anacreontic ballet in two acts. Music: Cavos; scenery: Corsini and Condratiev; machines: Thibeault. August 30.

Holiday in the Seraglio. Grand divertissement. September 6.

Aline, Reine de Golconde. Opera in 3 acts. Music: Boieldieu; ballets: Didelot. October 4.

Belmonte and Constanze (Die Entführung aus dem Serail). Opera in three acts. Music: Mozart; ballets: Didelot. December 18.

Marguerite D'Anjou. Historic drama, translated from French by Shiriaev. Ballets: Didelot. December 29.

1817 *The Unexpected Return, or Evening in the Garden.* Divertissement. First Russian debut of Karl Didelot, the son. January 11.

Le Sacrifice Interrompu. Heroic opera in three acts. Music: Winter; dances: Didelot. January 31.

Divertissement. February 3.

The Young Milkmaid, or Nicette and Luke. Comic ballet in one act. Music: Antonolini; scenery: Condratiev. April 10.

Télémaque Dans L'Isle de Calypso. Opera in three acts. Music: Boieldieu; ballets: Didelot. June 23.

Divertissement. July 13.

Apollo and the Muses. Grand divertissement. August 19.

Don Carlos and Rozalba, or The Lover, the Doll, and the Model. Comic ballet in three acts. Music: Cavos; scenery: Condratiev; costumes: Babini. August 30.

Le Prince de Catane. Opera in three acts. Music: Isouard; ballets: Didelot. September 19.

La Caravane du Caire. Comic opera in three acts. Music: Grétry; ballets: Didelot. November 5.

Theseus and Ariadne, or The Defeat of the Minotaur. Grand tragic-heroic ballet in four acts. Music: Antonolini; combats by Valville; scenery: Condratiev; machines: Dranché; costumes: Babini. November 22.

La Chaumière Hongroise, ou Les Illustres Fugitifs. Grand tragic-comic ballet in four acts. Music: Venua; combats: Valville; scenery: Condratiev; costumes: Babini. December 17.

1818 *Zéphire et Flore.* Anacreontic ballet in two acts. Music: Venua; scenery: Condratiev; costumes: Babini; machines: Thibeault. Hermitage Theater, January 26.

Apollon and Pallada in the North. Prologue, verses of A. Sheller. Music: Cavos; ballets: Didelot; new scenery: Martinov. Opening of Bolshoi Theater (St. Petersburg), February 3.

Semélé, ou La Vengeance de Junon. Mythological presentation. Libretto: A. A. Zhandr; music: Cavos and Antonolini; ballets: Didelot. February 7.

The Young Island Girl, or Leon and Tamaida. Ballet in two acts. Music: Cavos; scenery: Condratiev; costumes: Babini. February 14.

Divertissement, June 11.

Roxus Pumpernickel, or He Came to Get Married and Didn't. Comic opera in three acts. Ballets: Didelot. July 17.

The Caliph of Bagdad, or The Youthful Adventures of Harun Al-Rashid. Ballet in two acts. Music: Antonolini; combats: Valville; scenery: Canoppi, Martinov, and Condratiev; costumes: Babini. August 30.

Lodoiska, ou Les Tartares. Opera in three acts. Music: Kreutzer. September 9.

Zoraïme et Zulnare. Opera in three acts. Music: Boieldieu. October 2.

Strange Encounters, or Confusion at the Masquerade. Original comedy in three acts. Compiled by Didelot. October 28.

The Ruins of Babylon, or The Triumph and Fall of Giafar Barmecide. Historic opera in three acts. Music: Cavos; artists: Canoppi, Martinov, Condratiev; ballets: Didelot. November 6.

Dobrynia Nikitich, ou Le Château Terrible. Opera in three acts. Music: different composers, including Cavos and Antonolini. November 25.

A Hunting Adventure. Ballets in three acts. Music: Cavos; scenery: Condratiev and Tozelli. December 2.

1819 *Medée et Jason.* Grand tragic pantomime ballet of Noverre in four acts. Presented in St. Petersburg by Le Picq, all dances redone by Didelot. January 9.

La Vestale. Opera. Music: Spontini; ballets: Liustikh; divertissement: Didelot. April 28.

Raoul de Créquis, or Return From the Crusades. Grand pantomime ballet in five acts. Music: Cavos and his pupil Zhuchkovsky; scenery: Condratiev, Dranché and Canoppi; combats: Gomburov; machines: Biurse; costumes: Babini. May 5.

The Sea Victory (La Victoire Naval), or Liberation of the Captives. Divertissement in one act. Music: Antonolini and different composers; combats: Gomburov. July 18.

Bazaar. Divertissement, July 24.

Le Marchand de Smyrne. Opera-vaudeville in one act, translated from the French. July 29.

Divertissement. Didelot. July 29.

Le Petit Chaperon Rouge. Fairy opera in three acts. Music: Boieldieu. August 16.

Ken-Si and Tao, or The Beauty and the Beast. Grand Chinese ballet in

four acts. Music: Antonolini; scenery: Canoppi, Tozelli and Condratiev; machines: Biurse; costumes: Babini. August 30.

La Clochette. Fairy opera in three acts. Music: Hérold. October 8.

Laura and Henry, or The Troubadour. Fairy heroic ballet in three acts.
Music: Cavos; scenery: Condratiev, Tozelli; combats: Gomburov;
machines: Biurse; costumes: Babini. November 3.

Raoul Barbe-Bleue. Grand tragic ballet in four acts by Val'berkh.
Renewed by Auguste, in which tournament and feast of third act
were composed by Didelot. Music: Cavos and Antonolini. November 19.

Pretended Bandits, or Confusion in the Apartment. Opera-vaudeville in
one act, taken from the French by L. Titov. Music: Sapienza; tartar
dance by Didelot. December 8.

1820   *Ferdinand Cortes, or The Conquering of Mexico.* Lyric opera in three
acts. Music: Spontini, January 9.

The Dog of Aubri, or The Forest of Bondy. Historic-romantic melodrama
by Pixérécourt. April 26.

Inès de Castro. Tragic ballet in five acts. Music: Boieldieu. Renewed by
Auguste, dances in festive scene redone by Didelot. May 24.

The Abduction, or Robert, Ataman of the Robbers. Pantomime ballet in
three acts with combats. Mounted: Auguste; dances: Didelot. June
16.

Karl et Lisbeth, ou Le Déserteur Malgré Lui. Demi-character and military ballet in five acts. Music: Turik; scenery: Condratiev. July 7.

Cora and Alonzo, or The Virgin of the Sun. Grand heroic ballet in five
acts, adorned with games, ritual dances, combats, marches etc.
Music: Antonolini; decorations: Condratiev, Tozelli, Martinov, and
Canoppi. August 30.

Summer Ball. Divertissement. September 1.

The Fortune Teller, or Dances of Spirits. Original comedy-vaudeville by
Shakhovskoi. Music: different composers; divertissement: Didelot.
September 21.

Les Bayadères. Opera in two acts. Music: Catel, with several musical
numbers by Cavos. October 18.

Euthyme et Eucharis, or The Vanquished Shade of Libas. Music: Jomas;
scenery: Canoppi; machines: Biurse; costumes: Babini. December
8.

1821   *The Banquet of John Lackland.* One-act analogical prologue in verses of
P. A. Katenin. Divertissements: Didelot. January 21.

Alcestis, or The Descent of Hercules into the Underworld. Heroic ballet
in five acts. Music: Antonolini; scenery: Canoppi and Gonzaga; new
machines: Grif (Grieve?); costumes: Babini. February 7.

The Judgment of King Solomon. Historic drama in three acts, translated
from the French by R. Zotov. Music: Titov. April 25.

Christophe Colomb, ou La Découverte du Nouveau Monde. Translated

from the French (of Pixérécourt?). Music: arranged and in part
newly composed by Turik. Pantomime ballets and dances of wild
islanders by Didelot. May 14.

Roland and Morgana, or The Destruction of the Enchanted Isle. Heroic
fairy ballet in five acts. Music: Antonolini; scenery: Condratiev and
Canoppi; properties: Natier; machines: Grif (Grieve?); costumes:
Babini. August 30.

The Tempest. Fairy-romantic presentation of Shakhovskoi (from Shakespeare). Music: Cavos, using music of Cherubini and Steibelt;
divertissements and dances: Didelot. September 28.

The Return from India, or The Wooden Leg. Comic-romantic ballet in
the Scotch genre, taken from a Florentine tale. Music: Venua;
scenery: Condratiev; costumes: Babini. November 14.

Alexander of Macedon in India. Heroic opera in one act. Music:
Neukomm. November 21.

Algerian Bandits. Demi-character ballet in one act, with sea combat and
ship blown into pieces. December 14.

Living Pictures, or Ours Is Bad: Someone Else's Is Good. Vaudeville in
one act. Divertissement and pictures by Didelot. December 14.

1822   *L'Offrande à l'Amour.* Anacreontic ballet in one act. January 18.

Crazy in the Mind. Comedy-vaudeville in one act of Shakhovskoi,
translated from the French. January 30.

Toberne, ou Le Pêcheur Suédois. Opera in two acts, translated from the
French by P. Arapov. Music: Bruni. July 17.

The Princess of Trebizond, or The Island of the Dumb. Fairy-comic ballet
with songs, music, dances, pantomimes, divertissements and machines. Produced by Shakhovskoi and Didelot. Music: Cavos;
decorations: Gonzago. October 9.

Naina, or The Magic Rose-Leaf. Fairy opera in one act. Music:
Boieldieu, Isouard, and Cavos. October 16.

Secretive Carlo, or The Valley of the Black Stone. Romantic comedy in
five acts in the English form with songs, choruses, dances, old
Scotch games and feast, compiled by Shakhovskoi. Music: Leseur;
divertissements: Didelot. October 23.

The Fire-bird, or The Adventures of Tsarevich Ivan. Fairy opera in three
acts. Text from Russian folktale and poem *Levsil, Russian Bogatyr.*
Music: Cavos, with Antonolini; scenery: Condratiev, Canoppi and
Tozelli; machines: Thibeault. Persian and Tartar ballet in 2nd act:
Didelot. November 6.

Svetlana, or A Hundred Years in One Day. Fairy opera ballad in two
acts, from Zhukovsky. Music: Catel. December 29.

1823   *Charade in Action.* Presentation in completely new form. Music:
Verstovsky and Maurer; flights and machines: Thibeault; dances
and groups: Didelot. January 3.

Lily of Narbonne, or The Knight's Vow. Romantic comedy ballet in three acts with choruses, singing, divertissements, pantomimes, combats, duels, knight's consecration. Produced by Shakhovskoi and Didelot. January 8.

The Prisoner of the Caucasus, or Shade of the Bride. Grand pantomime ballet in four acts, from Pushkin. Music: Cavos, orchestrated by his pupil Zhuchkovsky; scenery: Condratiev; costumes: Babini; machines: Natier. January 15.

Anacreon and Cupidon. Theatrical spectacle with singing of anacreontic ode of Lomonosov. Music: Cavos; scenery: Condratiev; divertissements: Didelot. February 12.

Spanish Diversion, or Masks. Divertissement. February 15.

Jeanne D'Arc, or The Maid of Orléans. Heroic opera in three acts. Music: Carafa. February 26.

The Abduction. Ballet in three acts with combats compiled by Auguste and Didelot. Music: different authors. May 24.

The Visitation of the Prince, or The Warrior and the Merchant. Opera-vaudeville in one act, translated from the French by Shakhovskoi. Music: Turik. July 30.

The Falcon of Prince Yaroslav of Tver, or The Promised Husband on a White Horse. Russian tale in four acts with singing, choruses, military amusements, games and fights, compiled by Shakhovskoi. Music: Cavos; Tartar games with bows and arrows by Didelot. October 18.

The Genie Iturbiel, or The Thousand Years in Two Days of Vizier Haroun. Opera in three acts. Music: Cavos, Antonolini, Méhul, and Isouard. November 5.

The Pirate. Romantic comedy in five acts in prose and verse, taken from Scott's novel, compiled by A. A. Zhandr. Ballets and fist-fights by Didelot. December 3.

1824 *The European Saved by a Savage, or The Broken Idol.* Ballet in one act. Music: Turik; scenery: Condratiev; costumes: Babini. January 8.

Roger de Sicile. Opera in three acts. Music: Berton. January 14.

Baba-Yaga, or The Wedding of Tsarevich Ivan. Magical presentation in one act. Composer of chorus: A. Kukolnikov. February 5.

The Magic Mirror, or The White Dove. Fairy vaudeville in one act from Arabian tale. Divertissements and dances: Didelot. February 11.

New Slavic Folk Dance and Comic Harlequin Scene by Didelot. February 17.

Cendrillon. Pantomime ballet in four acts. Composition of Val'berkh and Auguste. Music: Cavos; dances: Didelot. June 9.

Journey to Kronstadt. Vaudeville in three acts, altered from the French by A. Pisarev. Turkish dance for Istomina by Didelot. August 25.

La Forêt Noire (The Black Forest). Pantomime ballet in three acts. Composition: Auguste; music: A. Paris; dances: Didelot. October 8.

The Thunder Clap, or The Terrible Secret. Romantic melodrama in three acts in imitation of the French by Veshniakov. Ballets, consisting of Scotch national dances, by Didelot. October 17.

Finn. Comedy in verse by Shakhovskoi from an episode of the poem *Ruslan and Liudmila* (Pushkin) in the form of a Greek trilogy: I) A Shepherd; II) The Hero; III) The Witch. Music: Cavos; scenery: Condratiev; flights etc.: Thibeault; new ballets, Russian rites, and games: Didelot. November 3.

Ruslan and Liudmila, or The Overthrow of Chernomor the Evil Sorcerer. Heroic fairy ballet in five acts spectacularly adorned with combats, marches, transformations, flights, machines. Based on Glushkovsky's version of Pushkin's poem. Altered and mounted: Auguste and Didelot; music: Sholtz; combats: Gomburov; decorations: Condratiev and Fedorov; machines: Thibeault and Natier; costumes: Babini. December 8.

Romance in Action. Pictures and pantomimes compiled by Didelot. December 11.

1825 *Aristophanes, or Presentation of the Comedy "The Horsemen."* Historic comedy in ancient form. Mounted: Shakhovskoi; music: Cavos; intermediate dances: Didelot. January 19.

The Secret Patron. Opera in two acts. Music: Kreutzer. January 26.

The Dream of Svetlana, from the ballad of Zhukovsky. Fairy-allegorical presentation with singing and combats. Ballets: Auguste and Didelot. January 30.

Diadima. Historical, romantic melodrama in four acts, translated from the German. Music: actor Shreintser. Three living pictures by Didelot. July 13.

Preciosa. Drama in four acts, translated from the German. Music: Weber. September 21.

Phaedra. Grand tragic heroic ballet in four acts. Special effects: Ippolite; music: Cavos and his students Turik and Shelikhov; decorations: Canoppi and Condratiev; machines: Natier; costumes: Babini. September 24.

Kerim-Girei. Romantic trilogy in five acts by Shakhovskoi. Content taken from Pushkin's *Fountain of Bakhchisarai.* Music: Cavos; scenery: Gonzago and Gerlini; costumes: Babini; divertissement, representing harem festival in third part, by Didelot. September 28.

Satan and All His Devices, or The Lesson of the Sorcerer. Analogical fairy ballet in three acts. Content from the opera *Le Diable à Quatre.* Mounted: Auguste; music: Cavos, Turik, and Shelikhov; new scenery: Fedorov, pupil of Canoppi. Divertissement in first act and final ballet by Didelot. October 29.

1826 (after a nine-month period of mourning for the death of Emperor Alexander I)

The Return of Prince Pozharsky to His Estate. Analogical divertissement with choruses, couplets, military evolutions and festive marches.

Music: Cavos; Russian dances: Auguste; various character dances: Didelot. August 26.

La Neige. Opera in two acts. Music: Auber.

The Dream Realized. National divertissement. Various character dances compiled by Didelot. December 30.

1827 *The Island of Trials.* Grand adagio. January 31.

Fête Villageoise. Grand divertissement, ornamented with various character dances compiled by Auguste. Music: Cavos, arranged by Turik and Shelikhov. Groups and pictures by Didelot. Kamenny Island Theater, July 1.

Miroslava, ou Le Bûcher de la Mort. Heroic fairy opera with choruses, ballets, combats, great spectacles. Music: from Antonolini, Cavos and his pupil Shelikhov; scenery: Canoppi, Condratiev, and Fedorov; machines: Thibeault. Ballets composed by Didelot. October 3.

Liza and Colin, or Vain Precautions. Ballet in two acts by Dauberval. Mounted: Didelot. October 11.

1828 *Joy of the Moldavians, or Victory.* Theatrical presentation in three acts. Music: Cavos and Eizerich; ballets: Didelot and Auguste. May 25.

Dido, or The Destruction of Carthage. Grand tragic ballet in five acts by Le Picq. Mounted: Didelot and Auguste; music: Martin i Soler and several others; compiled by Cavos; combats: Gomburov; scenery: Canoppi; machines, fire, and destruction of Carthage: Thibeault. October 24.

1829 *The Mad Woman, or The Coming of the New Lord (La Somnambule?).* New pantomime ballet in three acts by Scribe and Aumer. Music: Hérold; scenery: Ciceri; costumes: Lecomte; mounted: Auguste; dances: Didelot. April 29.

Beneficiant. Vaudeville in five divisions, translated from the French by Shakhovskoi. New dance for Istomina by Didelot. May 13.

The New Heroine, or The Cossack Woman. Grand pantomime ballet in three acts. Music: reworking of Titov and different authors. Mounted: Auguste; dances: Didelot. September 2.

Piramo e Tisbe. Grand heroic ballet in four acts. Music: Canziani, renewed by Auguste; dances: Didelot. September 16.

Notes

CHAPTER I. OPENING STEPS

1. The French word "marmotte" has often been translated as "monkey" in works dealing with Didelot. It could have been a monkey; however, *The Penny Cylopaedia* (London, 1839), in describing Alpine marmots says clearly, "they are taken by the Savoyards and others principally that they may be exhibited by those itinerants," p. 517.

2. This information comes from a biography of Didelot by N. P. Mundt, "Karl Ludovik Didlo, byvshii baletmeister imperatorskikh Sanktpeterburgskikh Teatrov," *Repertuar russkogo teatra* (tom 1, bk. 3, 1840) pp. 1–8. Starting in 1829 Mundt was a secretary to the directorship of the Russian Imperial Theaters. Iurii Slonimskii, author of the Russian biography, *Didlo* (Moscow, 1956), asserts that the trustworthiness of much of Mundt's information remains unshakeable. Slonimskii's own notes, however, contain certain mistakes e.g. in dates of sources (some may be typographical errors). A small Czech biography by Ian Rey, *Charles Louis Didelot, 1767–1837* (Prague, 1937) seems to be a summary of available Russian material. Vera Krasovskaia's *Russkii baletnyi teatr. Ot vozniknoveniia do serediny XIX veka* (Moscow-Leningrad, 1958), is both interesting and accurate on Didelot's work in Russia. Arthur Saint-Léon's, *La Sténochorégraphie, ou l'art d'écrire promptement la danse* (Paris, 1852), contains much of the same information as the Russian sources.

3. Programs: *Télémaque dans l'isle de Calipso. Ballet sérieux, héroi-pantomime and composition du Sr. Pitrot, Maître des Ballets*. (Paris, 1759). *Les Amants introduits au sérrail* [sic], *ou Le Sultan généreux. Ballet héroi-pantomime de l'invention and composition du Sr. Pitrot* (Paris, 1759). Material in Dance Collection, Lincoln Center.

4. Frederik August Dahlgren, *Förteckning öfver Svenska Skådespel Uppförda på Stockholms Teatrar 1737–1863 och Kongl. Teatrarnes Personal (1773–1863)* (Stockholm, 1866), p. 511.

5. Baron Melchior Grimm, "Du Poème lyrique," in *Correspondance littéraire, philosophique et critique par Grimm, Diderot, Raynal, Meister, etc.* (Paris, 1882), 16:398–9.

6. *Reminiscences of Michael Kelly of the King's Theatre, and Theatre Royal of Drury Lane* (New York, 1826), p. 233. Arnold Haskell, *Ballet Retrospect* (New York, 1965), p. 24.

7. Meaudre de Lapouyade, "Un Portrait de Madame Dauberval par Lonsing," *Revue historique de Bordeaux et du Département de la Gironde* (July-August, 1915), p. 205.

8. Nérée Désharbes, *Deux Siècles à l'Opéra* (Paris, 1868), p. 151. Louis Bachaumont, *Mémoires secrets, pour servir à l'histoire de la république des lettres en France, depuis MDCCLXII jusqu'à nos jours* (London, 1777–1788), 6:178; 7:133; and 27:145, 214, 249–52.

9. Émile Campardon, *L'Académie royale de musique au XVIIIè siècle. Documents inédits découverts aux Archives nationales* (Paris, 1884), 1:328.

10. Mundt, p. 2.

11. *La Métamorphose. Ballet épisodique en un acte* (Lyon, République Frimaire, an IV.) Program in Bibliothèque de l'Arsenal, Paris. Auguste Rondel Collection. The dedication was repeated verbatim in the libretto from his London production of *L'Amour vengé, ou La Métamorphose, 1796.*

12. *Psyché et l'Amour. Ballet érotique en cinq actes de la composition de M. Didelot* (St. Petersburg, 1809), p. 8. Program in Lunacharsky Memorial Theatrical Library, Leningrad.

13. Bachaumont, 6:7. Charles Hervey, *The Theatres of Paris* (London, 1846), p. 325.

14. Georges Cain, *Anciens théâtres de Paris. La Boulevard du crime. Les Théâtres du boulevard* (Paris, 1906), pp. 29–31.

15. Bachaumont, 6:7.

16. Mundt, p. 2.

17. Dahlgren, p. 572.

18. J.-G. Noverre, *Lettres sur les arts imitateurs en général et sur la danse en particulier* (Paris, 1807), 2:115.

19. Mundt, p. 2.

20. *Les Spectacles de Paris, ou calendrier historique et chronologique des théâtres pour l'année 1782,* p. 63.

21. Bachaumont, 33:65.

22. *Les Spectacles de Paris ou calendrier historique et chronologique des théâtres pour l'année 1783,* p. 18.

23. A. Geffroy, *Gustave III et la cour de France* (Paris, 1867), 2:29.

24. Adam P. Glushkovskii, *Vospominaniia baletmeistera* (Leningrad-Moscow, 1940), p. 190.

25. *Orphée et Euridice, Opera i Tre Acter* (Stockholm, May 11, 1786). Program-libretto in Royal Library, Stockholm.

26. *Armide. Opera i Fem Acter. . . .* (January 24, 1787). Program-libretto in Royal Library, Stockholm.

27. *Frigga. Opera i En Act. . . .* (May 31, 1787). Program-libretto in Royal Library, Stockholm.

28. *Almanach général des spectacles de Paris et de la Province pour l'année 1792,* p. 103.

29. Gaston Capon, *Les Vestris. Le "Diou" de la danse et sa famille 1730–1808* (Paris, 1908), p. 264.

30. Bachaumont, 33:65.

31. Campardon, 1:263–4. Capon, p. 267.

CHAPTER II. *English Growing Pains*

1. N. P. Mundt, "Karl Ludovik Didlo, byvshii baletmeister imperatorskikh Sanktpeterburgskikh Teatrov," *Repertuar russkogo teatra* bk. 3, (1840), 1:3. Deryck Lynham, *The Chevalier Noverre: The Father of Modern Ballet* (London, 1950), p. 106.

2. "On Two Italian Dancers," *The Gentleman's Magazine and Historical Chronicle* (1741), p. 30.

3. T. C. Hansard, *The Parliamentary History of England from the Earliest Period to the Year 1803* (London, 1814), 21:1243–4.

4. Gaston Capon, *Les Vestris. Le "Diou" de la danse et sa famille 1730–1808.* (Paris, 1908), pp. 266–7.

5. *The Morning Chronicle* (April 30, 1798).

6. *Les Spectacles de Paris, ou calendrier historique et chronologique des théâtres pour l'année 1785.*

7. *Public Advertiser* (January 3, 1788).

8. *Ibid.* (January 12, 1788).

9. *Ibid.* (February 5, 1788).

10. *Ibid.* (February 4, 1788).

11. *Ibid.* (February 21, 1788).

12. *Ibid.* (March 1, 1788 and March 13, 1788).

13. *General Advertiser* (April 5, 1788).

14. *Public Advertiser* (May 22, 1788).

15. *Ibid.* (May 29 and June 3, 1788).

16. Martin Cooper, *Opéra comique* (New York, 1949), p. 27.

17. *Journal de Paris* (September 14, 1788).

18. Mundt, p. 3. *The Morning Post* (February 26, 1789).

19. *The Morning Post* (January 10, 1789). *The Morning Herald* (January 12, 1789).

20. *The Morning Post* (February 24, 1789).

21. *The Times* (January 19, 1789).

22. *The Morning Herald* (January 26, 1789).

23. *The Morning Post and Daily Advertiser* (January 26, 1789).

24. *Ibid.* (February 4, 1789).

25. *The Times* (February 9, 1789).

26. *The Morning Herald* (February 9, 1789). Also *The World* (February 9, 1789).

27. *The World* (February 10 and 11, 1789).

28. *The Times* (February 16, 1789).

29. *Ibid.* (February 16, 1789).

30. *Ibid.* (February 14, 1789).

31. *Ibid.* (February 23, 1789).

32. *The Morning Post* (March 4, 1789).

33. *Ibid.* (February 19, 1789).

34. *The World* (March 9, 1789).

35. *The Morning Herald* (March 9, 1789).

36. *The Morning Post* (March 9, 1789).

37. *The Morning Post and Daily Advertiser* (March 19, 1789).

38. *The Morning Post* (March 31, 1789).

39. *Ibid.* (April 29, 1789).

40. *Ibid.* (May 13, 1789).

41. *Ibid.* (June 18–19, 1789).

42. *Ibid.* (June 29, 1789).

43. *Ibid.* (July 1, 1789).

44. *Ibid.* (July 6, 1789).

45. Eugène Lewenhaupt, ed., *Bref Rörande Teatern under Gustaf III* (Upsala, 1891), pp. 90–1.

46. *Ibid.* p. 56.

CHAPTER III. *Faux Pas in Bordeaux*

1. M. [Aurélien] Vivie, *Histoire de la terreur à Bordeaux* (Bordeaux, 1877), pp. 2–8.

2. F. A. Boisson, *Les Douze Colonnes de Louis. L'Histoire inconnue du Grand-Théâtre de Bordeaux* (Bordeaux, 1964), p. 43.

3. Hippolyte Minier and J. Delphil, *Le Théâtre à Bordeaux* (Bordeaux, 1883), p. 27.

4. Carlo Blasis, *Traité élémentaire, théorique et pratique de l'art de la danse* (Milan, 1820), p. 10.

5. J.-G. Noverre, *Lettres sur les arts imitateurs en général et sur la danse en particulier* (Paris, 1807), 1: v.j.

6. Meaudre de Lapouyade, "Un Portrait de Madame Dauberval par Lonsing," *Revue historique de Bordeaux et du Département de la Gironde* (July-August, 1915), p. 203. The letter from Mme. Théodore to Rousseau is of doubtful authenticity. *Correspondance Générale de J. J. Rousseau* (Paris, 1934), 20:348–9.

7. *Relation des cérémonies religieuses des indiens qui sont prisonniers à bord de l'Amiral dans le port de Bordeaux, adressé par Made. Dauberval aux ames généreuses.* (Bordeaux, Le 17 Prairial, an cinquième de la République), pp. 20–21.

8. *Oeuvres complètes de Pierre Bernadau de Bordeaux. Tom 5, Premier Recueil des Tabelettes Manuscrites. March 1787–Nov. 1789*, entries for October 14, 1789 and November 15, 1788. A helpful secondary source is Paul Courteault, *La Révolution et les théâtres à Bordeaux* (Paris, 1926).

9. Noverre (1807), 2: 119.

10. Vivie, p. 8. Minier, p. 52.

11. Carlo Blasis, *The Theory of Theatrical Dancing* (London, 1888), p. 76.

12. Minier, p. 26. Arnaud Detcheverry, *Histoire des théâtres de Bordeaux* (Bordeaux, 1860), p. 156.

13. Boisson, p. 42.

14. *Oeuvres complètes de Pierre Bernadau*, entries for March 29, 1788; February 10, 1788; and February 17, 1788.

15. *Ibid.*, entry for October 10, 1788.

16. *Journal de Guienne* (November 5 and 11, 1788).

17. *Oeuvres complètes de Pierre Bernadau*, entries for December 4 and 18, 1788.

18. *Ibid.*, entry for February 12, 1789.

19. The *lettre de cachet* is in the Archives Municipales de Bordeaux.

20. *Oeuvres complètes de Pierre Bernadau*, entry for April 20, 1789.

21. *Ibid.*, entry for May 13, 1789.

22. *Ibid.*, entry for July 3, 1789.

23. Archives Municipales de Bordeaux.

24. *Journal de Guienne* (October 14, 1789).

25. *Ibid.* (October 21–22, 1789).

26. *Oeuvres complètes de Pierre Bernadau*, entry for October 25, 1789.

27. "État des représentations de tragédies, comédies, opéras bouffons, grands opéras et ballets, joués à Bordeaux pendant l'année 1789 et qui a fini le 27 Mars 1790." Manuscrit de Lecouvreur. Bibliothèque de la Ville de Bordeaux.

28. *Journal de Guienne* (January 15, 1790).

29. *Ibid.* (March 20, 1790).

30. "Mémoire pour le Sieur Chevalier Peicam Danseur, attaché au spectacle de Bordeaux" (Bordeaux, April 9, 1790). Archives Municipales de Bordeaux.

31. Boisson, p. 50.

32. *Journal de Bordeaux et du Département de la Gironde* (June 9, 1790).

33. *Ibid.* (June 10, 1790).

34. *Journal de Guienne* (July 20, 1790).

35. *Ibid.* (July 8, 1790).

36. Eugène Lewenhaupt, ed., *Bref Rörande Teatern under Gustaf III* (Upsala, 1891), 1:50.

37. *Ibid*, p. 155.

38. *Ibid.*, p. 220–1.

39. *Ibid.*, p. 238.

40. *Les Spectacles de Paris, ou calendrier historiques at chronologique des théâtres* (Paris, pour l'année 1790), p. 16.

41. *Chronique de Paris* (January 30, 1791).

42. *Journal patriotique* (August 6, 1791).

43. *Ibid.* (April 14, 1791).

CHAPTER IV. *Revolutionary Ballet*

1. Joseph Grego, *Rowlandson the Cartoonist* (London, 1880), 1:283–6. Grego believes that Didelot is also in the first cartoon. This is questionable. Information is also contained in Mary D. George's *Catalogue of Political and Personal Satires Preserved in the Department of Prints and Drawings of the British Museum*, 6:863; *The School for Scandal. Thomas Rowlandson's London* (Lawrence, Kansas, 1967), pp. 67–8.

2. Charles Beecher Hogan, ed., *The London Stage 1660–1800* (Carbondale, Illinois, 1968), part 5, p. 1323.

3. *The Morning Chronicle* (February 21 and 23, 1791); *The Morning Post* (February 18 and 23, 1791).

4. *The Morning Chronicle* (March 21, 1791).

5. *The Morning Post* (May 9, 1791).

6. J.-G. Noverre, *Lettres sur les arts imitateurs en général et sur la danse en particulier* (Paris, 1807), 2:159.

7. *Chronique de Paris* (September 4, 1791).

8. *Ibid.* (November 26, 1791).

9. *Ibid.* (November 30 and December 3, 1791). *Gazette nationale* (December 1, 1791).

10. *Chronique de Paris* (December 31, 1791).

11. *Ibid.* (December 11, 1791) gives letter from Gallet to public. His grievances against the administration are voiced by Adolphe Jullien, *L'Opéra secret au XVIIIè Siècle* (Paris, 1880), pp. 212–4. Noverre (1807), 2:145.

12. *Mercure de France* (December 31, 1791).

13. J. Maudit-Larive, *Cours de déclamation prononcé à l'Athenée de Paris* (Paris, 1810), 2:397.

14. Émile Dacier, "Une Danseuse française à Londres au debut du XVIIIè siècle," extrait du *Mercure Musicale*, no. 5 (1907), p. 764. F. de Menil, *Histoire de la danse* (Paris, 1905), p. 294.

15. M. A. Baron, *Lettres à Sophie sur la danse* (Paris, 1825), p. 235. Arthur Saint-Léon, *La Sténochorégraphie, ou l'art d'écrire promptement la danse* (Paris, 1852), p. 14.

16. N. P. Mundt, "Karl Ludovik Didlo, *byvshii baletmeister imperatorskikh Sanktpeterburgskikh Teatrov*," *Repertuar russkogo teatra* (tom 1, bk. 3, 1840), p. 3–4.

17. *Chronique de Paris* (December 21, 1791).

18. *Ibid.* (May 12, 1792).

19. *Ibid.* (July 1, 1792).

20. Mundt, p. 4.

21. Louis Bachaumont, *Mémoires secrets, pour servir à l'histoire de la république des lettres en France, depuis MDCCLXII jusqu'à nos jours* (London, 1777–78), 13:114. Edmond de Goncourt, *La Guimard d'apres les registres des menus-plaisirs de la Bibliothèque de l'Opéra* (Paris, 1893).

22. Meaudre de Lapouyade, "Un Portrait de Madame Dauberval, par Lonsing," *Revue historique de Bordeaux* (July-August, 1915), p. 204.

23. Raymond de Pezzer, *L'Opéra devant la loi et la jurisprudence* (Paris, 1911), pp. 23–4. William F. Crosten, *French Grand Opera* (New York, 1948), p. 12.

24. Georges Cain, *Anciens théâtres de Paris. Le Boulevard du crime. Les Théâtres du boulevard.* (Paris, 1906), p. 30.

25. Crosten, p. 12. Max Aghion, *Le Théâtre à Paris au XVIIIè siècle* (Paris, 1926), pp. 255–6.

26. Castil-Blaze, *Théâtres liriques de Paris* (Paris, 1855), 2:29.

27. Pierre Bossuet, *Histoire des théâtres nationaux* (Paris, 1910?), pp. 71–2.

28. Henri Welschinger, *Le Théâtre de la Révolution 1789–1799* (Paris, 1880), p. 100.

29. Castil-Blaze, 2:25; Crosten, p. 13; Welschinger, p. 29; de Pezzer, p. 26.

30. Paul d'Estrée, *Le Théâtre sous la terreur* (Paris, 1913), p. 385.

31. Hannah Winter, *The Theatre of Marvels* (New York, 1964), p. 84.

32. Castil-Blaze, 2:8–9.

33. *Gazette nationale* (March 24, 1793). Review also in *Journal de Paris* (March 8, 1793).

34. *Chronique de Paris* (March 8, 1793).

35. *Les Spectacles de Paris et de toute la France . . . pour l'année 1792*, p. 41.

36. *Journal de Paris* (August 15, 1793).

37. *Ibid.* (August 17, 1793).

38. *Ibid.; Journal des spectacles; Chronique de Paris* (August 17, 1793).

39. Louis H. LeComte, *Histoire des théâtres de Paris. Le Théâtre national. Le Théâtre de l'égalité 1793–1794* (Paris, 1907), p. 83.

40. *Journal de Paris* (no. 281, 17th of 1er Mois, 2è année républicaine) and LeComte, pp. 29–30. *Journal des spectacles* (October 7, 1793).

41. *Journal de Paris* (November 16, 1793). Victor Couailhac, *Grandes et Petites Aventures de M-lle Montansier* (Brussels, n.d.), pp. 93–6. LeComte, p. 40. *Gazette nationale* (November 16, 1793).

42. *Journal de Paris* (November 20, 1793).

43. *Ibid.* (November 21, 1793).

44. LeComte, pp. 106–9.

45. *Ibid.*, pp. 112–4.

46. *Papiers inédits trouvés chez Robespierre, Saint-Just, Payan etc.* [*sic*] (Paris, 1828), 1:334–5.

47. *Journal de Paris* (March 19, 1794). *Journal des théâtres* (22 Vendemiaire, l'an 3) also had a favorable review.

48. L. Henry LeComte, *La Montansier, ses aventures, ses entreprises* (Paris, n.d.), p. 209.

49. Louis Trénard, *Histoire sociale des idées Lyon* (Paris, 1958), 1:149. M. Fuchs, "Les Danseurs des théâtres de Province au XVIIIé Siécle," *Archives internationales de la danse*, (no. 4, 1934), p. 140.

50. *Journal de Lyon* (September 15, 1795).

51. *Anacreon, Thomas Stanley's Translation* (New York, 1899), p. 7.

52. Noverre, 2:75.

53. *La Métamorphose. Ballet épisodique en un acte* (Lyon: République Frimaire, an IV). Bibliothèque de l'Arsenal, Paris, program in August Rondel Collection.

CHAPTER V. *Lofty Flights in Britain*

1. *The Morning Chronicle* (January 8, 1796).

2. *Ibid.* (February 8 and 11, 1796).

3. *The Morning Chronicle* (March 7, 1796). This was probably Pierre Germain Parisau, executed 21 Messidor, an II. Émile Campardon, *Les Spectacles de la foire* (Paris, 1877), p. 213.

4. *The Morning Chronicle* (February 11, 1796).

5. *True Briton* (February 22, 1796) and *The Morning Chronicle* (February 20, 1796).

6. *The Morning Chronicle* (February 22, 1796).

7. *True Briton* (February 22, 1796).

8. *The Morning Chronicle* (May 10, 1796).

9. *Ibid.* (March 2, 1796).

10. *Ibid.* (March 4, 1796).

11. *True Briton* (March 8, 1796).

12. *The Morning Chronicle* (April 13, 1796).

13. Mary D. George, *Catalogue of Political and Personal Satires Preserved in the Department of Prints and Drawings of the British Museum*, 7:301.

14. *Ibid.*, p. 302.

15. *The Morning Chronicle* (April 13, 1796).

16. *True Briton* (April 25, 1796).

17. *The Morning Chronicle* (April 23, 1796).

18. *Ibid.* (May 21, 1796).

19. *True Briton* (June 3, 1796).

20. *The Morning Chronicle* (June 3, 1796).

21. *Ibid.* (June 6, 1796).

22. Iurii Slonimskii, *Didlo* (Moscow, 1956), p. 11.

23. *Flore et Zéphire. Ballet Divertissement en un acte* (London, 1796). Program-libretto in Harvard Theatre Collection. *The Morning Chronicle* (June 6, 1796).

24. *True Briton* (July 9, 1796).

25. *L'Heureux Naufrage, ou Les Sorcières écossaises. Ballet dramatique en trois actes* (London, 1796). Program-libretto in Harvard Theatre Collection.

26. *The Morning Chronicle* (July 8, 1796).

27. *True Briton* (July 9, 1796).

28. *Ibid.* (July 25, 1796).

29. *The Morning Chronicle* (November 28, 1796).

30. *Ibid.* (November 24, 1796).

31. *True Briton* (November 28, 1796).

32. *The Morning Chronicle* (November 29, 1796).

33. *Ibid.* (December 14, 1796) and *True Briton* (December 13, 1796).

34. *The Morning Chronicle* (December 16, 1796).

35. *True Briton* (December 13, 1796).

36. *The Morning Chronicle* (December 29, 1796).

37. *Ibid.* (February 9, 1797).

38. *Ibid.* (March 13, 1797).

39. *Ibid.* (April 3, 1797).

40. *Ibid.* (April 7, 1797).

41. *Sappho et Phaon. Grand Ballet érotique en quatre actes* (London, 1797). Program-libretto in Folger Library, Washington, D.C.

42. *The Morning Chronicle* (April 7, 1797).

43. *The Monthly Mirror* (April 1797).

44. *The Morning Chronicle* (May 6, 1797).

45. *The Monthly Mirror* (May 1797).

46. *The Morning Chronicle* (June 16, 1797).

47. *The Monthly Mirror* (June 1797).

48. *The Morning Chronicle* (November 30, 1797).

49. *True Briton* (January 27 and 29, 1798).

50. *The Morning Chronicle* (January 3, 1798).

51. *Ibid.* (February 7, 1798).

52. *Ibid.* (March 3, 1798). A Russian visitor's account of the scandal is given by Vl. R. Zotov, "Obshchestvennaia zhizn' v anglii v kontse proshlago veka," *Istoricheskii vestnik* (April 1886), pp. 210–12. Parliamentary accounts in *Journal of the House of Lords Beginning Anno Tricesimo Sexto Georgii Tertii 1796*, 41: 485; "Journal of the Proceedings of the Second Session of the Eighteenth Parliament of Great Britain. House of Lords," *The European Magazine and London Review* (April 1798), p. 265.

53. *The Morning Chronicle* (March 3, 1798).

54. *Ibid.* (March 9, 1798) and *The Monthly Mirror* (March 1798).

55. *London Chronicle* (March 3–6, 1798), p. 219. *True Briton* (March 5, 1798).

56. *The Morning Chronicle* (March 9, 1798).

57. *Ibid.* (March 7, 1798).

58. *Ibid.* (March 13, 1798).

59. George, 7:507–9.

60. *The Morning Chronicle* (March 17, 1798).

61. *Ibid.* (March 26, 1798).

62. *Ibid.* (March 22, 24, and 26, 1798).

63. *Ibid.* (April 19, 1798).

64. *The Monthly Mirror* (May 1798).

65. *Ibid.* (June 1798).

66. *True Briton* (April 8, 1799).

67. *Ibid.* (March 27, 1799).

68. *Ibid.* (April 18, 1799).

69. *Ibid.* (January 13, 1800).

70. *Laura et Lenza, ou Le Troubadour. A Grand Ballet in Two Acts* (London, 1800). Program-libretto in Harvard Theatre Collection.

71. *The Monthly Mirror* (April 1800).

72. *True Briton* (May 26, 1800).

73. *The Morning Chronicle* (January 3, 1801).

74. *Ibid.* (April 8, 1801).

75. *Ken-si and Tao. A Grand Chinese Ballet in Three Acts.* (London, 1801). Program-libretto in Bibliothèque de l'Arsenal, Paris. August Rondel Collection.

76. *The Morning Chronicle* (May 15, 1801).

Chapter VI. *Loftier Flights in Russia*

1. "Perepiska mezhdu Grafami N. P. Sheremetevym i S. R. Vorontsovym," *Russkii arkhiv*, no. 2 (1897), pp. 181–6.

2. On serf theaters, see N. A. Elizarova, *Teatry sheremetevykh* (Moscow, 1944) and Tatiana Dynnik, *Krepostnoi teatr* (Moscow, 1933).

3. P. A. Karatygin, *Zapiski* (Leningrad, 1929), 1:112.

4. *Teatral'naia entsiklopediia*, 2:1036.

5. Pimen' Arapov, *Letopis' russkago teatra* (St. Petersburg, 1861), p. 308.

6. K. Waliszewski, *Paul the First of Russia* (Hamden, Conn., 1969), p. 152.

7. *Souvenirs de Madame Vigée-LeBrun* (Paris, n.d.), 2: 30.

8. S. P. Zhikharev, *Zapiski sovremennika* (Moscow-Leningrad, 1955), p. 735 and C. Joyneville, *Life and Times of Alexander I* (London, 1875), 1:134.

9. Comte Fédor Golovkine, *La Cour et la règne de Paul Ier* (Paris, 1905), p. 185. The other two were said to be Paul's favorite, Anna Lopukhina, and Mme. Greber, Anna's *dame de compagnie*.

10. *Biographie universelle et portative des contemporains* (Paris, 1836), 1:957.

11. *Memoirs of Countess Golovine. A Lady at the Court of Catherine II* (London, 1910), p. 225. See also Waliszewski, p. 152 and Zhikharev, p. 735.

12. M. L'Abbé Georgel, *Mémoires pour servir à l'histoire des evenemens [sic] de la fin du dix-huitième siècle* (Paris, 1820), 6:360.

13. Adam P. Glushkovskii, *Vospominaniia baletmeistera* (Leningrad-Moscow, 1940) p. 146.

14. Auguste de Kotzbuë, *L'Année la plus remarquable de ma vie* (Paris, 1802), p. 23.

15. R. A. Mooser, *Annales de la musique et les musiciens en russie* (Geneva, 1951), 3:736.

16. *Arkhiv direktsii Imperatorskikh Teatrov* (St. Petersburg, 1892), 2:561, 624, 643; 3:223–5.

17. V. Svetlov, "Pridvornyi balet v rossii ot ego vozniknoveniia do votsarenia Imperatora Aleksandra I," *Ezhegodnik Imperatorskikh Teatrov. Prilozhenie sezon 1901–1902,* pp. 28–9.

18. *Biographie universelle,* 1:957.

19. N. I. Grech, *Zapiski Moei Zhizni* (St. Petersburg, 1886), p. 160.

20. "Zapiski R. M. Zotova," *Istoricheskii vestnik* (no. 8, 1896), 65:303.

21. Ivan Val'berkh, *Iz arkhiva baletmeistera* (Moscow-Leningrad, 1948), pp. 73–6.

22. *Ibid.,* pp. 100–1, 106.

23. *Psyché et l'Amour. Ballet érotique en cinq actes de la composition de M. Didelot* (St. Petersburg, 1809), p. 14. Program in Lunacharsky Memorial Theatrical Library, Leningrad.

24. *Ibid.,* p. 10.

25. Glushkovskii, *Vospominaniia baletmeistera,* p. 147. Same opinion is expressed in V. S., "Iziashchnyia iskusstva o sanktpeterburgskom rossiiskom teatre," *Syn otechestva,* (no. 42, 1820), p. 57.

26. Zhikharev, p. 285.

27. [Konstantin Skal'kovskii] *Tantsy, balet. Ikh istoriia i mesto v riadu iziashchnykh iskusstv* (St. Petersburg, 1882), p. 165.

28. A. Pleshcheev, *Nash' balet, 1673–1899* (St. Petersburg, 1899), p. 80.

29. *Vospominaniia F. F. Vigelia* part III, (Moscow, 1864), p. 118.

30. Glushkovskii, *Vospominaniia baletmeistera,* p. 175.

31. *Psyché et l'Amour,* p. 14.

32. Faddei Bulgarin, "Teatral'nyia vospominaniia," *Panteon* (1840), part I, 88.

33. [Skal'kovskii], p. 166. Also Vl. Mikhnevich, *Russkaia zhenshchina XVIII stoletiia* (Kiev, 1895), p. 283.

34. [Alexandra Asenkova], "Kartiny proshedshago," *Teatral'nyi i muzykal'nyi vestnik* (no. 50; December 22, 1857), p. 709.

35. Glushkovskii, *Vospominaniia baletmeistera,* pp. 163–4.

36. Zhikharev, p. 285.

37. Karatygin, 1:54.

38. Glushkovskii, *Vospominaniia baletmeistera,* p. 164.

39. Arapov, p. 162. *Roland et Morgane, ou La Déstruction de l'île enchantée* (St. Petersburg, 1821). Program in Leningrad Public Library.

40. *Psyché et l'Amour,* pp. 20–1.

41. Ernest Daudet, *Une Vie d'ambassadrice au siècle dernier. La Princesse de Lieven* (Paris, 1903), p. 57.

42. Mikhnevich, p. 282.

43. Vera Krasovskaia, *Russkii baletnyi teatr. Ot vozniknoveniia do serediny XIX veka* (Moscow-Leningrad, 1958), p. 117.

44. Glushkovskii, *Vospominaniia baletmeistera*, p. 147.

45. *Ibid.*, pp. 88, 148.

46. *Ibid.*, p. 148.

47. *Ibid.*, p. 184.

48. Krasovskaia, p. 103.

49. Val'berkh, p. 67.

50. Iurii Slonimskii, *Didlo* (Moscow, 1956), p. 47.

51. M. V. Borisoglebskii, *Materialy po istorii russkogo baleta* (Leningrad, 1938), 1:54.

52. *Ibid.*, pp. 44–5.

53. *Ibid.*, p. 59.

54. *Ibid.*, p. 60.

55. *Psyché et l'Amour*, p. 20.

56. Karatygin, 1:57. Borisoglebskii, 1:91.

57. Vl. Mikhnevich, *Istoricheskie etiudi russkoi zhizni* (St. Petersburg, 1882), 2:357.

58. A. I. Vol'f, *Khronika Petersburgskikh Teatrov s kontsa 1826 do nachala 1855* (St. Petersburg, 1877), 1:11.

59. Avdot'ia Iakovlevna Panaeva, *Vospominaniia* (Moscow, 1956), pp. 30–1. Borisoglebskii, 1:55.

60. *Vospominaniia F.F. Vigelia*, 2:52.

61. Karatygin, 1:58.

62. Fedor Koni, "Biografiia Nikolai Osipovich Diura," *Repertuar russkago teatra* (1839), 2:8.

63. R[afail]. Zotov, "I moi vospominaniia o teatre," *Repertuar russkago teatra* (Bk. 7, 1840), 2:34.

64. Leonid Grossman, *Pushkin v teatral'nykh kreslakh* (Leningrad, 1926), pp. 117–8.

65. Krasovskaia, p. 113.

66. "Moskovskiia Zapiski," *Vestnik evropy* (no. 21, November, 1809), p. 79.

67. Zhikharev, p. 285.

68. *Zapiski Filippa Filippovicha Vigelia* (Moscow, 1892), part III, 121.

69. Karatygin, 1:152.

70. Zotov, "I moi vospominaniia," p. 35.

71. Karatygin, 1:152–3. Serge Lifar, *A History of Russian Ballet from Its Origins to the Present Day* (London, 1954), pp. 64–5.

72. N. Mundt, "Biografiia znamenitoi russkoi artistki Mar'i Danilovoi," *Panteon russkago i vsekh evropeiskikh teatrov* (1840), 1:88.

73. Bulgarin, p. 88.

74. [Alexandra Asenkova], "Kartiny proshedshago," *Teatral'nyi i muzykal'nyi vestnik*, (no. 44; November 10, 1857), p. 606.

75. Iurii Bakhrushin, *Istoriia russkogo baleta* (Moscow, 1965), p. 74. Ivor Guest also indicates that early evidence of the use of *pointes* in Paris relates to *Zéphire et Flore* in his book *The Romantic Ballet in Paris* (London, 1966), p. 18.

76. Mundt, "Biografiia Danilovoi," p. 123.

77. Pierre D'Alheim, *Sur les pointes* (Paris, 1897), p. 176.

78. "Herr Duport," *Ruthenia* (November 1808), pp. 248–9.

79. *Zapiski F.F. Vigelia*, 3:121.

80. Bulgarin, p. 89.

81. Glushkovskii, *Vospominaniia baletmeistera*, p. 175.

82. Krasovskaia, p. 118, quoting *Dramaticheskii vestnik* (no. 85, 1808), part IV, 51–2.

83. *Vospominaniia F.F. Vigelia*, 3:118.

84. Arapov, p. 188.

85. Mundt, "Biografiia Danilovoi," p. 125. Also [Asenkova], "Kartiny proshedshago," *Teatral'nyi i muzykal'nyi vestnik* (no. 44; November 10, 1857), p. 606.

86. "Na Smert' Danilovoi," *Polnoe sobranie poeticheskikh sochinenii i perevodov N. I. Gnedicha* (St. Petersburg, 1905), 1:54.

87. *Psyché et l'Amour*, pp. 18–20.

88. Slonimskii, p. 51.

89. V. Vsevolodskii [Gerngross], *Teatr v rossii v epokhu otechestvennoi voiny* (St. Petersburg, 1912), p. 137.

90. Bakhrushin, p. 54.

91. *Severnaia pchela* (no. 47, April 19, 1828).

92. U. Freyh. v. Schlippenbach, "Erinnerungen aus St. Petersburg," *Ruthenia* (May 1807), pp. 69–70. Quoted by Slonimskii, p. 54.

93. Glushkovskii, *Vospominaniia baletmeistera*, p. 171.

94. R. Zotov, "I moi vospominaniia," p. 36.

95. Glushkovskii, *Vospominaniia baletmeistera*, pp. 179–80.

96. [Asenkova], "Kartiny proshedshago," *Teatral'nyi i muzykal'nyi vestnik* (no. 44; November 10, 1857), p. 607.

97. *Psyché et l'Amour*, p. 13.

98. [Asenkova], "Kartiny proshedshago," (no. 44, November 10, 1857) p. 607.

99. Slonimskii, p. 55.

100. "Zapiski R.M. Zotova," *Istoricheskii vestnik* (no. 8, 1896), 65:303.

101. *Psyché et l'Amour*, p. 17.

102. Slonimskii, p. 69.

103. *Ibid.*, p. 69.

CHAPTER VII. *The Uproar House*

1. *Zefir i Flora. Anakreonticheskii balet v 2-kh deistviakh* (St. Petersburg, 1818). Program in Leningrad Public Library.

2. John Ebers, *Seven Years of the King's Theatre* (London, 1828), p. 120.

3. Mary D. George, *Catalogue of Political and Personal Satires Preserved in the Department of Prints and Drawings in the British Museum*, 9:314.

4. *The Times* (January 2, 1812).

5. *The Morning Chronicle* (January 15, 1812).

6. *The Times* (January 16, 1812).

7. *Ibid.*

8. *The Morning Chronicle* (January 16, 1812).

9. *The Times* (January 16, 1812).

10. *The Morning Chronicle* (February 10, 1812).

11. *The Times* (February 10, 1812).

12. *The Times* (April 9, 1812).

13. *The Morning Chronicle* (April 8, 1812).

14. *Ibid.* (January 16, 1812).

15. *Zefir i Flora.*

16. *The Times* (April 9, 1812).

17. *Ibid.*

18. *Ibid.*

19. *The Morning Chronicle* (June 6, 1812).

20. "Aline, Reine de GoncOnde," in *Oeuvres choisies de Bouffleurs* (Paris, 1832), pp. 7–24.

21. *The Times* (June 29, 1812).

22. *The Morning Chronicle* (June 5, 1812).
23. *The Times* (June 22, 1812).
24. *Satirist* (September 1, 1812), p. 269.
25. *The Morning Chronicle* (July 27, 1812).
26. *Ibid.*
27. *The Morning Chronicle* (January 20, 1813).
28. *The Times* (February 8, 1813).
29. *The Morning Chronicle* (February 10, 1813).
30. *The Times* (February 15, 1813).
31. *Satirist* (March 1, 1813), p. 262.
32. *Ibid.* (February 1, 1812), p. 161.
33. *The Morning Chronicle* (March 1, 1813). *Satirist*, (March 1, 1813), p. 263.
34. *The Morning Chronicle* (March 1, 1813).
35. *Ibid.* (March 12, 1813).
36. *Ibid.*
37. *Satirist* (April, 1813), pp. 389–91.
38. *The Morning Chronicle* (April 21, 1813).
39. The plot is given on the music score in the British Museum: *La Chaumière hongroise, ou Les Illustres Fugitifs* [*sic*] by F. Venua (London, n.d.).
40. *Satirist* (May 1, 1813), p. 484.
41. *The Times* (May 3, 1813). On Coates, see H. Barton Baker, *History of the London Stage* (New York, 1904), pp. 227–8.
42. *The Times* (May 4, 1813).
43. *Satirist* (June 1, 1813), p. 491.
44. *The Times* (May 4, 1813).
45. *Ibid.* (May 17, 1813).
46. *Ibid.* (May 5, 1813).
47. Description is in George, 9:313.
48. *The Times* (May 13, 1813) called it *Les Époux péruviens*; on May 14 and thereafter it was called *Les Amants péruviens. Satirist* (June 1, 1813) p. 495.
49. *The Times* (May 27, 1813).
50. *The Morning Chronicle* (May 29, 1813).
51. *Satirist* (July 8, 1813), p. 89.
52. *The Morning Chronicle* (July 3, 1813).
53. *Ibid.* (July 12, 1813).
54. *The Times* (April 18, 1814).
55. *The Times* (April 29, 30, and May 2, 1814).
56. *Ibid.* (May 19, 1814).
57. *The Morning Chronicle* (July 4, 1814).
58. *Ibid.* (July 14, 1814).
59. *Ibid.* (August 8, 1814).
60. *Ibid.* (July 22, 1814).
61. August Bournonville, in *Mit Theaterliv*, quoted in *Klassiki khoreografii* (Leningrad-Moscow, 1937), p. 261.
62. N. P. Mundt, "Karl Ludovik Didlo," *Repertuar russkogo teatra* (bk. 3, 1840), 1:6.
63. Iurii Slonimskii, *Didlo* (Moscow, 1956), p. 84.
64. Castil-Blaze, *Théâtres liriques de Paris* (Paris, 1855), 2:144.
65. Letter in Bibliothèque de l'Opéra, Paris.
66. Arthur Saint-Léon, *La Sténochorégraphie, ou l'art d'écrire promptement la danse* (Paris, 1852).

67. Mundt, "Karl Ludovik Didlo," p. 6.

68. *Zéphire et Flore. Ballet anacréontique* (Paris, 1816). Program in Bibliothèque de l'Opéra, Paris.

69. *Journal des débats* (December 14, 1815).

70. Information supplied by Ivor Guest.

71. *Flore et Zéphyre. A-propos Vaudeville en un acte* (Paris, 1816).

72. *Flore et Zéphyr. Ballet mythologique par Théophile Wagstaff* (London, 1836).

73. Saint-Léon, *La Sténochorégraphie.*

CHAPTER VIII. *Soulful Flights in Russia*

1. "Zapiski R. M. Zotova," *Istoricheskii vestnik* (no. 8, 1896), 65:303.

2. Vera Krasovskaia, *Russkii baletnyi teatr. Ot vozniknovenia do serediny XIX veka* (Moscow-Leningrad, 1958), p. 139.

3. Iurii Slonimskii, *Didlo* (Moscow, 1956), p. 82.

4. *Ibid.,* p. 87.

5. Krasovskaia, pp. 140–1.

6. "Zapiski R. M. Zotova," p. 303.

7. Pierre D'Alheim, *Sur les pointes* (Paris, 1897), p. 183.

8. Pimen' Arapov, *Letopis' russkago teatra* (St. Petersburg, 1861), p. 291.

9. Krasovskaia, p. 159. M. V. Borisoglebskii, *Materialy po istorii russkogo baleta* (Leningrad, 1938), 1:110.

10. Arapov, p. 291.

11. "Zapiski Grafa F.T. Tolstogo," *Russkaia starina* (1873), 6:29.

12. Arapov, p. 227.

13. "Iz Zapisok Ippolita Ozhe," *Russkii arkhiv* (Moscow, 1877), 1:243.

14. "Zapiski R. M. Zotova," p. 305.

15. *Acis et Galathée. Ballet anacréontique* (St. Petersburg, 1816). Program in Leningrad Public Library.

16. Adam P. Glushkovskii, *Vospominaniia baletmeistera* (Leningrad-Moscow, 1940), p. 183. Glushkovsky gives a complete account of the plot, pp. 180–3.

17. R[afael]. Zotov, "I moi vospominaniia o teatre," *Repertuar russkago teatra* (1840), 2:35.

18. *Ibid.*

19. M.Z., *Severnyi nabliudatel'* (no. 4, 1817), p. 143.

20. Borisoglebskii, 1:58.

21. Ivan Val'berkh, *Iz arkhiva baletmeistera* (Moscow-Leningrad, 1948), p. 166. ·

22. R[afai]l Z[oto]v, "Alina Koroleva Golkonskaia," *Syn otechestva* (bk. 3, 1818), p. 124.

23. *Neozhidannoe vozvrashchenie ili vecher v sadu* (St. Petersburg, 1816). Program in Leningrad Public Library.

24. Fedor Koni, "Biografiia Nikolai Osipovich Diura," *Repertuar russkago teatra,* (1839), 2:8–9.

25. M.Z., "Niseta i Luka," *Severnyi nabliudatel'* (no. 3, 1817), p. 106. *Molodaia moloshnitsa ili Nisetta i Luka* (St. Petersburg, 1817). Program in Leningrad Public Library.

26. *Don Karlos i Rozal'ba* (St. Petersburg, 1817). Program in Leningrad Public Library. Also, "Karlos i Rozal'ba," *Severnyi nabliudatel'* (no. 10, 1817), p. 326.

27. *Tezei i Arianna ili porazhenie minotavra* (St. Petersburg, 1817). Program in Leningrad Public Library.

28. Iuv. Pr., "Tezei i Arianna," *Syn otechestva* (bk. 48, 1817), p. 127.

29. *Severnyi nabliudatel'* (no. 2, 1817), p. 279.

30. Iurii Slonimskii, "Baletnoe stikhotvorenie Pushkina," *Neva* (no. 8, 1964), p. 208.

31. Joan Lawson, "Masters of the Russian Ballet of the Nineteenth Century," *Dancing Times* (December 1939), p. 123.

32. Glushkovskii, *Vospominaniia baletmeistera*, p. 165.

33. *Severnyi nabliudatel'* (no. 25, 1817), p. 359.

34. Krasovskaia, p. 148.

35. Arapov, p. 259.

36. V. S[ots], "O Sanktpeterburgskom Rossiiskom Teatre," *Syn otechestva* (bk. 42, 1820), p. 45.

37. Vladimir Nabokov, in notes to *Eugene Onegin: A Novel in Verse by Aleksandr Pushkin* (New York, 1964), 2:93.

38. A. Gozenpud, *Muzykal'nyi teatr v Rossii* (Leningrad, 1959), p. 479.

39. Arapov, pp. 262, 266.

40. *Zefir i Flora. Anakreonticheskii balet v 2-kh deistviakh* (St. Petersburg, 1818). Program in Leningrad Public Library.

41. Krasovskaia, pp. 110–11.

42. Glushkovskii, *Vospominaniia baletmeistera*, p. 179.

43. A. S. Rabinovich, *Russkaia opera do Glinki* (Leningrad, 1948), p. 150.

44. K. Didlo, "Otvet na stat'iu Iuv. Pr.," *Syn otechestva* (bk. 51, 1817), p. 252.

45. *V pamiat' 50-letiia stsenicheskoi deiatel'nosti artista baletnogo truppy N. O. Goltsa* (St. Petersburg, 1872), p. 20.

46. Glushkovskii, *Vospominaniia baletmeistera*, p. 166.

47. Borisoglebskii, 1:56. Avot'ia Iakovlevna Panaeva, *Vospominaniia* (Moscow, 1956), p. 34. Joan Lawson, "Pages from the History of the Russian Ballet," *Dancing Times* (April 1941), p. 385. Serge Lifar, *A History of Russian Ballet from Its Origins to the Present Day* (London, 1954), p. 53.

48. V. Vsevolodskii [Gerngross], *Teatr v Rossii v epokhu otechestvennoi voiny* (St. Petersburg, 1912), p. 122. P. A. Karatygin, *Zapiski* (Leningrad, 1929), pp. 54–7.

49. Glushkovskii, *Vospominaniia baletmeistera*, p. 173.

50. *Ibid.*, p. 183.

51. Nikolai Ramazanov, *Materialy dlia istorii khudozhestv v Rossii* (Moscow, 1863), p. 234.

52. Slonimskii, *Didlo*, p. 124.

53. Glushkovskii, "Iz vospominanii o znamenitom khoregrafe K. L. Didlo," *Moskvitianin* (no. 4, 1856), Bk. 2, pp. 394–412.

54. *Ibid.*, p. 409.

55. Grigorii Blok, "K. A. Kavos," *Ezhegodnik Imperatorskikh Teatrov* (Sezon, 1896). Supplement to bk. 2, p. 17.

56. "Zapiski R. M. Zotova," *Istoricheskii vestnik* (no. 11, 1896), p. 403.

57. *Blagonamerennyi* (1819), p. 208.

58. Glushkovskii, "Iz Vospominanii, pp. 401–2.

59. *Ibid.*, p. 404.

60. *Ibid.*, p. 393.

61. *Ibid.*, p. 410.

62. Arapov, p. 289.

63. Glushkovskii, *Vospominaniia baletmeistera*, p. 171.

64. Krasovskaia, p. 145.

65. Zotov's two accounts differ in details, but the air of general chaos is conveyed in essence in both: "I moi vospominaniia o teatre," p. 36 and "Zapiski R. M. Zotova," *Istoricheskii vestnik* (no. 11, 1896), p. 403.

66. V. Tomashevskii, *Pushkin* (Moscow-Leningrad, 1956), 1:266–7.

67. "Zapiski R. M. Zotova," *Istoricheskii vestnik* (no. 11, 1896), p. 403.

68. V. S[ots], p. 59.

69. Glushkovskii, *Vospominaniia baletmeistera*, p. 170.

70. *Kora i Alonzo ili Deva Solntsa* (St. Petersburg, 1820). Program in Leningrad Public Library.

71. *Ibid.*

72. Arapov, pp. 299, 329.

73. Adam Glushkovskii, "Balet v Rossii. Vospominanie o znamenitom khoregrafe K. L. Didlo," *Panteon* (no. 12, 1851), 6:6–9.

74. Peter Brinson, *Background to European Ballet* (Leyden, 1966), p. 151.

75. Glushkovskii, *Vospominaniia baletmeistera*, p. 168.

76. Borisoglebskii, 1:85. Panaeva, p. 40.

77. Arapov, p. 238.

78. *Ruskaia Talia* (St. Petersburg, 1825), p. viii.

79. Arapov, p. 308.

80. *Ibid.*, pp. 335–52.

81. Aleksandr Pleshcheev, *Nash balet* (St. Petersburg, 1899), pp. 76–7. "Duel' Sheremeteva s zavadovskim," in *Ocherki iz zhizni i byta proshlago vremeni S.I. Shubinskago* (St. Petersburg, 1888), pp. 157–62.

82. D. S. Mirsky, *History of Russian Literature* (New York, 1961), pp. 112–4. Nabokov, 2:86–90.

83. A. S. Pushkin, *Polnoe sobranie sochinenii v shesti tomakh* (Moscow-Leningrad, 1932), 4:708–15, 738. Also M. Zagorskii, *Pushkin i teatr* (Moscow-Leningrad, 1940), pp. 62–3.

84. All selections from *Eugene Onegin* have been translated by Babette Deutsch, in *The Works of Alexander Pushkin* (New York, 1936), pp. 119–26.

85. A. S. Pushkin, *Sobranie sochinenii* (Moscow, 1962), 6:247–8. *Pushkin i teatr* (Moscow, 1953), p. 323.

86. *Eugene Onegin*, p. 120.

87. A. S. Pushkin, *Polnoe sobranie sochinenii* (Moscow-Leningrad, 1949), 5:192.

88. *Eugene Onegin*, p. 120.

89. Glushkovskii, *Vospominaniia baletmeistera*, p. 183.

90. *Eugene Onegin*, p. 119.

91. *Ibid.*, p. 126.

92. *Aftografy A.S. Pushkina. Reproduktsii prilozhenie k knige B. Meilakh. Khudozhestvennoe myshlenie Pushkina kak tvorcheskii protsess.*

93. Iu[rii]. Slonimskii, "Baletnye uchitel'ia Pushkina," *Neva* (no. 2, 1969), p. 213.

94. Arapov, p. 259.

95. *Kavkazskii plennik ili ten' nevesty* (St. Petersburg, 1823). Program in Leningrad Public Library.

96. Sergei N. Durylin, *Pushkin na stsene* (Moscow, 1951), p. 20.

97. Glushkovskii, *Vospominaniia baletmeistera*, p. 170.

98. Durylin, p. 19.

99. *Damskii zhurnal* (no. 20, 1827), p. 61.

100. Arapov, p. 336.

101. J. Thomas Shaw, ed., *The Letters of Alexander Pushkin* (Bloomington, Ind., 1963), 1:104.

102. E. Surits, *Vse o baleta* (Moscow-Leningrad, 1966), p. 368.

103. A. G. Movshenson and Iu[rii]. I. Slonimskii, "Novoe o poslednikh godakh deiatel'nosti Didlo," *Teatral'noe nasledstvo* (Moscow, 1956), p. 70.

104. F. Inok [Koni] "Benefis G–zh Glushkovskoi," *Molva* (no. 20, 1831), pp. 10–11.

105. *Ruskaia Talia*, p. ix.

106. R[afail]. Zotov, "I moi vospominaniia o teatre," p. 42.

107. A. S. Griboyedov, *Polnoe sobranie sochinenii* (St. Petersburg, 1911), 1:14.

108. Movshenson and Slonimskii, p. 70.

109. Arapov, p. 373.

110. *Ibid.*, pp. 379, 382.

111. Slonimskii, *Didlo*, p. 234.

112. Vera Krasovskaia, "Sumbeka, ili pokorenie kazanskogo tsarstva," *Teatr i dramaturgiia* (Leningrad, 1967), p. 200.

113. A. I. Vol'f, *Khronika, Petersburgskikh Teatrov s kontsa 1826 do nachala 1855* (St. Petersburg, 1877), 1:29.

114. Arthur Saint-Léon, *La Sténochorégraphie, ou l'art d'écrire promptement la danse* (Paris, 1852).

115. Krasovskaia, "Sumbeka," p. 190.

116. A. Pravdukhin, *Literaturnye pribavleniia k russkomu invalidu* (no. 32, 1833), p. 255, quoted by Krasovskaia, "Sumbeka," p. 189.

CHAPTER IX. *The Master's Wing-Clipping*

1. A. I. Vol'f, *Khronika Petersburgskikh Teatrov s kontsa 1826 do nachala 1855 goda* (St. Petersburg, 1877), 1:29.

2. A. G. Movshenson and Iu[rii]. I. Slonimskii, "Novoe o poslednikh godakh deiatel'nosti Didlo," *Teatral'noe nasledstvo* (Moscow, 1956), p. 69.

3. *Ibid.*, p. 72.

4. M. V. Borisoglebskii, *Materialy po istorii russkogo baleta* (Leningrad, 1938), 1:95. Borisoglebskii states, however, "From documents of the archives of the Directorate it turns out that the new agreement was only minimal of those demands which Didelot presented. The ordinary earnings of Didelot and his wife came to thirty-nine thousand rubles a year," p. 80.

5. Movshenson and Slonimskii, pp. 72–3.

6. *Ibid.*, p. 73. Borisoglebskii, 1:116.

7. Leonid Grossman, *Pushkin v teatral'nykh kreslakh* (Leningrad, 1926), p. 120.

8. Borisoglebskii, 1:116.

9. N. P. Mundt, "Karl Ludovik Didlo, byvshii baletmeister imperatorskikh Sanktpetersburgskikh Teatrov," *Repertuar russkogo teatra* (bk. 3, 1840), p. 8.

10. Borisoglebskii, 1:106.

11. Movshenson and Slonimskii, p. 81.

12. Faddei Bulgarin, "Teatral'nyia vospominaniia," *Panteon russkago i vsekh evropeiskikh teatrov* (1840), 1:89.

13. Borisoglebskii, 1:107. Movshenson and Slonimskii, p. 78.

14. Movshenson and Slonimskii, pp. 78–9.

15. *Ibid.*, p. 76.

16. Borisoglebskii, 1:114.

17. V. P. Pogozhev, *Stoletie organizatsii Imperatorskikh Moskovskikh Teatrov* (St. Petersburg, 1908), p. 75.

18. Pierre d'Alheim, *Sur les pointes* (Paris, 1897), p. 184.

19. Vol'f, 1:29.

20. D'Alheim, p. 184.

21. Movshenson and Slonimskii, p. 90. Borisoglebskii, 1:120.

22. Vol'f, 1:29.

23. Borisoglebskii, 1:120.

24. Movshenson and Slonimskii, p. 91.

25. Borisoglebskii, 1:120–1.

26. Vol'f, 1:29.

27. Ia. Nazakulisnyi, "Teatral'naia khronika," *Molva* (no. 21, 1824), p. 325.

28. Grossman, p. 120.

29. V.V.V., *Severnaia pchela* (October 4, 1835).

30. *Severnaia pchela* (June 17, 1838). The reference is to Schneitzhoeffer's *La Sylphide.*

31. Glushkovskii, *Vospominaniia baletmeistera* (Leningrad-Moscow, 1940), p. 188.

32. Borisoglebskii, 1:103. A. Platov, *Istoricheskii ocherk obrazovaniia i razvitiia artilleriiskogo uchilishcha 1820–1870* (St. Petersburg, 1870), pp. 107–8, 136.

33. Samuel H. Cross, "The Russian Ballet before Diagilev," *The American Slavic and East European Review* (1944), 3:31.

34. August Bournonville, *Mit Theaterliv.* Translated in *Klassiki khoreografii* (Leningrad, 1937), p. 261.

35. Slonimskii, *Didlo,* p. 102.

36. R[afail]. Zotov, "I moi vospominaniia o teatre," *Repertuar russkago teatra* (1840), 2:37.

37. *Les Oeuvres melées de Mr de Rémond de Saint-Mard* (The Hague, 1742), vol. 2.

38. P. M., *Severnaia pchela* (December 3, 1859).

39. Cross, p. 23.

40. Vera Krasovskaia, *Russkii baletnyi teatr. Ot vozniknoveniia do serediny XIX veka* (Moscow-Leningrad, 1958), p. 107.

41. Borisoglebskii, 58. Serge Lifar, *A History of Russian Ballet* (London, 1954), pp. 50–1. Glushkovskii, *Vospominaniia baletmeistera,* p. 164.

42. G. Danilevskii, "A. E. Martynov," *Panteon* (bk. 6, 1852), 3:48.

43. A. Glushkovskii, "Iz vospominaniia o znamenitom khoragrafe K. L. Didlo," *Moskvitianin* (no. 4, bk. 2, 1856), p. 390.

44. Serge Kara-Moura, "Charles-Louis Didelot," *Archives internationales de la danse* (April 15, 1934), p. 54.

Index